Marrakesh: through writers' eyes

MARRAKESH
through writers' eyes

Edited by Barnaby Rogerson
and Stephen Lavington

London

This arrangement, biographical notes and introduction © Eland Publishing 2003
Text © Contributors as acknowledged 2003
The six linocuts that illustrate the chapter headings
were executed by Mungo McCosh specifically for this book
though he controls all rights as artist and for their further use.
First published in May 2003 by Sickle Moon Books, part of Eland Publishing Ltd,
61, Exmouth Market, Clerkenwell, London ECIR 4QL
ISBN 0 907871 99 2
Cover image: Street of the Dyers © Robert Holmes/CORBIS
Typesetting and text layout by Antony Gray

Contents

Illustrations

Preface

Tahir Shah

Six days ago I saw a man sitting in J'ma al Fna, the vast central square of Marrakesh. He was bald, with a long tatty beard and a single silver earring reflecting the light. I knew he wasn't a Moroccan because of the look in his eye. He looked as if he had seen a miracle. I was waiting for a friend to turn up and we got talking. The man was a German called Casper. He told me he had travelled for sixteen years. It seemed to him that every inch of the world had passed beneath his feet. Sapphire eyes wide with wonder, hands out, fingers splayed, he told me that every minute until then had been the preparation – the preparation for that sight.

'This is the world,' he said in a soft Bavarian voice.

I asked him what he meant. He smiled.

'You don't feel it?'

I didn't reply.

'You don't feel it?' he repeated.

'What? Feel what?'

'The humanity,' he said.

Casper stood to his feet and staggered away, mumbling something about a drink of cold water. Then he was gone. I stood there, gazing out at the square's stew of human life – snake handlers and fortune-tellers, healers and madmen, door-to-door dentists, witches, water-sellers, and a single blind man waiting for a coin to be pressed into his palm. Casper from Bavaria was right. There is perhaps no spot on Earth so alive, so human, as J'ma al Fna, the 'Place of Execution'.

Like almost everyone else who has ever been there, I have tried to understand Marrakesh. I have sat in Aghana, my favourite café overlooking the square, and I have watched, listened, and pondered. Is it Africa? Is it Morocco? Is it a tourist destination *par excellence*? Or is it a strange kind of paradise, a paradise for the senses? The answer is that Marrakesh is all of these things, and a great deal more.

My only grumble is that these days the Red City is far too easy to arrive at. You fly in, and half an hour later you can be embedded in the medina or lazing by a pool, wondering where on earth you are. Look at the map. Study it, and you see that you are deep in the desert, with the Atlas Mountains rising up behind you. If I had my way, you would still have to struggle to get to Marrakesh – to really earn it, like every other traveller in history. For there is nothing like perspiration to make one appreciative.

With the afternoon heat too suffocating in the square, the light too bright for any but a Marrakeshi's eyes, I slipped into the labyrinth of the medina. Cool vaulted stone, courtyards latticed with bamboo staves, casting zebra stripes across the merchants and their stalls. What an emporium – mountains of turmeric, paprika, salted almonds and dates, yellow leather slippers laid out in rows, ostrich eggs and incense, chameleons in wire cages, and beef tenderloins nestled on fragrant beds of mint.

Roam the medina's narrow passages and you are dragged back in time. Marrakesh may be prosperous these days, bolstered by tourist wealth, but the medina is still intact, vibrant, raging with life, as it's been for centuries. There may be Chinese plastic dolls on offer, and second-hand TVs stacked up by the dozen, and racks of mobile phones, but don't be deceived. Marrakesh moves to an ancient rhythm. The decoration comes and goes, as do the wares, but the soul does not alter.

Of all the stalls and shops, there is one that I visit on every journey to the Red City. It is the *Maison de Mèknes*, a low-fronted place, on a side street off a side street. There are steps going down, rounded by decades of eager feet. Inside, the ceiling is low, cobwebbed, and the shelves beneath it cluttered with treasure. There are ancient Berber chests, silver teapots, ebony foot-stools, swords once used by warring tribes, and cartons of postcards left by the French, Box Brownie cameras, candle-sticks, silk wedding belts, and camel headdresses crafted from indigo wool.

The proprietor is a smug-faced man with tobacco-coloured eyes called Omar bin Mohammed. He is always perched on a stool behind a pool of light just inside the door. You don't see him at first, not until your eyes have become accustomed to the darkness. Omar is greedy for business, but there is one thing that he enjoys more than loading tourists up with loot. He loves to tell stories. Visit his shop and you can't leave until you have sat a while on a low leather-topped stool, quaffed a glass of boiling mint tea, and listened.

The first time I stepped into the shop was to ask for directions. It was early in the morning, before the crowds of tourists had begun to ramble through. None of the other emporia were open, and Omar was still only preparing, washing the steps leading down into his lair. I had asked him the way to the main square. Before I knew it I had been lured inside. I spent all day in there, listening. The first thing Omar told me when I crossed the threshold was that nothing – absolutely nothing – was for sale. However much I wanted one of the ancient Berber boxes, or the rough Saharan shields, or the amber necklaces, I was out of luck, he said.

'Is it a museum, then?' I asked.

Omar bin Mohammed clawed a hand through the scrub of grey beard on his cheek.

'My shop isn't like the others in the medina,' he hissed. 'The others, they're charlatans. They'll eat you up, sell you their mothers.'

'Then how is your place different? Is your merchandise of higher quality?'

Omar blew his nose into an oversized handkerchief, and rubbed his thumbs to his eyes.

'No, no,' he said. 'All this stuff I'm selling is worthless. It may look nice to you, because you don't know. The light's bad in here. An empty tin can would look like treasure in this light. Take something away and the first time you'd realise it's rubbish is when you are home.'

'I really don't understand why you're telling me this.'

Omar held his right palm out in the air.

'There's a problem,' he said. 'I have endured it since my youth.'

I wondered what the shopkeeper was talking about. People I've just met are always offloading their troubles on me. I braced myself to be petitioned for charity.

'We all have problems,' I said.

'You understand,' came the reply. 'And my problem is that I can't help but tell the truth.'

'That doesn't sound like a problem. Quite the opposite in fact.'

Omar the shopkeeper blinked hard.

'You have no idea. When you're a salesman here in the Marrakesh medina, lying is the first thing you learn. Generation after generation, they pass it on. It's the secret ingredient, the frame for a salesman's life. Lie well and you can make a fortune every day. Only then will your wife be happy, only then will your children walk with pride.'

'Can't you just pretend to lie?'

'That's it,' said Omar. 'The other shopkeepers say I'm a fool, that I should simply trick the tourists like everyone else. After all most of them will never be back. And what are tourists for but for tricking?'

'*So?*'

'So in my shop nothing's for sale.'

'Ah,' I said.

Omar paused, flexed his neck, and smiled.

'Nothing's for sale…' he repeated. 'Instead, it's all free. Absolutely free!'

I looked greedily at the shelves. One of the ancient Berber coffers had caught my eye. The thought of getting it for nothing was suddenly very pleasing.

'Can I have that, then?'

'Of course you can,' said Omar.

'Without charge? Can I just take it?'

'I told you,' he said, 'I give the objects away.'

'I'm so glad I came inside here.'

'I'm glad you did, too,' said the shopkeeper.

I stood up and moved over to the Berber chest. Omar encouraged me to pull back the lid, revealing a felt-trimmed interior.

'Oh, there's something I should tell you,' he said gently.

'What?'

'That to every item in here there's something attached.'

Again, I didn't quite understand.

'What's that?'

'A story.'

I glanced over at the shopkeeper and narrowed my eyes.

'Huh?'

'If you want to take an item,' he said, 'then you have to buy the story attached to it.'

Omar blinked. Then I blinked. He rubbed a hand to his face again, and I pondered the arrangement. In a city where competition for tourist dollars had reached fever pitch, Omar bin Mohammed had come up with a ruse like none other. He grinned hard, then tried to look meek.

'What story is attached to that chest?'

'It's called "The Horseman and the Snake".'

'How much does it cost to hear it?'

'Six hundred dirhams.'

'That's forty pounds,' I said. 'That chest isn't worth that.'

'I told you, the objects I'm giving away are not special at all. The chest looks nice but it's worthless.'

'Then why should I fork out six hundred dirhams for something of such little value?'

Omar bin Mohammed wove his fingers together and bowed them towards the floor.

'For the story,' he said.

I pulled out three high denomination bills.

'Here's the money.'

A moment later the bills had been tucked beneath layers of clothing, and the Berber chest had been wrapped in newspaper.

'It's a good choice,' said Omar.

'But I thought you said you were dealing in rubbish.'

'That chest may be rubbish,' he said, 'but "The Horseman and the Snake" is worth three times the money I'm charging you for it.'

Leaning back on his stool, Omar bin Mohammed stared hard into the pool of light just inside his door, and he began:

'Once upon a time,' he said, 'long ago and many days travel from where we sit, there was a kingdom called the Land of Pots and Pans. Everyone there was happy, and everyone was prosperous, made so by their thriving business of selling pots and pans to the other kingdoms all around.'

Omar the salesman paused to pass me a glass of sweet mint tea.

'Now,' he said, 'in the Land of Pots and Pans there were all sorts of animals, except for snakes. No one had ever seen a snake, and no one had ever imagined such a creature. One day a woodcutter was asleep in the forest, when a long green serpent slithered up to him and slid into his open mouth and down his throat. The woodcutter woke up, as the snake suffocated him. Panicking, he managed to stand up and flap his arms all around, moaning as loudly as he could.

'As luck would have it, a horseman was riding by at that precise moment. He saw the woodcutter waving his arms in distress. Having come from the neighbouring land where snakes were plentiful, he realised immediately what had happened. Pulling out his whip, he leapt from his steed and began to whip the poor woodcutter's stomach with all his strength.

'The woodcutter tried to protest, but half-suffocated by the serpent and wounded from the horseman's seemingly unprovoked attack, he could do nothing except fall to his knees. Displeased at the discomfort of its hiding place, the snake reversed up out of the woodcutter's throat and slithered away. Seeing this, the horseman jumped back onto his mount and rode off without a word. Hailing from a land where such attacks were frequent, he didn't give the matter another thought. As he caught his breath, the woodcutter began to understand what had happened, and that the horseman had attacked him in silence because time was of the essence, before the reptile had injected venom into his bloodstream.'

Omar bin Mohammed held up the Berber chest wrapped in newspaper and grinned.

'Don't forget the story,' he said. 'You will appreciate it all the more because you have paid to hear it. Allow it to move around your head, the more it does so, the more its real value will become apparent.'

These days Marrakesh seems to charging ahead, like a stagecoach hurtling into the night. I can think of few places that are quite so alive, quite so popular. There are people everywhere, all of them doing something, selling something, or waiting for something to happen. In most other cities the combination would be asphyxiating, but not in Marrakesh. I think it's because everyone living in or visiting the city understands that they are there at a particular time. There's a sense that the cocktail of life is just right, that it's something which occurs very seldom.

For centuries Marrakesh has been a remote staging post, a frontier before the desert. The intrepid have passed through en route south into the Sahara, or eastwards towards Mecca. It's always been a caravanserai, where possessions have been bought and sold, and stories swapped: a place where people live on the edge, thankful that they are there.

As I stroll through the central square of J'ma al Fna, I often find myself pondering how Marrakesh has become what it has – the world's most celebrated desert destination. I find myself wondering what my grandfather, the Afghan writer Ikbal Ali Shah, would have thought of the city now. He first visited it back in the 1930s, shortly before Winston Churchill brought Franklin D. Roosevelt to stay at The Mamounia during the War, to soak up the light. On the face of it, the change has been extraordinary – a surge of people, cars and buildings. But look in a different way. Close your eyes and let the city touch your other senses, and you begin to appreciate that Marrakesh is today what it has always been – a crucible of all that is exotic.

ABOUT THE AUTHOR

Tahir Shah is the author of *The Caliph's House: A Year in Casablanca.* He is currently working on a new book about Morocco, *In Arabian Nights.*

Introduction

The City of Youssef ibn Tachfine

Barnaby Rogerson

The Red City of Marrakesh has always been a place of multiple identities. It is the drum that beats an African and a specifically Saharan identity into the complex soul of Morocco. It is the city that keeps alive an imperial dream. It is one of the triumphant citadels of the Muslim world underwritten by an epic history and the deeds of five dynasties of Sultans. It is a place of sumptuous secret garden palaces, yet keeps a true regard for the poverty of sainthood. It is a city that is possessed by its southern horizon, by the lofty blue peaks of the High Atlas mountains. Beyond those snow-capped summits beckons the vast desert, waiting like an implacable sea to consume or to be crossed.

The Red City of Marrakesh has always been thought to encapsulate the very essence of Moroccan individuality. Indeed the very name Morocco was created by European travellers from out of their mangling of the word 'Marrakesh'. Similarly Turkish maps still mark the country as 'Fas' from the time when Ottoman ambassadors were despatched to the city of Fez.

The city walls, overlooked by the minaret of the Koutoubia Mosque, at first seem to frame nothing more than a vast transitory souk fronted by the celebrated animation of the J'ma al Fna square. Off to one corner of this square lies one of the historical lodestones of the city, the small tomb of the founder of Marrakesh – Youssef ibn Tachfine. In another hidden corner can be found a small domed washing room, which is all that remains of the beautiful first city built by his son Ali.

Marrakesh first arose to the sound of one man's command, to be the advance base of an Empire of Faith then being forged by blue-veiled Muslim knights from the Sahara. The secret desert headquarters of this league of holy warriors has never been found, though their ribat (their fortress of the faith) is believed to have been established on an isolated cliff-fringed promontory lashed by both the desert winds and the rolling surf of the Atlantic on the coast of the Western

Sahara. After twenty years of desert warfare this group of jihadists – named *al-murabitun* (the men of the ribat) had seized control over all the desert valleys, oases and trade routes of the Sahara.

In 1059 the general in command of these *al-murabitun*, Abu Bakr was in a position to lead an expedition over the High Atlas into central Morocco. Marrakesh was at first no more than one of their many marching camps, defined by a wall of thorn bushes, which marked the rapid progress of the *al-murabitun* army. At that time there was nothing special to mark it out as a place of historical destiny for it guarded neither a river crossing nor a mountain pass and boasted no ancient temple or royal tomb. While the name of the camp itself had little dignity, for 'Marrakesh' derives from 'to cross and hide', probably a Saharan reference to its role as their base 'beyond' the mountains. However this military camp site was well placed to prosper as a regional centre for it stood at the conjunction of three different geographical zones: the arid plateau, the High Atlas mountains and lush stream-fed oasis plantations. It was also roughly equidistant from the three pre-existing Berber market towns in the region as well as the three most important routes across the High Atlas. However the garrison camp of Marrakesh was soon to be emptied of practically all of its troops as the *al-murabitun* army was led north to attack the Berghouata, a confederation of Berbers who were sworn enemies of the *al-murabitun* due to their heretical beliefs. The Berghouata, based on the rough hills around the modern cities of Rabat and Casablanca, were to prove themselves the toughest and most resourceful of all the adversaries of the *al-murabitun*. Indeed in one of the early battles between these two Berber powers, the founding guru and spiritual leader of the *al-murabitun* (Ibn Yasin) was killed and the whole edifice of *al-murabitun* power seemed to be on the point of collapse as a revolt broke out in their Saharan homeland. Abu Bakr made a quick decision to nip this rebellion in the bud and in 1060 rushed back to the Sahara with the bulk of his army, leaving a young cousin from his own tribe (the Lamtuna of the Sahara) to hold the northern frontier from the base camp of Marrakesh. It was probably about then that the first permanent structure, the Ksar el Hajar – the tower of stone – rose to watch over the camp. Nothing remains of this, though I imagine it to be a smaller, slightly more severe version of the Koutoubia.

The young cousin Youssef ibn Tachfine was more than equal to his cousin's charge for instead of merely holding his position he launched upon the conquest of Morocco the very next year. He had learned much from the debacle of the previous campaign against the Berghouata. The mountain and hill tribes of Morocco were isolated, the towns and cities were liberated and befriended while the real rivals to *al-murabitun* power, the nomadic Berber tribes of the plans, were defeated in battle and their cavalry assimilated into his army. Having successfully seized Fez, the three-hundred-year-old capital of Islamic Morocco in 1069, Youssef ibn Tachfine moved immediately to secure the eastern frontier by conquering the tribes of Western Algeria, then in 1082 switched his attention to the famously bellicose Rif mountains of northern Morocco. Six years later, on the invitation of the embattled Muslims of Spain, he took his desert legions across the Mediterranean and defeated the Christian Castilians at the battle of Zallaqa. Ibn Tachfine's imposition of his version of true Islam soon had the Muslim princes of Spain appealing to their old Christian enemies for help. One by one their 'treason' was discovered and they were dethroned so that within a few years all of Muslim Spain was administered by the governors of ibn Tachfine. The most famous of these dethroned rulers, El-Mutamid, the poet prince of Seville, was sent into internal exile at El-Aghmat just outside Marrakesh, where the view of the High Atlas mountains taunted him with cherished memories of his Spanish home.

In 1087 Ibn Tachfine's elder cousin, Abu Bakr, died. (As a given name Abu Bakr has powerful associations within Islam for it is the name of the Prophet Muhammad's first adult disciple who rose to become the first Caliph after his death). Long before his own death, this Berber Abu Bakr from the Sahara had acknowledged a tacit division of power within the Empire with his young cousin. This is explained in a pleasing story in which one year Abu Bakr made a visit of inspection to Marrakesh. As the titular commander of the *al-murabitun* movement he was afforded every possible mark of honour and distinction. After three days he was also presented with a cascade of sumptuous gifts packed on a vast caravan of beautiful camels, so that in the words of Zaynab, the canny wife of Ibn Tachfine, 'he should be short of nothing in his desert home.' Abu Bakr accepted this courteous hint, and thereafter restricted his rule and his tours of inspection to the vast expanses of the Sahara, while Ibn Tachfine governed north of the High Atlas.

After Abu Bakr's death the *al-murabitun* Empire was reunited so that it stretched from the banks of the Niger to the foothills of the Pyrenees with Marrakesh as its acknowledged centre. Ibn Tachfine was nothing if not orthodox and at the time of his cousin's death humbly petitioned the distant, and near powerless Caliph at Baghdad, for recognition of his authority as *amir al-muslimin*, commander of the Muslims. For his part Ibn Tachfine also kept rigorously to the example of the Prophet. He wore only the woollen garments of a desert herdsman and had nothing to do with the silks, jewels and precious metals traditionally associated with royal power. Indeed his clothes came exclusively from his own flocks and had been spun and woven by the women of his household. His diet was the same as that of any desert shepherd: milk, barley bread and dates enlivened by feasts of camel meat and mutton. To make certain that the decisions of his government followed the example of the Prophet and were in accordance with the Koran and the collected sayings of the Prophet, salaried scholars of the religious texts were incorporated into every level of government. Even a provincial judge, a *Qadi*, was forbidden to pass judgement unless he was assisted by four such consultant scholars. The most revered of these scholars were appointed to a permanent council which accompanied the *amir* everywhere and was consulted before every major decision of state. It was as convincing an attempt to create a purely Islamic state as has ever been attempted and would be the model adhered to by all subsequent rulers of Morocco and North Africa for the next thousand years.

In 1106 the great desert warrior was succeeded by his son Ali ben Youssef. The new *amir* took the empire to its territorial apogee as first Lisbon and then the Balearic Islands were added to the *al-murabitun* Empire in Spain. Ali was also a great builder, and if the various *al-murabitun* castles that I have visited are his work – on mountains in the Rifs, Middle Atlas, Anti-Atlas as well as outside Zagora and atop a High Atlas foothill – he had an unerring eye for strategic position and the dignity of stone, routinely defying what would otherwise have been considered impossible. Ali was also the first to lay out the walls of Marrakesh, encircling a beautiful garden city enriched by the artisans of Andalucia, the wealth of Timbuctoo and a desert-born delight in water engineering. Nothing of this has survived, save the line of the walls and one small, domed washing room which was excavated from the ruins in 1948, about which one (admittedly over-enthusiastic) historian declared that 'the art of Islam has never exceeded the splendour of this extraordinary dome'. This is all we have with which to reconstruct an entire twelfth-century city, built at the same time that the Normans were triumphantly at work in Sicily, the Holy Land and England. The modest tomb of Youseff ibn Tachfine (as well as that of the poet prince El Mutamid) might be useful centres for our devotion but are no more than modern 'commemorations'. For the dynasty that replaced them – and who built the Koutoubia Mosque to mark their triumph as well as the minarets that still dominate the skyline of Seville and Rabat – obliterated every trace of their presence.

However even in defeat there is something triumphant about the *al-murabitun*. Amir Tachfine, fighting for his life outside the city of Oran in Western Algeria spurred his horse over the edge of a cliff rather than surrender. Two years later his younger brother Ishaq died at his post, defending the walls of Marrakesh to the last. The examples of their father Ali and of their grandfather Youssef ibn Tachfine have become embedded deep in the ethos of the city, the dreams, legends and aspirations of it citizens. Marrakesh remains a place where a shepherd may turn into a prince, because there are individuals whose manners, morality and culture prepare them to be either alone in contented poverty with their flocks on the hill or in absolute command of thousands of followers.

It has taken me many years to understand the defining dignity of the Moroccan historical identity, which is indistinguishably associated with the gifts of their Islamic faith and the example of the Prophet. It is however not always so easy to be enchanted with the present, day-to-day habits of the city.

I first came to Marrakesh as a child. I vividly recall those first sensations: of complete bewilderment, of heat and of being pinned down by the power of the sun, the footings of vast walls and the ferocious passion of young freelance guides desperate to earn a commission. I also remember being freed from all this oppression by a swim in an irrigation tank of green-coloured water later in the day. It was packed full of local children; a vast cauldron of jumping, leaping, fiercely animated faces. There was no barrier of language or religion then, only laughter.

As a young man I became a dedicated fact collector in the city, preparing a guide book by reading my way through the accounts of previous travellers and then trying to find my own route to every historical mosque and palace as well as discovering forgotten courtyards, ruined enclosures and my favourite places to picnic under the shade of palms. I remained an over-educated but complete outsider, always curiously restless in the city. For Marrakesh has this curious power to suggest that something very exceptional is about to happen just round the corner, or behind that high wall – some revelation, some new love or delight – later this evening . . . or perhaps this time tomorrow.

Over the years I added a little colour to the endless fact collecting. I befriended a transvestite hooker who used to sell bracelets to tourists in the square, collecting her stories over bowls of soup and cups of mint tea in the cafés. Years later we met again by chance. Overpowered by sniffing too much glue, she fell into the lap of my distinguished-looking friend from Casablanca who was beside me. He rose up, brushing away her old claims of friendship, to curse the place 'as a city without either religion or morals, a city that lives off strangers and forgets its past'.

I never sniffed glue though I found that it was impossible to appreciate the tortured paranoia of the best Moroccan short stories without some knowledge of hashish. I watched the Koutoubia tower grow dark and massive over a night spent on a hotel roof with two other awestruck friends. On another evening we transformed the whole teeming mass in the J'ma al Fna into a company of wolves, each one eyeing up their neighbour as either prey or predator. I was later told by a Moroccan friend that this is a common enough impression, which can be perceived by an indigène without the help of drugs.

Years later I spent part of the summer in the mountains to the south of the city, living in a borrowed house with a young family. I used to play with their two young boys in the nearby stream, building bridges and dams with the boulders of the river bed. One day we met a young snake charmer on the banks. He had come out of the city to wash his clothes and breathe the cool air for a day. He warned us to be a bit more careful, for our chosen playground was not only used as the village latrine but was also very popular with snakes. And to prove his point he carefully moved a couple of big stones and before long he plucked up a snake which writhed around his wrist and looking very startled in the sunlight. It was a harmless variety but he was clearly an expert handler. The boys were spell-bound and entranced by his skills, so a little while later he returned and showed us his travelling box, packed with squirming serpents. He even offered us a pair as pets. I was glad when their mother reluctantly refused this generous offer. He also told us that although he came from this valley he liked to dress as a city-boy in modern western clothing whenever he visited so that they could see he was an outsider but when he was in Marrakesh he always wore the woollen homespun cloak of a Berber hillsman, 'so that there too I can always be a stranger'.

It was excellent advice. For despite the trains, the planes, the tourist buses and the ever-expanding litany of sumptuous hotels, bars and restaurants,

Marrakesh remains compellingly different. This collection of travel writing relishes the 'otherness' of Marrakesh, the place to cross and hide.

BARNABY ROGERSON

EDITOR'S NOTE

It is said that Britain shares three things with Morocco. Both know what it is to live beside the Atlantic, to live under a monarchy and how to make peace with France. We share but little else. Our climates are an inversion of each other, one a green island patrolled by rain, the other an elemental mass of continental mountains ruled by the sun. Our national characteristics are in comic reversal of one another. The warm familial hospitality of Morocco has always been favourably compared to the cold reserve of the British, while the incremental prosperity of a well-run British business is inconceivable in a land that has had to believe (from the brutal evidence of its capricious climate) in both boom and bust. The British, though they delight in drama, also like to restrict it to the auditorium of a theatre, a television screen or the covers of a book while in Morocco they live it triumphantly on a public stage – be it in the street, café, home or bedroom. However if a neighbourly dispute is culminating in violence in Morocco, a dozen individuals will rush forward to arbitrate a settlement, while in a similar situation the British would rather stand back and watch the blood flow. But if Britain and Morocco stand poles apart in these ways, this difference has also been unusually creative. Into this gulf of difference generation upon generations of travel writers have poured forth their interpretations. There have been few attempts to bridge the cultural gap, instead they appear to have relished and exaggerated the differences. It makes for a compelling and fascinating collection of tales.

We have sorted the travel writing into half a dozen chapters to enhance the different moods, and we have not copy-edited the various texts so there is an impressive range of variant spelling.

Spirit of Place

In the Back Streets

from *Voices of Marrakesh* by Elias Canetti

The Cries of the Blind

Here I am, trying to give an account of something, and as soon as I pause I realize that I have not yet said anything at all. A marvellously luminous, viscid substance is left behind in me, defying words. Is it the language I did not understand there, and that must now gradually find its translation in me? There were incidents, images, sounds, the meaning of which is only now emerging; that words neither recorded nor edited; that are beyond words, deeper and more equivocal than words.

A dream: a man who unlearns the world's languages until nowhere on earth does he understand what people are saying.

What is there in language? What does it conceal? What does it rob one of? During the weeks I spent in Morocco I made no attempt to acquire either Arabic or any of the Berber languages. I wanted to lose none of the force of those foreign-sounding cries. I wanted sounds to affect me as much as lay in their power, unmitigated by deficient and artificial knowledge on my part. I had not read a thing about the country. Its customs were as unknown to me as its people. The little that one picks up in the course of one's life about every country and every people fell away in the first few hours.

But the word 'Allah' remained; there was no getting round that. With it I was equipped for that part of my experience that was most ubiquitous and insistent, and most persistent: the blind. Travelling, one accepts everything; indignation stays at home. One looks, one listens, one is roused to enthusiasm by the most dreadful things because they are new. Good travellers are heartless.

Last year, approaching Vienna after a fifteen-year absence, I passed through *Blindenmarkf* – in English 'Blind Market', as one might say 'Slave Market' – a place whose existence I had never previously suspected. The name struck me like a whiplash, and it has stayed with me since. This year, arriving in Marrakesh, I suddenly found myself among the blind. There were hundreds of them, more than one could count, most of them beggars. A group of them, sometimes eight, sometimes ten, stood close together in a row in the market, and their hoarse, endlessly repeated chant was audible a long way off. I stood in front of them, as still as they were, and was never quite sure whether they sensed my presence. Each man held out a wooden alms dish, and when someone tossed something in the proffered coin passed from hand to hand, each man feeling it, each man testing it, before one of them, whose office it was, finally put it into a pouch. They *felt* together, just as they murmured and called together.

All the blind offer one the name of God, and by giving alms one can acquire a claim on him. They begin with God, they end with God, they repeat God's name ten thousand times a day. All their cries contain a declension of his name, but the call they have once settled on always remains the same. The calls are acoustical arabesques around God, but how much more impressive than optical ones. Some rely on his name alone and cry nothing else. There is a terrible defiance in this; God seemed to me like a (wall that they were always storming in the same place. I believe those beggars keep themselves alive more by their formulas than by the yield of their begging.

Repetition of the same cry characterizes the crier. You commit him to memory, you know him, from now on he is there; and he is there in a sharply defined capacity: in his cry. You will learn no more from him; he shields himself, his cry being also his border. In this one place he is precisely what he cries, no more, no less: a beggar, blind. But the cry is also a multiplication; the rapid, regular repetition makes of him a group. There is a peculiar energy of asking in it; he is asking on behalf of many and collecting for them all. 'Consider all beggars! Consider all beggars! God will bless you for every beggar you give to.'

It is said that the poor will enter paradise five hundred years before the rich. By giving alms you buy a bit of paradise from the poor. When someone has died you 'follow on foot, with or without trilling mourners, swiftly to the grave, in order that the dead shall soon achieve bliss. *Blind men sing the creed.*'

Back from Morocco, I once sat down with eyes closed and legs crossed in a corner of my room and tried to say 'Alláh! Alláh! Alláh!' over and over again for half an hour at the right speed and volume. I tried to imagine myself going on saying it for a whole day and a large part of the night; taking a short sleep and then beginning again; doing the same thing for days and weeks, months and years; growing old and older and living like that, and clinging tenaciously to that life; flying into a fury if something disturbed me in that life; wanting nothing else, sticking to it utterly.

I understood the seduction there is in a life that reduces everything to the simplest kind of repetition. How much or how little variety was there in the activities of the craftsmen I had watched at work in their little booths? In the haggling of the merchant? In the steps of the dancer? In the countless cups of peppermint tea that all the visitors here take? How much variety is there in money? How much in hunger?

I understood what those blind beggars really are: the saints of repetition. Most of what for us still eludes repetition is eradicated from their lives. There is the spot where they squat or stand. There is the unchanging cry. There is the limited number of coins they can hope for. Three or four different denominations. There are the givers, of course, who are different, but blind men do not see them, and their way of expressing their thanks makes sure that the givers too are all made the same.

The Marabout's Saliva

I had turned away from the group of eight blind beggars, their litany still in my ear, and gone only a few steps farther when my attention was caught by a white-haired old man standing quite alone with his legs slightly apart; he held his head a little on one side and he was chewing. He too was blind and, to judge from the rags he was dressed in, a beggar. But his cheeks were full and red, his lips healthy and his mouth closed and the expression on his face was a cheerful one. He chewed thoroughly, as if following instructions. It evidently gave him much pleasure, and watching him I was put in mind of his saliva and the fact that he must have a great deal of it. He was standing in front of a row of stalls on which mountains of oranges were banked up for sale; I said to myself that one of the stall-keepers must have given him an orange and that he was chewing that. His right hand, stood a little way away from his body. The fingers of that hand were all widely splayed. It looked as if they were paralysed and he could not close them.

There was quite a lot of free space around the old man, which in this busy spot I found surprising. He gave the impression that he was always alone and did not wish it otherwise. I resolutely watched him chewing, intending to wait and see what happened when he had finished. It took a very long time; I had never seen a man chew so heartily and so exhaustively. I felt my own mouth begin to move slightly although it contained nothing that it could have chewed. I experienced something akin to awe at his enjoyment, which struck me as being more conspicuous than anything I had ever seen in association with a human mouth. His blindness failed to fill me with compassion. He seemed collected and content. Not *once* did he interrupt himself to ask for alms as the others all did. Perhaps he had what he wanted. Perhaps he did not need anything else.

When he had finished he licked his lips a few times; stretched his right hand with the splayed fingers a little farther forward, and in a hoarse voice said his piece. I went up to him rather shyly and laid a coin on his palm. The fingers remained stretched; he really could not close them. Slowly he raised the hand towards his face. He pressed the coin to his protruding lips and took it into his mouth. Hardly was it inside before he began chewing again. He pushed the coin this way and that in his mouth and it seemed to me I could follow its movements: now it was on the left, now on the right, and he was chewing as exhaustively as before.

I was amazed and I was dubious. I wondered whether I was not mistaken. Perhaps the coin had meanwhile disappeared somewhere else and I had not noticed. I waited again. When he had chewed with the same enjoyment and was finished, the coin appeared between his lips. He spat it into his left hand, which he had raised. A great deal of saliva streamed out with it. Then he slipped the coin into a pouch that he wore on his left.

I tried to dissolve my disgust at this proceeding in its outlandishness. What could be filthier than money? But this old man was not I; what caused me disgust gave him enjoyment, and had I not sometimes seen people kissing coins? The copious saliva undoubtedly had a role to play here, and he was clearly distinguished from other beggars by his ample generation of saliva. He had put in long practice before ever asking for alms; whatever he had eaten before, no one else would have taken so long over it. There was some kind of meaning in the motions of his mouth.

Or had he only taken my coin in his mouth? Had he felt in the palm of his hand that it was of a higher denomination than he was usually given and wanted to express his special thanks? I waited to see what would happen next, and I did not find waiting difficult. I was bewildered and intrigued and would certainly not have been able to give my attention to anything but the old man. He repeated his formula a few times. An Arab came past and laid a much smaller coin on his palm. He lifted it to his mouth without hesitating, put it in, and began chewing exactly as before. Possibly he did not chew quite as long this time. He spat the coin out, again with a great deal of saliva, and slipped it into his pouch. He was given other coins, some of them quite small, and the same proceeding was repeated several times. I became more and more perplexed; the longer I looked on, the less I understood why he did it. But one thing there was no doubting any more: he always did it, it was his habit, his particular way of begging, and the people who gave him something expected this expression of interest on the part of his mouth, which seemed to me redder every time he opened it.

I did not notice that people were also looking at me, and I must have presented a ridiculous spectacle. Possibly, who knows, I was even gaping open-mouthed. Then suddenly a man came out from behind his oranges, took a few steps towards me, and said soothingly: 'That's a marabout.' I knew that marabouts were holy men and that special powers were attributed to them. The word aroused awe in me and I felt my disgust immediately dwindle. I asked diffidently: 'But why does he put the coins in his mouth?'

'He always does that,' said the man, as if it had been the most natural thing in the world. He turned away from me and resumed his post behind his oranges. Only now did I notice that behind every stall there were two or three pairs of eyes trained on me. The astonishing creature was myself, who stood so long uncomprehending.

With this information I felt I had been dismissed and stayed no longer. The marabout is a holy man, I told myself, and everything about this holy man is holy, even his saliva. In bringing the givers' coins in contact with his saliva he confers a special blessing on them and thus enhances the merit they have acquired in heaven through their almsgiving. He was sure of paradise, and himself had something to give away that men needed much more than he needed their coins. Now I understood the cheerfulness that was in his blind face and that distinguished him from the other beggars I had seen hitherto.

I went away, but with him so much in mind that I talked about him to all my friends. None of them had ever noticed him and I sensed that they doubted the truth of my words. The next day I went back to the same spot but he was not there. I looked everywhere; he was not to be found. I looked every day; he did not come again. Perhaps he lived alone somewhere in the mountains and only rarely came to the city. I could have asked the orange vendors about him but I was ashamed to face them. He did not mean the same to them as he did to me, and whereas I was not in the least averse to talking about him to friends who had never seen him I tried to keep him separate from people who knew him well and to whom he was a familiar and natural figure. He knew nothing of me and they might perhaps have talked to him about me.

I saw him once more, exactly a week later, again on a Saturday evening. He was standing in front of the same stall, but he had nothing in his mouth and was not chewing. He said his piece. I gave him a coin and waited to see what would happen to it. He was soon chewing it assiduously again, but while he was still busy doing so a man came up to me and said his nonsense: 'That's a marabout. He's blind. He puts the coin in his mouth to feel how much you've given him.' Then he said something to the marabout in Arabic and pointed to me. The old man, his chewing finished, had spat the coin out again. He turned to me, his face shining. He said a blessing for me, which he repeated six times. The friendliness and warmth that passed across to me as he spoke were such as I had never had a person bestow on me before.

The Silent House and the Empty Rooftops

In order to feel at home in a strange city you need to have a secluded room to which you have a certain title and in which you can be alone when the tumult of new and incomprehensible voices becomes too great. The room should be quiet; no one should see you make your escape there, no one see you leave. The best thing is when you can slip into a cul-de-sac, stop at a door to which you have the key in your pocket, and unlock it without a soul hearing.

You step into the coolness of the house and close the door behind you. It is dark, and for a moment you can see nothing. You are like one of the blind men in the squares and passages you have just left. But you very soon have your eyesight back. You see a stone stairway leading to the first floor, and at the top you find a cat. The cat embodies the noiselessness you have been longing for. You are grateful to it for being alive: a quiet life is possible, then. It is fed without crying 'Allah' a thousand times a day. It is not mutilated, nor is it obliged to bow to a terrible fate. Cruel it may be, but it does not say so.

You walk up and down and breathe in the silence. What has become of the atrocious bustle? The harsh light and the harsh sounds? The hundreds upon hundreds of faces? Few windows in these houses look onto the street, sometimes none at all; everything opens onto the courtyard, and this lies open to the sky. Only through the courtyard do you retain a mellow, tempered link with the world around you.

But you can also go up on the roof and see all the flat roofs of the city at once. The impression is one of levelness, of everything being built in a series of broad terraces. You feel you could walk all over the city up there. The narrow streets present no obstacle; you cannot see them, you forget that there are streets. The Atlas gleam close and you would take them for the Alps were the light on them not brighter and were there not so many palm trees between them and the city.

The minarets that rise here and there are not like church spires. They are slender, but they do not taper; they are the same width top and bottom, and what matters is the platform in the sky from which the faithful are called to prayer. A minaret is more like a lighthouse, but with a voice for a light.

The space above the rooftops is peopled with swallows. It is like a second city, except that here things happen as fast as they happen slowly in the human streets below. They never rest, those swallows, you wonder if they ever sleep; idleness, moderation, and dignity are qualities they lack. They snatch their prey in flight; maybe the roofs in their emptiness look like a conquered land to them.

You see, you do not show yourself on the roof. Up there, I had thought, I shall feast my eyes on the women of fable; from there I shall overlook the neighbours' courtyards and overhear their goings-on. The first time I went up on the roof of my friend's house I was full of expectations, and as long as I continued to gaze into the distance, at the mountains and out over the city, he was content and I could sense his pride at being able to show me something so beautiful. But he started to fidget when, tiring of the far off, I became curious as to the near at hand. He caught me glancing down into the courtyard of the house next door, where to my delight I had become aware of women's voices speaking Spanish.

'That's not done here,' he said. 'You mustn't do that. I've often been warned against it. It's considered indelicate to take any notice of what goes on next door.

It's considered bad manners. In fact one oughtn't to show oneself on the roof at all, and a man certainly not. Sometimes the womenfolk go up on the roofs, and they want to feel undisturbed.'

'But there aren't any women up here at all.'

'We may have been seen,' said my friend. 'One gets a bad name. One doesn't address a veiled woman on the street, either.'

'What if I want to ask the way?'

'You must wait till a man comes along.'

'But surely you can sit up on your own roof, can't you? If you see someone on the next roof it's not your fault.'

'Then I must look away. I must show how uninterested I am. A woman's just come up on the roof behind us, an old servant. She has no idea I've seen her, but she's already going down again.'

She was gone before I could turn round.

'But then one's less free on the roof than one is on the street,' I protested.

'Certainly,' he said. 'One wants to avoid getting a bad name with one's neighbours.'

I watched the swallows and envied the way they went swooping at their ease over three, five, ten roofs at a time.

The Woman at the Grille

I was passing a small public fountain at which a youth was drinking. I turned off to the left and heard a soft, tender, caressing voice coming from above me. I looked up at a house opposite and saw, at first-floor level, behind a woven grille, the face of a young woman. She was unveiled and dark and held her face right up to the grille. She was pouring out a gentle stream of phrases, and all those phrases consisted of endearments. I was puzzled that she wore no veil. Her head was tilted slightly, and I sensed that she was speaking to me. Her voice never rose but remained uniformly soft, and with so caressing a quality in it that she might have been holding my head in her arms. But I could see no hands, she showed no more than her face; perhaps her hands were secured somewhere. The room she stood in was dark; in the street, where I was standing, the sun shone harshly. It was as if her words issued from a fountain, flowing into one another. I had never heard endearments in that language, but I sensed that that was what they were.

I wanted to go over and look at the door of the house the voice came from, but

I was half afraid that a movement on my part might frighten the voice away like a bird, and what would I do if it fell silent? I tried to be as gentle and soft as the voice itself; I have never stepped so warily. And I managed not to frighten it. I could still hear the voice when I was right up to the house and could no longer see the face at the grille. The narrow building gave the impression of a ruined tower. There was a hole in the wall where the stones had fallen out. The completely plain door, consisting of a few wretched planks, was fastened with wire and looked as if it were not often opened. It was not an inviting house: you could not get in, and inside it was dark and very likely dilapidated. Just around the corner was a cul-de-sac, but it was deserted and silent there and I could see no one I might have asked. Even in the cul-de-sac I could still hear the fountain of the caressing voice; round the corner it was like a far-off murmuring. I went back, again took up, a position at some distance from the house, looked up, and there was the oval face pressed to the grille and the lips moving to the tender words.

It seemed to me that they now had a slightly different quality; a vague pleading was audible in them, as if she had been saying: don't go away. Perhaps she had thought I had gone for good when I disappeared to examine house and door. Now I was back and I was to stay. How can I describe the effect that an unveiled female face, looking down from the height of a window, has on one in this city, in these narrow streets? There are few windows on the street and never anyone looking out of them. The houses are like walls; often you have the feeling of walking for a long time between walls, although you know they are houses: you can see the doors and the sparse, unused windows. It is like that with the women. They are shapeless sacks walking down the street; you can make out nothing, guess at nothing, and soon grow weary of the effort of trying to arrive at a firm idea of them. You dispense with women. But you do so reluctantly, and a woman who then appears at a window and even speaks to you and inclines her head slightly and does not go away, as if she had always been there waiting for you, and who then goes on speaking to you when you turn your back on her and steal away, who would so speak whether you were there or not, and always to you, always to everyone – such a woman is a prodigy, a vision, and you are inclined to regard her as more important than anything else that this city might have to offer.

I would have stood there much longer, only it was not an entirely unfrequented quarter. Veiled women coming up the street towards me took no exception whatever to their compeer at the grille. They passed the tower-like house as if no one had been speaking. They neither stopped nor looked up. Never changing their pace they approached the house and turned, right under the speaker's window, into the street where I was standing. I did sense, though, that they gave me disapproving looks. What was I doing there? Why was I standing there? What was I staring up at?

A group of schoolchildren came past. They were playing and joking as they went past and behaved as if they did not hear the sounds coming from above. They examined me: I was a less familiar figure to them than the unveiled woman. I was slightly ashamed of my standing there and staring. I sensed, however, that I would disappoint the face at the grille by going away; those words flowed on like a little river of bird sound. But now between them came the shrill cries of the children, who were slow in going. They had their satchels with them and were on the way home from school; they were trying to draw out the journey by inventing little games, one of the rules of which entailed their running forwards a little way, and then backwards. As a result they progressed at a snail's pace and made listening an ordeal to me.

A woman with a very small child halted beside me. She must have come up from behind; I had not noticed her. She did not stay long; she gave me a venomous look; behind the veil I made out the features of an old woman. She grasped the child as if my presence constituted a threat to it and shuffled on without a word to me. Feeling uncomfortable, I left my post and slowly followed her. She went a few houses farther down the street and then turned off. When I reached the corner round which she had disappeared I saw, at the bottom of a cul-de-sac, the dome of a small koubba. A koubba is a shrine in which a saint is buried and to which people make pilgrimages with their wishes. The old woman stopped in front of the closed door of the koubba and lifted the tiny child up, pressing its mouth to a object that I could not make out from where I was standing. She repeated this movement several times, then set the child down, took its hand, and turned to go. At the end of the cul-de-sac she had to pass me again, but this time she did not even give me a venomous look before going off in the direction we had both come from.

I went up to the koubba myself and saw, halfway up the wooden door, a ring wound round with old rags. It was these the child had kissed. The whole episode had taken place in complete silence, and in my embarrassment I had failed to notice that the schoolchildren were standing behind me and watching me. Suddenly I heard their ringing laughter as three or four of them made a rush for the door, seized the ring, and kissed the old rags. Laughing loudly, they repeated this ritual from all sides. One hung from the right side of the ring, another from the left, and their kisses were like a series of loud smacks. Soon they were shoved aside by others behind them. They all wanted to show me how it should be done; perhaps they expected me to imitate them. They were clean children, all of them, and well looked-after; I was sure they were washed several times a day. But the rags looked as dirty as if the alley had been wiped with them. They were supposed to be shreds of the saint's own robe and for the faithful there was something of his holiness in them.

When the boys had had their fill of kissing them they came after me and milled around me. One of them attracted my attention by his intelligent face and I saw he would have liked to speak to me. I asked him in French whether he could read. He answered with a well-mannered 'oui, monsieur'. I took a book from under my arm, opened it, and held it out to him; slowly but faultlessly he read the French sentences aloud. It was a work on the religious customs of the Moroccans, and the passage I had opened it at dealt with the veneration of the saints and their koubbas. You can call it an accident if you like, but he now read out to me what he and his friends had just demonstrated to me. Not that he gave any indication of being aware of this; perhaps in the excitement of reading he did not take in the meaning of the words. I praised him, and he accepted my tribute with the dignity of an adult. I liked him so much that I involuntarily associated him with the woman at the grille.

I pointed in the direction of the half-ruined house and asked: 'That woman at the grille up there – do you know her?'

'Oui, monsieur,' he said, and his face became very serious.

'Elle est malade?' I went on.

'Elle est très malade, monsieur.'

The 'very' that reinforced my question rang like a complaint, but a complaint about something to which he was wholly resigned. He was perhaps nine years old, but he looked then as if he had been living for twenty years with a chronic invalid, well knowing how a person ought to conduct himself in such a case.

'Elle est malade dans sa tête, n'est-ce pas?'

'Oui, monsieur, dans sa tête.' He nodded as he said 'in the head', but instead of pointing to his own head he pointed to that of another boy, who was exceptionally beautiful: he had a long, pale face with large, dark, very sad eyes. None of the children laughed. They stood there in silence. Their mood had changed: the moment I had started talking about the woman at the grille.

A Visit to the Mellah

On the third morning, as soon as I was alone, I found my way to the Mellah. I came to a cross-roads where there were a great many Jews standing about. The traffic streamed past them and round a corner. I saw people going through an arch that looked as if it had been let into a wall, and I followed them. Inside the wall, enclosed by it on all four sides, lay the Mellah, the Jewish quarter.

I found myself in a small, open bazaar. Men squatted among their wares in little low booths; others, dressed European style, sat or stood. The majority had on their heads the black skull-cap with which the Jews here mark themselves out, and a great many wore beards. The first shops I came to sold material. One man was measuring off silk. Another bent thoughtfully over his swiftly moving pencil, reckoning. Even the more richly-appointed shops seemed very small, many had callers; in one of the booths two very fat men were carelessly ensconced about a third, lean man – the proprietor – and were holding a lively yet dignified discussion with him.

I walked past as slowly as possible and looked at the faces. Their heterogeneity was astonishing. There were faces that in other clothing I would have taken for Arab. There were luminous old Rembrandt Jews. There were Catholic priests of wily quietness and humility. There were Wandering Jews whose restlessness was written in every lineament. There were Frenchmen. There were Spaniards. There were ruddy-complexioned Russians. There was one you felt like hailing as the patriarch, Abraham; he was haughtily addressing Napoleon, and a hot-tempered know-all who looked like Goebbels was trying to butt in. I thought of the transmigration of souls. Perhaps, I wondered, every human soul has to be a Jew once, and here they all are: none remembers what he was before, and even when this is so clearly revealed in his features that I, a foreigner, can recognize it, every one of these people still firmly believes he stands in direct line of descent from the people of the Bible.

But there was something that they all had in common, and as soon as I had accustomed myself to the rich variety of their faces and their expressions I tried to find out what it was. They had a way of swiftly glancing up and forming an opinion of the person going past. Not *once* did I pass unnoticed. When I stopped they would scent a purchaser and examine me accordingly. But mostly I caught the swift, intelligent look long before I stopped, and I even caught it when I was walking on the other side of the street. Even in the case of the few who lay there with Arab indolence, the look was never indolent: it came, a practised scout, and swiftly moved on. There were hostile looks among them; cold, indifferent, disapproving, and infinitely wise looks. But none of them struck me as stupid, they were the looks of people who are always on their guard but who, expecting hostility, do not wish to evoke it: no trace of a challenge; and a feat that is careful to keep itself hidden.

One is almost inclined to say that the dignity of these people lies in their circumspection. The shop is open on one side only and they have no need to worry about anything going on behind their backs. In the street, the same people feel less secure. I soon noticed that the 'Wandering Jews' among them, the ones who gave a restless, dubious impression, were always *passers-by;* people who carried all their wares with them and were obliged to force their way through the crowd; who never knew whether someone was not about to pounce on their wretched stock from behind, from the left, from the right, or from all sides at once. The man who had a shop of his own and spent his day in it had a quality almost of assurance.

Some, however, squatted in the street and offered bits and pieces for sale. Often these were miserable little heaps of vegetables or fruit. It was as if the vendors actually had nothing at all to sell but were merely clinging to the gestures of commerce. They looked neglected; there were a great many of them, and I did not find it easy to get used to them. Before long, though, I was prepared for anything, and it caused me no particular surprise to see an aged and infirm man squatting on the ground and offering for sale a single, shrivelled lemon.

I was now in a street that led from the bazaar at the entrance deeper into the Mellah. It was thronged with people. Among the innumerable men I noticed one or two women who went unveiled. An ancient, withered crone came shambling along, looking like the oldest thing on earth. Her eyes stared fixedly into the distance as if she saw exactly where she was going. She stepped aside for no one; where others described curves to get through, she always had room around her. I believe people were afraid of her: she walked very slowly and would have had time to throw a curse on every living creature. It was probably the fear she inspired that gave her the strength for this walk. When at last she had gone by me I turned to look after her. She felt my eyes on her, because she slowly swivelled round, as slowly as she walked, and turned her gaze full on me. I hurried on; and so instinctive had been my reaction to her look that it was not for some time that I noticed how much faster I was now walking.

I passed a row of barber shops. Young men, the hairdressers, lounged outside. On the ground opposite a man offered a basket of roast locusts for sale. I thought of the famous plague of Egypt and was surprised that Jews too ate locusts. Squatting in a booth that lay higher than the others was a man with the features and colouring of a Negro. He wore the Jewish skull-cap, and he was selling coal. The coal was stacked up high all around him; he looked as if he was to be walled in with coal and was just waiting for the men to come along and complete the job. He sat so still that at first I did not see him; it was his eyes that caught my attention, shining in the middle of all that, coal. Next to him a one-eyed man was selling vegetables. The eye he could not see with was atrociously swollen; it was like a threat. He was fiddling confusedly with his vegetables. He pushed them gingerly across to one side, then pushed them gingerly back again. Another man squatted beside five or six stones lying on the ground. He picked one up, weighed it in his hand, inspected it, and held it up in the air for a moment. Then he put it back with the others, repeating the same ritual with these. He did not *once* look up at me, although I had stopped right in front of him. He was the only person in the entire quarter who disdained to look at me. The stones he was trying to sell took up his whole attention; he seemed to be more interested in them than in purchasers.

I noticed how, the deeper I penetrated into the Mellah, the poorer everything became. The beautiful woollens and silks were behind me. No one looked wealthy and princely like Abraham. The bazaar by the entrance gate had been a kind of posh quarter; the actual life of the Mellah, the life of the simple people, went on here. I came into a small square that struck me as being the heart of the Mellah. Men and women stood together around an oblong fountain. The women carried pitchers that they filled with water. The men were filling their leather water-containers. Their donkeys stood beside them, waiting to be watered. A few open-air cooks squatted in the middle of the square. Some were frying meat, others little doughnuts. They had their families with them, their wives and children; it was as if they had moved house out into the square and were living and cooking their meals here now.

Peasants in Berber costume stood around with live hens in their hands; they held them by the legs, which were tied together, their heads dangling down. When women approached they held the hens out to them to feel. The woman took the bird in her hand without the Berber's releasing it, without its altering its position. She pressed it and pinched it, her fingers going straight to the places where it ought to be meaty. No one said a word during this examination, neither the Berber nor the woman; the bird too remained silent. Then she left it in his hand, where it continued to dangle, and moved on to the next peasant. A woman never bought a hen without first examining a great many others.

The whole square was lined with shops; in some of them craftsmen were at work, their hammering and tapping sounding loud above the noise of voices. In one corner of the square a large number of men were gathered together in ardent debate. I did not understand what they were saying but to judge from their faces they were discussing the affairs of the world. They were of different opinions and they were fencing with arguments; it seemed to me that they laid into one another's arguments with gusto.

In the middle of the square stood an old beggar, the first I had seen here; he was not a Jew. With the coin he received he made immediately for one of the little doughnuts that were sizzling in the pan. There were a good many customers round the cook and the old beggar had to wait his turn. But he remained patient, even with his pressing desire on the threshold of fulfilment. When at last he had got his doughnut he took it back with him to the middle of the square and there ate it with mouth wide open. His relish spread like a cloud of contentment over the square. No one took any notice of him, but everyone absorbed the flavour of his contentment and he seemed to me to be extremely important for the life and wellbeing of the square – its eating monument.

But I do not think it was only him I had to thank for the happy enchantment of that square. I had the feeling that I was really somewhere else now, that I had reached the goal of my journey. I did not want to leave; I had been here hundreds of years ago but I had forgotten and now it was all coming back to me. I found exhibited the same density and warmth of life as I feel in myself. I was the square as I stood in it. I believe I am it always.

I found parting from it so difficult that every five or ten minutes I would come back. Wherever I went from then on, whatever else I explored in the Mellah, I kept breaking off to return to the little square and cross it in one direction or another in order to assure myself that it was still there.

I turned first into one of the quieter streets in which there were no shops, only dwelling-houses. Everywhere, on the walls, beside doors, some way up from the ground, large hands had been painted, each finger clearly outlined, mostly in blue: they were for warding off the evil eye. It was the sign I found used most commonly, and people painted it up for preference on the place where they lived. Through open doors I had glimpses of courtyards; they were cleaner than the streets. Peace flowed out of them over me. I would have loved to step inside but did not dare, seeing no one. I would not have known what to say if I had suddenly come across a woman in such a house.

I was myself alarmed at the thought of perhaps alarming someone. The silence of the houses communicated itself as a kind of wariness. But it did not last long. A high, thin noise that sounded at first like crickets grew gradually louder until I thought of an aviary full of birds. 'What can it be? There's no aviary here with hundreds of birds! Children! A school!' Soon there was no doubt about it: the deafening hubbub came from a school.

Through an open gateway I could see into a large courtyard. Perhaps two hundred tiny little children sat crammed together on benches; others were running about or playing on the ground. Most of those on the benches had primers in their hands. In groups of three or four they rocked violently backwards and forwards, reciting in highpitched voices: '*Aleph. Beth. Gimel.*' The little black heads darted rhythmically to and fro; one of them was always the most zealous, his movements the most vehement; and in his mouth the sounds of the Hebrew alphabet rang out like a decalogue in the making.

I had stepped inside and was trying to unravel the tangle of activity. The smallest children were playing on the floor. Among them stood a teacher, very shabbily dressed; in his right hand he held a leather belt, for beating. He came up to me obsequiously. His long face was flat and expressionless, its lifeless rigidity in marked contrast to the liveliness of the children. He gave the impression that he would never be able to master them, that he was too badly paid. He was a young man, but *their* youth made him old. He spoke no French, and I expected nothing of him. It was enough for me that I could stand there in the middle of the deafening noise and look around a bit. But I had underestimated him. Beneath his rigor mortis there lurked something like ambition: he wanted to show me what his children could do.

He called a little boy over, held a page of the primer up in front of him in such a way that I could see it too, and pointed to Hebraic syllables in quick succession. He switched from line to line, backwards and forwards across the page at random; I was not to think the boy had learned it by heart and was reciting blind, without reading. The little fellow's eyes flashed as he read out: '*La–lo–ma–nushe–ti–ba–bu.*' He did not make a single mistake and did not falter once. He was his teacher's pride, and he read faster and faster. When he had finished and the teacher had taken the primer away I patted him on the head and praised him - in French, but that he understood. He retired to his bench and made as if he could no longer see me, while the next boy took his turn. This one was much shyer and made mistakes; the teacher released him with a gentle spank and fetched out one or two more children. Throughout this proceeding the din continued unabated, and the Hebraic syllables fell like raindrops in the raging sea of the school.

Meanwhile other children came up to me and stared at me inquisitively, some cheeky, some shy, some flirtatious. The teacher, in his impenetrable wisdom, ruthlessly drove off the shy ones while letting the cheeky ones do as they liked. He was the poor and unhappy overlord of this part of the school; when the performance was over the meagre traces of satisfied pride disappeared from his face. I thanked him very politely and, to give him a lift, somewhat condescendingly, as if I were an important visitor. His satisfaction must have been obvious; with the clumsiness of touch that dogged me in the Mellah I determined to return next day and only then give him some money. I stayed a moment longer, watching the boys at their reciting. Their rocking to and fro appealed to me; I liked them best of all. Then I left, but the din I took with me. It accompanied me all the way to the end of the street.

This now started to become busier, as if it led to some important public place. Some way in front of me I could see a wall and a large gateway. I did not know where it led to, but the closer I got to it the more beggars I saw, sitting on either side of the street. I was puzzled by them, not having seen any Jewish beggars before. When I reached the gateway I saw ten or fifteen of them, men and women, mostly old people, squatting in a row. I stood rather self-consciously in the middle of the street and pretended to be examining the gate, whereas in reality I was studying the faces of the beggars.

A young man came over to me, pointed to the wall, said 'le cimetiere israélite', and offered to take me in. They were the only words of French he spoke. I followed him quickly through the gate. He moved fast, and there was nothing to say. I found myself in a very bare, open space where not a blade of grass grew. The gravestones were so low that you hardly noticed them; you tripped over them as if they had been ordinary stones. The cemetery looked like a vast heap of rubble; perhaps that was what it had been once, only later being assigned its more serious purpose. Nothing in it stood up to any height. The stones you could see and the bones you could imagine were all lying. It was not a pleasant thing to walk erect; you could take no pride in doing so, you only felt ridiculous.

Cemeteries in other parts of the world are designed in such a way as to give joy to the living. They are full of things that are alive, plants and birds, and the visitor, the only person among so many dead, feels buoyed up and strength-ened. His own condition strikes him as enviable. He reads people's names on the gravestones; he has survived them all. Without admitting it to himself, he has something of the feeling of having defeated each one of them in single combat. He is sad too, of course, that so many are no more, but at the same time this makes him invincible. Where else can he feel that? On what battlefield of the world is he the sole survivor? Amid the supine he stands erect. But so do the trees and gravestones. They are planted and set up there and surround him like a kind of bequest that is there to please him.

But in that desolate cemetery of the Jews there is nothing. It is truth itself, a lunar landscape of death. Looking at it, you could not care less who lies where. You do not stoop down, you make no attempt to puzzle it out. There they all lie like rubble and you feel like scurrying over them, quick as a jackal. It is a wilderness of dead in which nothing grows any more, the last wilderness, the very last wilderness of all.

When I had gone a little farther I heard shouts behind me. I turned round and stopped. On the inside of the wall too, on either side of the gate, stood beggars. They were bearded old men, some of them on crutches, some blind. I was taken aback; I had not noticed them before. My guide having been in such a hurry, a good hundred paces lay between them and me. I hesitated to cross that stretch of wasteland again before I had penetrated farther. But *they* did not hesitate. Three of them detached themselves from the group by the wall and came hobbling over in a tremendous hurry. The one in front was a broad-shouldered, heavy man with a huge beard. He had only one leg and hurled himself forward with mighty thrusts of his crutches. He was soon far ahead of the others. The low gravestones were no obstacle to him; his crutches always found the right spot on the ground and never skidded. Like some threatening animal he came hurtling at me. In his face as it drew rapidly closer there was nothing to arouse sympathy. Like his whole figure it expressed a single, violent demand: 'I'm alive! Give!'

I had an inexplicable feeling that he wanted to slay me with his bulk; it was uncanny. My guide, a light, slim person with the movements of a lizard, pulled me swiftly away before he reached me. He did not want me giving anything to these beggars and shouted something at them in Arabic. The big man on crutches tried to follow us, but when he saw that we were faster he gave up and came to a standstill. I could hear his angry cursing for some time, and the voices of the others who had fallen behind joined with his in a chorus of ill will.

Relieved to have escaped them, I was at the same time ashamed of having roused their expectations in vain. The one-legged old man's onslaught had been foiled not by the stones, with which he and his crutches were familiar, but by the quickness of my guide. And God knows, victory in so unequal a contest was nothing to be proud of. Wanting to find out something about our wretched enemy, I questioned the guide. He did not understand a word, and instead of an answer a half-witted smile spread over his face. 'Oui,' he said, over and over again; 'oui.' I had no idea where he was leading me. After the episode with the old man, however, the wilderness was no longer quite so desolate. He was its rightful occupant, keeper of the bare stones, the rubble, and the invisible bones.

But I had overstated his importance, for before long I came upon an entire population domiciled here. Beyond a small rise we turned into a hollow and were suddenly standing in front of a tiny house of prayer. Outside it, in a semicircle, perhaps fifty beggars had taken up residence, a jumble of men and women afflicted with every infirmity under the sun, an entire tribe almost, except that the aged predominated. They had installed themselves in colourful groups on the ground and they now, by degrees, not too hastily, moved into action. They began muttering benedictions and stretching out their arms. But they did not approach too close before I had visited the house of prayer.

I looked into a very small oblong room in which hundreds of candles were burning. They were stuck in little glass cylinders and swimming in oil. Most of them were ranged on tables of normal height and you looked down on them as if they had been a book you were reading. A smaller number hung from the ceiling in large vessels. On either side of the room stood a man who was obviously appointed to say prayers. A few coins lay on the table near them. I hesitated on the threshold because I had nothing to cover my head with. The guide took off his skull-cap and handed it to me. I put it on, not without a certain awkwardness because it was very dirty. The prayer leaders were beckoning me and I stepped inside among the candles. They did not take me for a Jew and I said no prayer. The guide pointed to the coins and I understood what was now expected of me. I did not stay for more than a moment. I was awed by this little room in the wilderness that was filled with candles, that consisted of nothing but candles. They radiated a quiet serenity, as if nothing was quite over as long as they still burned. Perhaps these frail flames were all that was left of the dead. But outside you became closely and densely aware of the passionate life of the beggars.

I was back among them and now they really moved into action. They pressed round me from all sides as if I might miss precisely *their* infirmity and brought it to my attention in an elaborate and at the same time extremely vigorous kind of dance. They clutched my knees and kissed the flaps of my jacket. They seemed to be blessing every bit of my body. It was as if a throng of people had brought their mouths and eyes and noses, their arms and legs, their rags and crutches, everything they had, everything they consisted of, to bear upon praying to you. I was frightened, but I cannot deny that I was also deeply moved and that my fright was soon lost in this emotion. Never before had people come physically so close to me. I forgot their dirt, I did not care, I forgot about lice. I could feel the seduction of having oneself dismembered alive for others. That terrible weight of worship seems to justify the sacrifice, and how could it not work miracles?

But my guide took care that I did not remain in the beggars' hands. His claims were older, and nothing had yet been done to satisfy them. I did not have enough change for everyone. He drove off the unappeased with a lot of yelping and barking and pulled me away by the arm. When we had the house of prayer behind us he said 'oui' three times with his half-witted smile, although I had not asked him anything. It no longer seemed the same rubble heap as I retraced my steps. I knew now where its life and light were gathered. The old man inside the gate who had thrown himself with such vigour into the race on his crutches gave me a dark look; he said nothing, however, and kept his curse to himself. I passed out through the gate of the cemetery and my guide disappeared as swiftly as he had come, and at the same spot. It is possible he lived in a crack in the cemetery wall and emerged only rarely. He did not go without first having accepted his due, and by way of farewell he said 'oui'.

ABOUT THE AUTHOR

ELIAS CANETTI was born in Russe, Bulgaria in 1905. After a peripatetic childhood spent in England, Austria, Germany and Switzerland, Nazi persecution forced Canetti's Jewish family (whose forebears had themselves fled the Inquisition of Spain) to settle in England. He produced works in all major genres except poetry and his two most famous books are the novel *Die Blendung* (1935, *Auto da Fe*) and the socio-political work *Masse und Macht* (1965, *Crowds and Power*). In 1981 Elias Canetti won the Nobel Prize for Literature. He died in Zurich in 1994. The extract reproduced here is taken from his 1967 work *Die Stimmen von Marrakesch*, translated into English, under the title *Voices of Marrakesh*, by J. A. Underwood. This extraordinarily beautiful collection of essays came about almost by chance, for Canetti only came to Morocco as a guest of Orson Welles, who was filming *Othello* at Safi, El Jadida and Essaouira.

'Aysha's *Dyafa*

from *A Year in Marrakesh* by Peter Mayne

'Aysha sent her daughter round this morning with a message. I supposed it was the girl employed at 'Aysha's *alma mater*, and when she had delivered the message (which I scarcely understood, as a matter of fact) I asked her if she worked.

'*Iyyeh*,' she said, nodding.

'Where?' I asked vaguely, pretending that it really didn't matter at all to me, though I longed to know. She looked so small to be working, even if she isn't allowed to do much more than the menial tasks of the household.

'*Ed-dar el-merhba*,' she said. The house of the Bienvenu. 'Abdeslem was peeping out of his charcoal-booth and called to her:

'You're getting quite big, aren't you?' and the girl nodded seriously. 'What have you come here for?'

I was glad of this question because I hadn't followed exactly what it was all about. The girl repeated what she had presumably told me, and 'Abdeslem looked at me in inquiry, as if to ask if I had understood.

' 'Aysha is giving a *dyafa* tonight. She asks you to come too.'

A *dyafa* is a party. 'A proper *dyafa*? With dancers?'

'Very proper. You will come? I will tell the girl you will come, *yak*?'

'Of course I will come!'

The child was following all this and directly she heard that I was coming too, *Insha'Allah*, she said something softly and quickly to 'Abdeslem. 'Abdeslem nodded and turned back to me.

'What will you bring?' he asked.

'I shall bring . . . Well, what shall I bring? Wine?'

'Not wine,' he said in the voice of one who has caught another out in a social gaffe. 'Not wine. You had better bring chickens.' He swung round to the girl, asking: 'Chickens?'

'Abdeslem was taking so keen an interest in 'Aysha's *dyafa* that I wondered

24

whether there had been a reconciliation between him and the hostess. I had heard nothing to that effect.

'Have you been reconciled to 'Aysha, then?' I whispered to him behind my hand. I have noticed that this is the polite way of exchanging a confidence in the presence of others who ought not to be allowed to hear. 'Abdeslem took up the pan from his charcoal scales to whisper behind and said:

'I shall come too, *Insha'Allah*. But don't tell them. I don't want her to make anything – *fahemti-ni*? You follow? – anything *spécial. Ti vois?*'

I said to the child: 'Thank you very much, and may the blessing of God be upon you, my little love. I will come, if God wills, and I will bring for you two chickens. Tell your noble mother that I ask God to bless her.' I said it in Arabic without a halt. I was rather pleased with myself, and I don't think I have ever before managed to say such a long sentence extempore.

She smiled, pretended to kiss my hand, started forward as if to kiss 'Abdeslem's and then didn't after all (so perhaps the reconciliation is still incomplete), and left us. I think I saw 'Aysha's head-scarf – the one with pictures of the Sultan printed on it in full colour – whisk back into her door as the girl went in. So probably 'Aysha had been watching the conversation. She generally watches everything that goes on in our *derb*, but I had the impression that this was important, because of 'Abdeslem.

'Who else is coming to the party?' I asked 'Abdeslem.

'I do not know. But I think there will certainly be the gentleman from the *Postes et Télégraphes* – the one who brings the letters. And his fiancée,' ("fiancée" is usually said in French, and means something less, and yet something more, than in French) 'and also perhaps Sidi Bou Djem'a. And others who 'Aysha has known. Will you wear the *costume gris*? Yes? I do not consider that the *cravate marron rayée vert* is quite good for that *costume*. I was seeing you two days ago so dressed and I was thinking, "*Tiens!* What *dommage!* That *cravate* does not at all go with that *costume*." '

'Do *you* want to wear the *cravate marron rayée vert* then?'

He had started to make a little pyramid of charcoal and now popped a big piece on top as a sort of cairn.

'*B-el-haqq*, I had not considered yet. But yes, if you wish. With my *veste en velours vert*? Is it that you propose?'

'I think *that* is what we had in mind, isn't it?'

It was the first time I had entered 'Aysha's house, and I was surprised to find how completely equipped it is for a party such as this. Of course she may have borrowed things too. The walls of the principal room were hung with *haitis* and wherever there was space on the little tables she had put vases filled with paper flowers. She had also made paper shades for the electric-light bulbs of which there were two in the room, and a third which came in on the end of a long flex from the patio and was hooked over a picture-frame.

When I got there I found 'Abdeslem already seated on one of the divans. The *'amara* and *siniya* and tea-things had been placed before him which most certainly means that he is back in favour. The senior guest is traditionally given the honour of making and pouring out the mint-tea. He was busy preparing the first brew, but he found time to look up and make me a dignified bow from the waist. 'Aysha was rapturous, in a succession of muslin dresses, each with its embroidered blazon of flowers. She also wore her gold-braid cordage and belts, a new *sibniya* with bobbles on it, and a good deal of golden jewellery on her arms and neck and ears and forehead, and some on the breast too. I had never seen her before like this and I thought she looked lovely. I told her so and she pinched me on the behind and said: '*Ma shufti shay!*' by which I suppose she meant 'Just wait! You haven't seen a thing.' Then she introduced me to Si Fulan (*Postes et Télégraphes*) and his fiancée, a girl named Zwina who was behaving very demurely and didn't want to take off her veil till 'Aysha insisted. She was not very pretty when she took it off. There were two or three other men as well, one of them a big negro dressed in a black-and-white striped *djellaba*. He said his name was Bou Djem'a. Everyone was very welcoming and nice, and 'Abdeslem was by now starting to serve the tea. He had already tasted the brew in the special tasting glass, nodded approvingly, poured what remained in the glass back into the tea-pot and looked round at us. A dozen little glasses of about the size and shape of the small tumblers used for claret in nineteenth-century England stood in front of him. They had rims decorated in various colours. 'Aysha came round with a plate of biscuits.

I dare say that parties of this kind always start very formally. Each talked to his neighbours, and I did the best I could with mine – the big negro Bou Djem'a on one side, the fiancée Zwina on the other. They were very patient with my Arabic, and spoke slowly and clearly – at least Bou Djem'a did – so that I might understand: or perhaps this is the way he ordinarily talks. More people came in and sat down, but 'Aysha did not always introduce new-comers. I think that some of them were not considered up to much socially. I thought I saw the water-carrier, for example, but when I looked again he had gone. Perhaps I was mistaken. 'Aysha's two children were acting as servitors and I expect there was some slaveling outside in the little patio, to keep the braziers going and help serve.

For the dinner we had to group ourselves round two or three circular tables drawn up to the divans, managing as best we might. I could see that with all the will in the world my two chickens could not feed the party, and when food came it proved to be a sort of *tajin* - beef stewed with black olives and *poivrons*. Not bad, but I wondered about my chickens. A second dish arrived after the *tajin* and this time it was my chickens: stewed with rounds of lemon. The other tables were being given something else which I could not clearly see. Finally *cous-cous*. I have eaten *cous-cous* in Paris and been told that it would be much better in North Africa. Now I have eaten it in Morocco and I think that it must probably be much better in Algeria or somewhere else. It seems to me that semolina is always less good than rice, even indifferent rice, and the meat accompaniment was unremarkable. We finished the dish all the same.

It was a filling meal all right. We sat back contentedly. We had eaten with our fingers in the ordinary way, the fingers of the right hand. Si Fulan's fiancée, beside me, had done so with tremendous gentility and when she had finished there was scarcely any grease on her at all. What there was she managed to clean off with no more than a couple of ladylike licks and then sat with her hands held together in front of her to let them dry out. Bou Djem'a was different. I watched entranced as he worked a huge pink tongue round and round his knuckles. He saw me watching and smiled comfortably.

'*Mezian*,' he remarked, examining his fingers.

Then sweets: big, black slabs like fudge, and a *gâteau* very similar to *mille-feuilles* but oozing with honey. The sweets were really the best part of the meal, I think, and I took more of the fudge, to Bou Djem'a's amusement.

'*Mezian oula la?*' he asked. It was good, and I said so. 'But I prefer when it is more sugared,' he went on. 'When you come to my house you shall see. My woman makes *nimero wahad*.' Number one: first class!' 'Abdeslem caught my eye from the next table, nodding as 'Aysha offered me still more. But there is a limit after all, and I said: 'No thank you. Later perhaps.' They were bringing

27

round an ewer and a basin with towels and soap and we all cleaned ourselves up.

Even before they served the next glass of mint-tea someone had taken out a stringed instrument and was tuning it. Nobody had asked him to play as far as I know, but it was reasonable that he should. It was a little two-stringed instrument, both strings tuned to the same note. The body was pendant-shaped, wood probably, covered with coarse hide. Si Fulan's fiancée leaned across me to say something confidential to Bou Djem'a and in doing so stamped on my foot. I moved it, and she stamped again, so I wondered if after all she had meant it the first time. Bou Djem'a whispered back to her and everyone looked their way. But Si Fulan seemed quite unperturbed about it. The musician had started to sing meanwhile.

It was less a song than a story, and the music was less music than an intermittent twanging to mark pauses between stanzas, or simply when the singer wanted a rest, like on the Djema'a el-Fna. Tea was on its way round again. Everybody sipped it with a great intake of breath, partly because it was so hot and partly because it is considered better taken this way – just a few drops at a time and a great deal of air.

In the middle of the song and the tea-drinking some more guests arrived, amongst them the night-watchman of our *derb* and a girl who, on taking off her *haik,* was so pretty that we all stopped sipping to look. The fiancée gave a tiny little snort. Even the singer stopped. Bou Djem'a quite frankly said, 'Ah–h . . . !' very loudly indeed, followed by some kissing noises.

'*Halwa? Zid, jbed shuwiya,*' the fiancee said softly, holding out the plate of sweetmeats. '*Hadak. El-kahla . . .*' She picked up a piece of the black fudge and gave it to me, smiling. I took it and thanked her. The singer had started a new song and Si Fulan stretched across the fiancée saying: '*C'est une autre chanson. Une nouvelle.* I will tell you what he is singing.' He speaks quite passable French and off he went, a sentence or so behind the singer.

'From a city of the cities of el-Moghreb a voyager set out on his way to Marrakesh. He was poor but vigorous, and he walked all day across plains and little hills with no thought for beasts or robbers because of the singing in his belly . . . '

'Do you like Si Fulan's fiancée?' Bou Djem'a whispered to me.

'No. Not much.'

'Neither do I. She is too thin. Look at her! Too thin.'

'I don't want to look at her.' I was looking at the new girl as a matter of fact, and Bou Djem'a noticed this.

'*That* is the good one. *Meziana! Hadak meziana*,' and he made more kissing noises. I tried to stop him, but he paid no attention, and Si Fulan was prodding at me across the fiancée. 'Listen,' he was saying:

' . . . But by eventide when the sun left the world and all became darkness the voyager was weary and perhaps frightened too . . . '

'Abdeslem had left the room a moment before and now returned, but instead of going back to his seat he shamelessly wedged himself in between the new girl and the night-watchman. I could see that 'Aysha was not pleased.

' . . . lamp-light flowing from a window,' continued Si Fulan, raising his voice slightly to drown the very indecent noises that Bou Djem'a was now aiming across to the far divan. 'The voyager entered. "I wish of God and of you," said he to the widow woman, "to eat and to drink and to rest for the night, for I have voyaged all day without sustenance." '

'Give me a *halwa*,' Bou Djem'a hissed at me but without looking. I stretched for the plate and he took two. One he popped straight into his own mouth and the second he thrust vaguely in the direction of mine, still without looking. I ate it out of politeness and then turned back to Si Fulan in answer to his tweaking. He seemed mildly annoyed at my divided attention and allowed it to show in his voice, though it did not at all suit the context:

' "Alas, I have nought but these chickens that you see," replied the widow woman, pointing about the hut, "and the three boiled eggs that even now complete their cooking upon the fire." "*Merci beaucoup*," remarked the voyager and he took and ate the three eggs.'

I saw with interest that 'Aysha had beckoned away the night-watchman and that he now came back to the divan, smacked the new girl on the leg and quickly slipped into the space beside her in the moment that she recoiled under the blow. It was stuffy in the room, but I was very content. In fact I felt wonderful, and I thought the new girl looked wonderful too, warm, and such big brown eyes – would they be brown? I was uncertain at that distance – big, anyway. I think I started to tell Bou Djem'a about it. I wanted to make some sort of plan, but Si Fulan was really being tiresomely exacting:

'You must listen. *Vous etes obligé a m'entendre! Voyons!*'

'He does not wish to listen,' the fiancée said coldly to him. 'He is watching that little *qahba*.'

'*Qahba*,' murmured Bou Djem'a contentedly.

'Next day the voyager thanked the widow woman, made his farewell and left on his journey to Marrakesh and after several years he became rich and important whereas the widow woman remained poor.'

'Good,' I said, without thinking.

'Good? What can you mean?' Si Fulan was indignant.

'I'm sorry,' I said. 'I meant "bad"; I'm very sorry.' I don't know what had come over me. I felt as if I was likely to start laughing soon and I searched my brain for the funny circumstance that was responsible. 'I can't think,' I said, or something of the sort.

'You have only to listen,' Si Fulan said sternly. 'You have eaten too much *halwa*. That's what it is.'

My brain was getting clearer and clearer. I saw exactly what sort of plan I had to make. I think I squeezed the fiancée a little in order to console her for being so thin and plain when the new girl was so beautiful and, momentarily inattentive, I did not notice that Bou Djem'a had slipped away on hands and knees. It was only when I turned to outline my plan to him that I found him gone. He was several yards distant by now and my blood was up. Treachery! I jumped up, flew across the room and brought him back. I was of course very powerful at the time.

'He is crying,' the fiancée said morosely, nodding towards Bou Djem'a, and it was true. 'I tire of these tears. Men,' she said. '*Men*. Even a little piece of *halwa* is stronger than a man.'

Si Fulan had been droning on all this time and suddenly realized that I had not heard. He was very angry.

'You are missing the fine part!' he cried. 'Have you heard how an enemy of the voyager-now-rich goes to the widow and causes her to complain to the Pasha? Have you heard?'

'No. I'm sorry. I seem to have been very busy lately. But what had she to complain of? And what have *you* to complain of, Si Fulan?' My voice sounded very loud.

'Hush,' he said placatingly. 'Nothing for me. But *she* had. The enemy of the now-rich voyager makes her to complain to the Pasha in this way: "O sir, think of my riches gone! Think of my three little eggs from which would have emerged chicks, and think of the eggs they too were waiting to lay, and the more chicks, and this throughout the years that this rich man is being rich in Marrakesh and me poor in my hovel. Think!" '

'The fine part is now coming,' said the fiancée.

Am I mistaken? Was she speaking French? Could she?

'Good,' I said politely. The new girl seemed to be looking up sideways at 'Abdeslem across the night-watchman, and 'Abdeslem's arm was stretched across the night-watchman's shoulders quite as far as her neck, which I was certain could mean no good for anyone. 'You had better tell 'Aysha,' I whispered to Bou Djem'a, but unfortunately Bou Djem'a was sleeping. We did not like to disturb him.

' . . . "Where is the defendant?" cried the Pasha?' Si Fulan was making a glorious effort. ' . . . "But where is the defendant?" A man stepped forward very neat and said: "By your leave I am sent by the defendant to say he is unable to come today." "And why?" asked the Pasha. "Because he is gone to his fields," the neat man replied. "What does he in those fields?" "I think, monsieur, that he is at planting out boiled beans so that he may reap a rich harvest in the years to come – richer even than from boiled eggs!" Thereupon the Pasha laughed heartily and dismissed the case.'

Bou Djem'a had woken and said: '*Halwa.*'

'Do not give,' the fiancée muttered. 'Already he is useless with *halwa.*'

Si Fulan was beaming at me through the mist that had come up in the last few minutes. 'Now tell me how you enjoyed the story, monsieur,' he said, but somehow, nice as he was, I had no wish to speak with him. I wished to speak to the new girl. I don't exactly remember the sequence of events – whether perhaps it was now that I danced a slow romantic valse in the costume of a Hussar; there was certainly a horse somewhere, and flashes of fire from the horse's nostrils, probably. And Bou Djem'a behaved rather badly in some way that I now forget, something to do with the fiancée, I fancy, though possibly that was later, and not Bou Djem'a at all. Much later. I am uncertain of the time . . .

I awoke late this morning, fresh as a daisy but disorientated. I am sorry to say that the fiancée was there, and that actually it was she who woke me. I don't really like her very much and I cannot think how it came about that she was in my house at all, but she was, and when she brought me my mint-tea, she gave a smacking kiss and said: '*Min daba kull sbah nesaub-lek atay, yak?*' which means that henceforth this fiancée whom I don't in the least care about intended to wake me each morning with a pot of mint-tea. I looked round for Si Fulan but he did not seem to be there.

'Where is Si Fulan?' I asked her reprovingly.

'*Min f-id-dar dyal-uh* . . . He must be in his house. I am your fiancée now!'

She looks awful in the light of day – but then I dare say that I do too. I didn't quite know what to do about it. And what about Si Fulan? Would he be pleased? I had to consult with 'Aysha quietly, perhaps with 'Abdeslem too. Between them they would know how to deal with such a situation. What had happened to the 'new girl', incidentally?

'Give me money and I will buy *svenj*,' the fiancée was saying. *Svenj* are little *beignets* in rings and I cannot say how much I disliked the thought of them. But I thought too that if once she were out of the house – on this loving errand, for example - perhaps it would be easier. So I gave her money.

'The *svenj* I prefer are to be purchased from a stall opposite the *tabac* on the Djema'a el-Fna,' I told her. Somehow my tongue did not seem to get round the Arabic words as well as it ought. Last night there had been no difficulty with it at all.

She had the effrontery to pout: 'What a long way . . . '

'Never mind, my little love,' I said. 'You have good strong legs.' She has, too. She had hitched up her overskirts, for housework I suppose, and I could see them. She took the money and went.

Directly I heard the front door shut, I hurried out of bed and ran downstairs. Bou Djem'a was lying asleep in the vestibule. On the floor. This was getting too much. I went into the alley. 'Abdeslem's charcoal-shop was shuttered. 'Aysha's door was closed too, but I crossed and knocked on it. Neighbours were passing and smiled at me, and one of them laughed outright. Then 'Aysha came to her door.

Thank God for 'Aysha! She is wonderful. She said that I might leave the fiancée to her – and Bou Djem'a too, and that would be the end of it, but . . . Her lips tightened.

'You know about 'Abdeslem?' she asked.

'No. What about him?'

'And that little *putain* who came with the night-watchman? You do not know?'

'How should I know?'

'That girl is already with the Pasha's police because she is entirely without authority and must be punished. And 'Abdeslem is . . . well, 'Abdeslem . . . I have had to give him some little possets . . . You are aware of these possets . . . ? Yes, I thought you would know. Possets, and some rather particular powders and . . . A Berber lady helped and advised. It was necessary to hold 'Abdeslem down like a chicken that is to be filled. Friends very kindly assisted. If you require charcoal today, *cher* Monsieur Peter, I must ask you to go to the *brave homme* at the end of our *derb*. It seems that 'Abdeslem's *boutique* is locked from the outside . . . ' Slowly she wiggled a key on the end of a string. 'You enjoyed the *dyafa*, yes? Bou Djem'a also makes good *halwa* – he uses the *hashish* from his *bled:* he pretends it is better. But mine also is good, yes?'

ABOUT THE AUTHOR

PETER MAYNE was born in 1908 in England. At the age of twenty he went to Bombay to work in a firm of merchant-shippers. As a businessman he was less than successful, though he enjoyed easy access to Indian society through his father (a schoolmaster who specialised in educating the sons of ruling Indian princes). In Kashmir at the time of partition, Mayne was offered a job in the Ministry of Refugees and Rehabilitation of the new Government of Pakistan. After two years he resigned and moved to Morocco in order to write. *A Year in Marrakesh* – from his journal – tells of his time spent in that city, of the friends he made, his trials and experiences. While the novel he also wrote in this period has not survived, this journal won much acclaim. As can be seen in this extract, Mayne was a gifted composer of prose: the subtle way he shapes the *hashish*-addled recollection of a party given by one of his friends is one of the highlights of a wonderful book.

The Couscous of the Dead

from *Women of Marrakesh* by Leonora Peets

When we settled in Marrakesh in 1929, I was told that some old women would stealthily disinter corpses in the cemetery for mysterious reasons. I refused to believe it. Having come from Estonia, with a European way of thinking, I could not countenance such acts. Such tales had to be invention, a fantasy of the Arab mind – maybe widespread in oral folklore, but lacking any basis in fact.

Some years later, in 1935, I happened to glance at the local newspaper and was startled. In a matter-of-fact style, the police were reported as having caught two women in the act of busily digging up a body in a graveyard. So these macabre happenings actually went on. It said so, in black and white.

I continued to be puzzled. Why should anyone want to mess around with corpses?

In a roundabout way, I sought information from those Arab acquaintances with whom we had established a certain tie of friendship. I received no satis-factory response, but soon became convinced that the oasis city of Marrakesh hardly sheltered a single person unaware of the practice. People were evasive about the reasons – they merely expressed awe at the perpetrators' stouthearted-ness. Those reckless ones were not afraid of Aisha Qandisha, the ogre who roamed the cemeteries at night. Taller than a man, she had a woman's torso, a camel's legs, and a bloody wound beneath each eye. Her eyes glowing like coals, she pursued all humans, but was particularly fond of catching men.

I began to look at cemeteries more attentively. When passing by, I would sometimes step over the crumbling wall and walk among the mounds. The Moroccan graveyards were – and still are – treeless and bushless patches of desert. Skies glassy with the glowing sun made cemeteries look like mazes of trash piles or junk heaps dug up by moles. No human hand ever cared for those haphazardly scattered mounds, and no flower ever decorated them: why be concerned about earthly remains destined by Allah to decay? Only some of the most recent barrows had a tilting tile stuck into the ground at either end. Bodies were buried only a few spans deep, usually without a coffin, wrapped in cheap muslin. Nothing of value could be sought or found on them.

As I gradually became familiar with the nuances of Arabic, my ear started to catch such strange comments as:

'Mohammed is going like mad after Lila, the dancing girl. She must be feeding him kneecap.'

Another time:

'What else could Mustafa have died of but swallowing a ground tooth? And it happened right after he brought a new wife into the house, a really young one, in addition to his first wife.'

More frequently, it was said:

'These ashes are extremely potent against such and such an ailment – unfortunately they are also expensive.'

But I also overheard whispers:

'As soon as he had finished eating his dish of couscous, his guts were contorted by cramps. They probably stretched him out right next to the one whose hand had rolled the couscous granules.'

Finding a single missing letter may solve a crossword puzzle, and a single word made me grasp, one day, the meaning of all these disparate utterances. Add the word 'corpse' to the teeth, kneecaps and ashes, and you had the answer - one sought help from the dead against ailments of body and of soul.

Dead bones were to repel disease, and to help ward off witchcraft, widely practised in Morocco at that time. This practice was usually harmless, but there were many serious consequences too. Polygamy bred intrigue and quarrelling among the wives, each of whom was on the look-out for her own interests and those of her children. Small wonder, then, that the more potent cures were brought in from the graveyard, when every other means had failed to soothe despair and rage.

Due to the shallowness of the graves, it wasn't actually very difficult to pull out a few bones. One only had to be sure to pick an old grave where the sun had baked the bones through the thin covering of earth to a state of brittleness. The kneecap could easily be extracted from between the thighbone and the shin-bone. It was also rather easy to crush it into powder in a mortar. The kneecap was harmless. Burned to ashes, it was suitable for controlling disease and regulating love affairs.

The tooth was more dangerous. At times, it could kill. Pound and crush it as you might, its enamel would not completely disappear. If swallowed, the slightest amount of these tiny splinters could cause lesions in the intestines, causing pain and eventually even death.

But why was the speaker's voice hushed into a whisper, at times, when mentioning couscous in my presence? Why was it called the 'couscous of the dead'? Foolishness. Couscous is the Moroccan national dish, a tasty food made of semolina and flour rolled together on a tray, using the palms of the hand and slowly adding water until larger granules form. What could this have to do with the dead?

In time this question was cleared up too. The granules of the 'couscous of the dead' were to be rolled not by living hands, but by those of a relatively fresh corpse. Deadly cadaver toxins were thus absorbed.

My newly acquired knowledge was to be supplemented almost at first-hand. While visiting the market in Gueliz, the European quarter of Marrakesh, I could not help noticing an unusual couple: a uniformed French captain and his Arab common-law wife, Lalla Fatima. I knew neither of them personally, yet I had come to hear quite a lot about this lady. Fate had put me in a house next to that of Lalla Setti, who was Lalla Fatima's bosom friend. Arab blood also flowed in Lalla Setti's veins, and she too was an unwed live-in companion to a French official.

How clever she was! Lalla Setti was supremely adept at bossing her man around. With her unsophisticated natural instincts, she discovered and defused all dangers that could beset her in European surroundings. And she had provided against a rainy day by taking a lover of her own race.

My relations with Lalla Setti were those of good neighbours. We often offered each other a glass of mint tea. Lalla Fatima was casually mentioned in many of our chats, but one day I found Lalla Setti in a state of feverish excitement: the captain had turned Lalla Fatima out of his house.

'But why?' I asked. 'He even has a daughter by this woman.'

The story that followed was extraordinary. Incensed by what had happened, but also proud of her own success based on wise and skillful handling of her mate, Lalla Setti forgot prudence. In her confusion she trusted me with a most intimate secret about Lalla Fatima.

It seems that the captain's relations with his mistress had got markedly worse some time ago. All Lalla Fatima's expedients had failed: he was turning ever more impatient and bad-tempered. Having tried everything else, Fatima finally resorted to the ultimate remedy – to use the dead as a means of instilling submissiveness in the officer. With her mother, she stole off to the cemetery in the dead of the night. They scraped the dirt off a newly buried body, and then lifting it up into a sitting position, they momentarily dressed it in the captain's uniform jacket. But inexplicably the corpse's coolness, thus stored in the coat, was of no use in cooling down the captain's soul. The act produced a contrary effect: the captain went utterly wild and turned both Lalla Fatima and her daughter out of his house.

The very next day I met the captain in the street. My feet gave a jerk, and blood rushed into my head. He walked wearily, and the look on his face was obtuse. Was the uniform coat he was wearing the one that had had the macabre baptism? Like some learner driver irresistibly mesmerised by oncoming head-lights, I could only look at that coat. I moved towards it until, at the last moment, disgust made me swerve to one side.

'If you only knew!' I felt like shouting at the captain. Fighting down nausea, I rushed home with my burden of secrecy. Later I heard that the captain had moved to France, where he was stricken with paralysis and soon died.

About a year later I made the acquaintance of yet another nightly visitor to graveyards, although I did not know it at first. Lalla Hedda immediately aroused my interest. She was still quite young, with a very fair complexion and a pleasant face, but some indefinable melancholy seemed to weigh her down. Although her smile was warm, her eyes remained sad.

I met Hedda in a friendly Moroccan home, where she used to drop in and assist the mistress of the house in working on wool. Her job was to wash the matted sheep wool of old sitting mattresses, pluck it loose, and refill the ticks with clean wool. I wondered why a Muslim woman was doing such furniture work; as a rule, it was the job of male Jews to handle those long and heavy sitting mattresses.

One day, while Lalla Hedda was working there, plucking tufts of wool apart in her usual withdrawn manner, I could not resist asking the hostess about Hedda's background.

'She's without husband or child.'

That was odd. Why would such a comely woman stay single, when ugly women, and even those with deformities, had procured a husband, making full use of the prevalent custom of not letting the groom see the bride before the wedding night?

And then the mistress of the house told me. Listening, I felt as if the words came directly from Hedda herself, at the only time when this human being had gathered enough courage to open her tormented heart to my hostess.

You know well, honourable mistress, that I am without kin. As a child, I was picked up from the street, during the Great Famine, by the widowed Lalla Tammou, so that I could run errands for her. As I grew up, I became her companion. My foster-mother evoked in me obedience and respect, which was not without fear. No one knew herbs better than she did. Making use of their beneficial or poisonous properties, she brewed remedies for various purposes. She dealt in witchcraft too, which is why I dreaded her. People came from far and near to seek her help, and the thump of the door-knocker frequently echoed in our patio.

Although two living rooms led off this patio, one of them was usually locked up. This was not done to spare the sitting mattress with its new multicoloured muslin cover; Tammou's chest of valuables was in there. It felt sinister, and I kept away from it. The chest contained potent materials like aloe and myrrh for subduing spirits, and coriander and leather shavings for conjuring demons. It also contained human hair, bits of nails, and urine – and even more efficacious ingredients out of which Tammou knew how to brew a sensational love potion by adding the right amount of finely-pestled Spanish flies.

At times my mistress would send me to work with Ba'aba Bohbot, a Jew who was buying up huge amounts of herbs to sell them overseas to the Christians. To clean and screen these herbs, the Jew needed many hands, especially in the spring, when the donkeys carried in entire loads of orange blossoms and rose buds, and when the poppy flowers were heaped high in the storage shed.

At home Lalla Tammou made me pestle strange mixtures in a mortar, and after dusk I had to pay strict attention not to step accidentally over the mortar. Lalla Tammou gave me a stern warning about that. You can well understand, honourable mistress, what untold misfortunes I, a parentless child, could suffer if I strode over all that witchcraft.

Lalla Tammou was often away from home. At times she even vanished at night, leaving me alone. I was scared and anguished when that happened.

When I had started to grow up, a new family moved in next to us. Their eldest son was called Larbi, and there was no handsomer young man in the world. He had a friendly look, and when he laughed his teeth flashed like chunks of sugar on the grocer's counter. I observed him through a door that I held scarcely open, as he strode to or from work, his bearing calm and self-assured. Although his job was irrigating the fields beyond the city walls, he wore city clothes. Once he removed his turban to rewrap it, and I noticed that the top of his head was not shaven clean: he followed the new fashion of letting the hair grow.

One day, coming from the public baking oven, a bread board with the hot loaf balanced on my head. I wanted to open our house door, but the corner of my *haik* got stuck round the knocker. The loaf almost fell off. As I grabbed the bread board with both hands, my *haik* unwrapped itself, uncovering my face. At that very moment the neighbour's door flew open, and Larbi almost bumped into me. He saw my naked countenance! Utterly ashamed, I escaped into the house. Yet from that day Larbi was different. It was odd how we now seemed to encounter each other more frequently, and I felt as if he was now keeping on the lookout. Then, as we passed in the street, he whispered:

'Oh gazelle! the light for my eyes!'

His voice, hot and sweet like mint tea, made my body glow. I began to hope that he might marry me, because his mother addressed me with increased kindliness. Pointing at me with her finger, she said meaningfully to Tammou: 'If my son wants to buy our own country's wheat, be it so! – even if it be but barley.'

Rumours flew that Larbi was saving for bride purchase money. My joy knew no bounds, and I was eagerly waiting for the matchmaker.

A haughty and corpulent lady, the oldest of the three wives of Berra'ada the merchant had become Lalla Tammou's most steadfast client. Tammou prepared charms for her to guard against her co-wives' evil eye. I once went with my foster-mother to the cemetery around noon. With her she took the merchant's slippers, one filled with grain, the other with salt. After pouring the contents on a mound and placing the slippers on top of it, Tammou kept circling the grave, spinning around herself and wildly waving her arms. As we went away, we left the slippers behind. I was quivering all over, thinking about the merchant. From now on he could no longer make love with his two younger wives – the grip of the dead had drained his bodily strength.

Lately that merchant's wife had become worried again, and her visits became more frequent. Then Tammou announced that we had to go to the graveyard once more to deal with the merchant – this time for good.

The fateful day arrived. Already in the morning, my foster mother made preparations, piling all sorts of stuff, even food, into the basket. We left in the late afternoon. To my astonishment, Tammou attached a short-handled hoe under both her caftan and mine, and, after we had gone out through the city gate, she led me to a place quite a long way from the cemetery. We sat down in, the shelter of some dense bushes and ate the bread and the dates we had brought with us. Only when night fell did Lalla Tammou initiate me into her plans, and I became filled with anxiety, as if someone had squeezed my entrails. I was to help her dig up a girl who had been buried only the day before. I was not to resist or even hesitate. Now I understood why Tammou had left home several days in succession: she had kept watch outside the city gate for a funeral procession to pass by.

We did not leave the bush until past midnight. There was no sound. A new moon lay over on its back, and one could easily find one's way about by its faint glow.

I was scared stiff, and walked close to my foster-mother. We stepped over the low graveyard wall, and then, stumbling in the maze of graves, we tried to make our way towards the dark mass of some date palms. Reaching the trees, Tammou searched until she located the mound – she had memorised where it was. Higher and more fresh than all others, anyone could tell that it was a recent one.

We took our hoes out from underneath our clothes, and on harsh command from Tammou I started striking the mound along with her to get the earth away. We soon reached the smooth surface underneath. In spite of the darkness Tammou found the contours of the actual pit. Its width towards each end was as usual – one span plus four finger-widths – and around the centre it corresponded to the width of an adult person. It did not take much effort to shovel the gravelly dirt out of that narrow ditch, since the grave had not yet settled. Soon my hoe banged against something hard – one of the bricks which were laid in two rows, tilting against each other and forming a sharp-ridged roof over the body. We put down our hoes and, kneeling, continued tossing the dirt out with our bare hands.

Removing the first brick was hard work, but the others came out easily. The whitish shimmer of the shroud was now visible, and the sight struck me with horror. Up to that point I had worked away as if I was in a daze, but now I stiffened, and a brick fell from between my fingers, landing on the corpse with a dark thud.

'May Allah punish you with fever!' Lalla Tammou hissed.

The roof over the corpse's head we left intact. Tammou cautiously lowered her legs into the pit, next to the shins, and barely had room to stand on one leg. From her bosom she pulled out a candle which she lit with a match, passed it all over the length of the body, and then directed the flickering light into the niche at the head. The human shape, wrapped in muslin, was wedged into the grave, lying on its right side, so that it looked towards Mecca. I was brought to my senses by Tammou's shouting for the rope. She pulled it through underneath the corpse's shins, then she tied a knot and threw one end to me.

'We'll soon have her out!' she mumbled, climbing out of the pit on all fours. 'She found favour with Allah: look how loosely she fits into the grave. There was no need to force her in. Now we just have to keep pulling!'

Our joint efforts made the body start to move. The smoothness of the palm-leaf mat at the bottom of the grave made it slide more easily. However, the last part of the operation was complicated by the fact that the corpse had been placed on its side. Again Tammou went down into the pit, and tried to turn it over on to its back. The ditch was so narrow that she barely succeeded, and then only because the girl was so small. We battled away until the legs surfaced. Tammou jumped into the pit a third time. Gasping from the strain, she heaved the corpse while I pulled at it by the legs. At last we made it, and the shrouded corpse was spread out at the edge of the grave like a serpent in its sheath.

I was at the end of my strength. Panting and shivering all over, I closed my eyes and sat down with cold sweat on my forehead. But there was little time for resting.

'Up you get!' Tammou snapped, and I staggered to my feet again.

Tammou had cut the shroud on each side, and pulled out the girl's hands – I stared at them with an indescribable sense of ghastliness, for they were not as one would expect a corpse to be, but gruesomely yellow. A woollen thread round the wrists denoted a bride. Finally it occurred to me that the yellow was caused by saffron, a solution used by those who wash corpses to rub over the hands and faces of virgins.

'Come on!' Tammou said hoarsely. 'Help me to sit her up!'

Lifted up by the shoulders, the corpse insisted on bending forwards, and it would have dropped back into the pit if Tammou had not pushed it to lean against me.

'Hold her up!' she hissed, piercing me with her vicious glance. 'May leprosy attack your heels if you let her go!' I did not doubt the seriousness of the threat or the potency of Tammou's curse.

The torso pressed with a leaden weight against my chest. Its icy cold came through my clothes, and into the very marrow of my bones. The stench was sickening. I wanted to jump up and run away, but Tammou had already placed the sowing tray in the corpse's lap, thrown in one fistful of couscous and another of flour, and sprayed water from a bottle over the top. Seizing the arms she began to revolve these lifeless hands in circles, against the bottom of the tray. They rustled softly.

How long did the preparation of couscous granules last? I have no idea because I was on the verge of fainting when Tammou finally allowed me to set the body down. I pulled my hands away so quickly that the corpse crashed on its back, and the sweatcloth unravelled itself, revealing the face – which was a grisly saffron yellow. My knees were bending, and I felt as if my feet were growing roots to stay forever in that graveyard.

Then a diffuse distant buzz roused me from my stupor. Tammou and I listened: there was no doubt it was human voices. By now we could also hear the sound of steps - and see the silhouettes of three men moving straight toward us. Were they some irrigators of the fields returning home from the night shift and emboldened by 'safety in numbers' to take a short cut through the cemetery?

They stopped. Had they been disturbed, by something? Had the faint glow of the candle deep down in the pit given us away? After hesitating a moment, they came on towards us. We panicked.

'Push!' said Tammou, 'push that offspring of dogs into the pit!'

We shoved with all our might, and down it went, head first and half-bent. Tammou pushed two candles into my hand: 'Light them!' She grabbed a hoe, covered it with her white *haik,* and lifted it high above her head. With the other hand she held the two candles in front of the *haik.* I got it: this object was to represent the fiery-eyed demon head turning Tammou into the high-necked Aisha-Qandisha.

In this guise, she reeled towards the intruders, and two of them immediately turned on their heels and ran. The third, more courageous, stood his ground. I heard him pronounce the formula to repel demons: '*Besmellah rahman rahim!*'

I knew this voice! Where had I heard it before? Allah, Allah, it could not be . . . Yes, it was Larbi.

Once more, Larbi implored God for help. Fear overcame him. The bogey woman was all set to drag him away, and satisfy her lust right there among the mounds. Never again would he see his home and his mother. The bogey would bury him alive in this graveyard.

'A tool made of steel!' The thought flashed simultaneously through my mind and Larbi's. Cutting steel – the only way to defeat Aisha-Qandisha!

It all happened fast as lightning. In a few bounds Larbi rushed up, something whistled through the air, and Tammou's fearful scream resounded through the cemetery. Struck down, she howled like a dog caught under a cartwheel. Her voice too must have sounded somewhat familiar, because Larbi stepped closer.

'You' he cried, appalled. 'Lalla Tammou!' The two neighbours stared at each other.

'So it's you, you damned bastard!' Tammou bawled. 'Curses to you! May a bullet strike you! May your guts be torn to pieces! You interrupted my work, and you cut my hand off with your spade!'

'And what are you doing here?'

'May hell's fires parch you!' Tammou writhed in pain. 'What was I doing? I was turning a child round in the right position. It had been buried carelessly, face down and so its mother could not bear other children. Out of the goodness of my heart I came to readjust that child – and now you have killed me. Curse you!'

But Larbi went to the pit. His glance took in the adult body, and the couscous tray – it was all as clear as daylight. At one swoop he tore off my *haik.* His face was hard and grim. Kicking the couscous aside, he jumped into the pit, and set the corpse on its side.

'Pull the legs straight!' he told me, and his words were like whiplashes.

And then the most horrible event of all . . . In my haste to obey Larbi's command, and confused as I was, I stepped over the grave. At once the consciousness of my terrible position pierced me like a red-hot skewer. Astride above an open grave, worthy mistress! Happiness was now to be excluded for ever from my life. There was no more point in pouring my heart out to Larbi – explanations and reconciliations were of no use when I could not any longer make a fitting wife for him, or for any other man. Striding over the grave had turned me barren. No child could ever be conceived in my womb. Never.

Larbi quickly filled in the pit and left. We hobbled home, I burdened by the basket full of tools and by my tormented soul, and Tammou moaning and nursing her hand.

The very next night I fled and sought shelter with Ba'aba Bohbot's wife to serve her in exchange for a crumb of bread. Living among the Jews – that's where I learned the wool trade. Lalla Tammou's hand shrivelled away. Now she begs on street corners.

And how could I, a minor slave, avoid the fate that Allah had assigned to me? Faced with the inevitable, I can only say: humans cannot escape the alternation of day and night, nor can they escape death. Let us be submissive to Him.

I should supplement the notes I made at that time by mentioning two much later events. Despite the fact that the graveyard walls had been raised higher and guards had been hired, a newspaper in Marrakesh reported in 1959 that a corpse had been dug out. The same year in March a human skeleton used for anatomy lessons at the French high school in Casablanca vanished from a classroom without a trace.

Are we entitled to react with contempt to such happenings? For we follow in the footsteps of those who use corpses for magic by exchanging our dimmed corneas for those of the dead, and by acquiring their hearts and other organs.

ABOUT THE AUTHOR

LEONORA PEETS spent forty-five years in Morocco with her husband, physician Rudolf Peets. She was born in Tannin, Estonia in 1899 and moved to Marrakesh in 1929. While there she had journal articles published, in Estonian, and a selection of these articles were collected and translated by her nephew, Rein Taagepera, in the volume *Women of Marrakesh* (1988). Though not a trained anthropologist, her episodic writings – prose snapshots, almost – show a deep interest in and enthusiasm for the lives and beliefs of Marrakeshis and at points – most notably in *The Couscous of the Dead* – she seems to manage a complete empathy with their mind-set.

Houses that Sang and Danced, Blossomed and Burgeoned

Christopher Gibbs

My friend Paul Getty came to Marrakesh on his honeymoon. His beautiful young bride Talitha shared with him a yearning for the exotic. Both had tasted the dolce vita life of Rome and the bliss and freak years of late 1960s London, so 'le plus proche des pays lointains' was a natural point of call, and, besides their old friend from Rome and London, Bill Willis, had just wintered in Tangier, so they scooped him up and descended on the Mamounia. It was 1967 and Marrakesh a much smaller, yet more charming city. The Pasha Glaoui had died disgraced and Muhammad V, grandfather of his present Majesty Muhammad VI (whom God preserve) had returned to the throne of his ancestors, succeeded within a very short time by his son Hassan II. The framework of the French administration over which the Pasha had so long presided was being subsumed into a new Moroccan bureaucracy, but many of the players in the old regime were still living in their shuttered villas and out-of-town orange groves.

After a few days unwinding in the cool walks and scented alleys of the Mamounia garden, they began to explore, aided by Bill Willis and a native courtier (an ambulant middleman who knows who owns what and what is for sale): discovering behind drab walls the many tumbledown palaces about the town, mostly empty and decayed with vines, jasmine and bougainvillea beginning to blur the architecture, pigeons cooing in the crumbling eaves, and ancient guardians – sebsis in hand – brewing tea at the gate.

Rejecting the vast palace of the Caid Ayadi by the Bab el Khemis, and other dauntingly decayed offerings near the Place Djemma el Fna, they fell for the Palais Zahia at Sidi Mimoun, within a stones throw of Bab Rob and open country, yet snug in the sainted corner of the city where Muhammad VI has now made his Marrakesh home. A short street runs west to the Hopital de la Mamounia with high walls masking a great tiled Riad and smaller courts including the old harem with its painted ceilings, old *zellij* and little fountain. They bought it from Monsieur Egret, its banished proprietor, for £7,000. The Monsieur was a French adventurer and Glaoui protégé whose life was ruled by the pendulum, which he would pass over menus and maps, to help him to decide what to eat today or where to buy land tomorrow.

Handsome green eyed Irish-American Bill Willis, a citizen of Memphis, New York, Rome and London, thought he was in heaven when he found himself in Marrakesh. The warmth of its people, the splendour of its landscape, the lamplit poetry of its dusty gamey fragrant streets moved him deeply as he got to know the town and discovered the many hidden wonders of its architecture. He discovered too, that craftsmen still lived, carving cedar wood, chipping out exploding starbursts of mosaic *zellij*, and chasing freehand Suras from the Qur'an along stucco friezes. Its hard to realise how things have changed in 35 years. Then only the Court and the Mosque employed a dwindling band of practictioners in their ancient skills. The *Riads* of the Medina and the Kasbah were falling down and most rich Moroccans ignoring the splendours of their past, were moving with relief into concrete villas in the leafy suburbs, where plumbing and electricity were better organised. Much of the revival – indeed survival – of these ancient skills is due to Willis, to his patrons and to his pasticheurs. His, though, the vision, the innate understanding, getting always to the essence of design, the just balance of sobriety and ornament, the true harmony of colours.

With Maalam Houman, a Marrakeshi builder of long experience and gentle wisdom, he built a team of craftsmen who transformed the seedy shambles into a house of gaiety and beauty with the good old elements cherished and freshened and much new work in the garden bright spirit of the old. Moulay Kebir, bearded, Senegalais *sebsi* at hand, sat on the wall and translated. Now my oldest and dearest Moroccan friend, Moulay Kebir was in those far off days swift to surprise: producing a snake charmer and a box of cobras to frighten a parcel of London ladies or munificently buying, from off their heads, the shell-covered caps of the dancing Gnaoua in the square.

The expatriate community was diverse as were its social interweavings with its Moorish hosts. At the Villa Taylor, Madame de Breteuil, patrician widow, slight, fair, blue-eyed and veined used to mix visiting grandees with the local gratin, entertaining deliciously on folding campaign chairs painted with gay arabesques. Smoke darkened portraits by Van Loo looked down on worn yet still glittering *zelij* and out through cool arcades to a jungly garden. Out at Dar Tunzi along a dusty track among olives and palm was the pisé farmhouse of the painter Ira Belin and her holy fool brother the bearded Ganya. Her salon, formed from rough earth walls and a ceiling of palm trunks, was dominated by a painted eighteenth-century Chinoiserie screen. Ira, hair scraped back and bound in a blue kerchief a la Russe, was Stravinsky's niece, had been Barbara Hutton's secretary, a Tangier art dealer and was a grand survivor. A corner of her farm was used by John Hopkins, blond American writer and his tousel-headed friend Joe MacPhillips, long since headmaster of the American School in Tangier. The Canadian Christopher Wanklyn lived deep in the *derb*, his little *Riad* alive with singing birds and tinkling fountains, his walls covered with small portraits of sloe eyed young men, whilst in a darkened room inside lay his friend Boujmaa, master and slave of *mahjoun*, connoiseur of Berber weavings, plump, sleek and dandified.

Nearer the square and the cafes and the cinemas he haunted was John Shepherd '*Monsieur John a changè ca siege douze fois cet apres midi*' – a son of Hampstead, actor, painter, gossip. In her husband's studio in the Jardin Majorelle was the painters model and widow Maiteé, a fleshy exotic odalisque - and *en face*, across the lane, the raffish Luigi, a hairdresser of uncertain origin in a garden. Loud with squawking peacocks, and in winter fragrant with narcissi thrusting pale heads through the rank grass.

Aloof from all this was Maurice, the Indochinese antiquaire and mystic, well drawn by Peter Mayne in his *A Year in Marrakesh*. With a vitrine in the Mamounia, and a wooden minzah in a garden off the Place Djemma el Fna where he sold needleworks, opaline sugar boxes and bottles, tiles and potiche, culled in daily takings and ramblings through all grades of stalls, markets and auctions. He made a very pretty house near the Bab Doukala, Derb es Hanch (Snake House) delicately recreating an agelessly refined yet simple setting for his solitary life. He showed me how to use the labrynth of lanes that abut the great square, how to move invisibly, and where to find the shrines or zaouias of the seven saints of Marrakesh.

At the angle of the city wall beyond the Mamounia garden, in rooms that looked towards the snowy backdrop of the High Atlas, lived Docteur Robin, the neat dedicated ornithologist who directed the poor peoples Hopital de la

Mamounia to his east. Collector of Berber woodwork and carpets, seasoned traveller in remotest Morocco, it was he who told us of Foum Tsguid, the great lake that wells up in the desert where millions of flamingo descend to feast on a crustacean that buries itself in the sand for seven years until the waters magically rise. And then of course there were the Krupps, Arndt and Hetty, living sometimes out at the Targa on a property given them by the King, two seemingly disparate beings against the betting, very happy together and bringing to Marrakesh her *hoch geborren* relations and his rackety camp followers.

The arrival, in the midst of all these, of a glamorous young couple, well travelled, civilised, spirited, amused, in a wonderful old palace brilliantly resurrected by the magician Wills, and with a raft of friends from all over the world to share with them the city's delights, was of course cause for rejoicing. Nowhere else might one find Dado Ruspoli, Mick Jagger, Harold Acton, Gore Vidal, Bill Burroughs, Brion Gysin, Robert Fraser, Moulay Aly, Moulay Abdullah, the young Benjellouns and Tazi's with General Oufkir dallying with Talitha, Victoria, Inez and Lola. For three or four years the house danced and sang, blossomed and burgeoned. Skinny little Boujmaa the crazy gardener pruned and planted, mulched and watered, Mahjoub the smiling willing footman, lit dozens of lanterns as dusk fell, and a procession of drunken cooks were marshalled first by Nicolette Meeres, English painter gone native, and later by Judith from Vienna, while from Monsieur Egret's time remained young Mohammed, a rheumy-eyed kif-smoking old soldier at the gate, and old Mohammed, a stately old pedcrast (and great-grandfather) who had been there since 1916. And as it later appeared two families of troglodytes who lived under the first courtyard, and only emerged when the drains were being re-rooted.

What years they were, when hippies took the Marrakesh Express; when Aids was unheard of: when there were frequent flights between Moroccan cities at sensible hours for a few pounds from rustic airports; when old style Moorish cafés with sparkling rills to cross, and chess played under ancient vines and clouds of jasmine were round every corner; when the *silham*, the *foukia,* the *burnous* and *babouches* were everyday wear; when Lucien Freud's children lived free range on the Djemma el Fna; when the Café Glacier was to Marrakesh as the Café Flore to Paris; where one could watch a half-naked French professor in rags bucking like bronco across the square, poisoned for his infidelities it was said with datura by his Moroccan wife; and when a turbaned dwarf, said to be a man of property, felt licenced to help himself from every stall in view; when Burroughs, Gysin and young Mikey Portman invoked the Abramelan demon in the Hotel Toulousain; and there were 23 egg dishes on the Mamounia's menu; and boys sold roses twisted with mint at the Kissaria gate, and one could swim in irrigation tanks among fields of flowers near the airport, and dance all night at the Bar Piscine next door.

Now, again the house at Sidi Mimoun shines anew as the home of Monsieur Bernard Henri Levy and his beautiful wife Ariel. Madame de la Rochefoucauld who succeeded the Gettys did much to spoil it. Monsieur Alan Delon and his beautiful wife did little. Boujmaa's trees make a sylvan glade within, and the King's guards at the head of the street insure you know it's palace territory.

I chose another of Egret's lairs, high in a mountain valley among orchards and olive groves, a country pendant to his town palace. 'Notre regretté Sir Winston Churchill' he wrote to me, would often paint in its garden. By the time we found it the house had been unvisited for years, dark and pokey inside and choked with looming pieces of casual furniture, its tiny windows made useless by screens of moorsherabaya. It was not until you clambered to the roof that you saw the silvery valley of the Ourika river curving north towards Marrakesh, and to the south the red heights of Jebel Yagour still capped with snow. To the west the mountain maquis rose and, beyond the gardens mud walls, a track wound snake-like out of sight leading to a network of distant villages, still on market days busy with heavy loaded mules and family's walking back for ten miles from the big Monday, or the small Thursday souks, where goods are traded, courtships are continued and teeth are extracted.

Masons and builders from the neighbouring village of Timskrine camp each day beside the house. (Master mason Lahcen, thirty years later, still maintains this tiny kingdom). Moulay Kebir sat again in a cool corner interpreting what Maalam Willis and Maalam Hounian had decreed. The warren of little rooms upstairs became our big salon with an obelisk fireplace of blue river stones opposite stout shelves of palm-wood to receive my 1960s reading, I Ching, Thomas Mann, Crowley, Ouspensky, Gerard Manley Hopkins, Evelyn Waugh. A little *kouba* rose alongside, with another blue river chimney. One spring we made a pool three terraces below the house, to catch the water that cascades through every garden in the valley twice a week, when we get our share of the river that's drawn up the mountainside by a labyrinth of contour canals or seghias. Lahcen and his men delved, and at the end, against the red mountain backdrop, up rose a little Zigarat tower to change in (and to dry onions and peppers in winter) with a battlemented roof, where one may lie on Berber rugs, take sun, breathe sparkling mountain air and contemplate the patchwork of tiny fields and olive groves, knit by shady lanes that curl round boulders too vast to shift. In the summer thousands come, escaping the baking plain below, and nights are alive with song, flute and drum but for the rest of the year its Arcadia, and the coarseness of the modern world's at bay and the ancient rythmns reign. Sound now wild, now gentler of the river, the shrill song of girls in gaudy dresses tending the beasts of the field, the nightly boom of frogs, the braying of the ass, and the call of the muezzin once the strong reedy voice of my neighbour across the valley – now alas 'une disque'.

ABOUT THE AUTHOR

CHRISTOPHER GIBBS, born 1938, is a London antiques dealer, with a heart torn between Morocco and England.

The Oral Patrimony of Humanity

Juan Goytisolo

As Bakhtin shows in his remarkable study of the world and writing of Rabelais, there was a time when the real and the imaginary mingled, names supplanted the things they designated and newly invented words were wholeheartedly put to use: they grew, broadened out, shacked up, gave birth like creatures of flesh and blood. Markets, squares, public spaces, constituted the ideal place for their festive germination. Discourses entangled, legends lived, the sacred was the target of wiseacres but remained sacred, the bitterest parodies rubbed shoulders with liturgy, a well-knit story kept its audience in suspense, laughter preceded the prayers to reward the bard or showman as the plate was handed round.

The universe of cheapjacks and charlatans, beggars and water-sellers, tinkers and artisans, cutpurses at their nimble-fingered knavery, street urchins, lunatics, women of scant virtue, rustics as keen as mustard, striplings not tarrying to prosper, *pícaros*, cartomancers, quacks, preachers, doctors of homespun science, that entire motley world of free-and-easy commerce, once the succulent marrow of Christian and Islamic society – much less differentiated than people think - in the days of the Archpriest of Hita, was swept away gradually or at one foul swoop by a nascent bourgeoisie whose State gridironed cities and lives, lingering on as a hazy memory in their technically advanced and morally empty nations. The empire of cybernetics and the audiovisual flattens minds and communities, Disney-ises children, atrophies their powers of imagination. Today only one city upholds the privilege of sheltering the extinct oral patrimony of humanity, labelled contemptuously as 'Third World' by many. I refer to Marrakesh and the Square of Djemaa el Fna, next to which, on and off, for some twenty years, I have joyously written, meandered and lived.

Its bards, performers, acrobats, comedians, story-tellers are, more or less, equal in number and quality as on the day when I arrived, at the time of

Canetti's fertile visit or as in the Tharaud brothers' travel account written sixty years earlier. If we compare its present appearance with photographs taken at the beginning of the Protectorate, the differences are few: buildings are more solid, still modest; an increase in wheeled transport; a vertiginous proliferation of bicycles; identical work-shy horses and traps. The groups around horse-traders still mix with the *halca* framed by the steam wafting hospitality from the cooking-pots. The immutable minaret of the Koutubia surveys the glories of the dead and the helter-skelter of the living.

In the brief lapse of a few decades the wooden huts with bazaars, cold drinks and second-hand book stalls appeared and disappeared: finished off by a fire, they were moved to the burgeoning New Market (only the booksellers suffered cruel exile to Bab Dukala where they withered and died). The coach companies located on the vertex of Riad Zitun – a ceaseless bustle of travellers, traders and hawkers of tickets, cigarettes and sandwiches – also departed elsewhere with their musical incentives: to the orderly, spick and span bus station. In honour of GATT, Djemaa el Fna was tarmacked, swept, spruced up: the stalls that punctually invaded its space and vanished in a trice after a glimpse of the watch, migrated to more favourable climes. The Square lost a little of its hassle and hullabaloo, but retained its authenticity.

Death in the meantime brought natural losses to the ranks of its most distinguished offspring. First went Bakshish, the clown with the tasseled bonnet, whose daily performances drew to the insular orb of his *halca* a tightly-packed ring of onlookers, adults and children. Then, Mamadh, the bike artiste, springing from handle-bars to seat, spinning swiftly round in his magical balancing-act. Two years ago it knocked on the door of Saruh (the Rocket), majestic seer and wily Goliard, reciter of tasty stories of his own creation about the innocent and cunning Xuhá: deployer of a broad, unblushing language, his allusive and elusive tropes quivered like arrows round their unnamable sexual bull's eye. His imposing figure, shaven skull, pontifical paunch, were inscribed in an ancient tradition of that place, incarnated years ago by Berghut (the Flea) and their origins go back to rougher, harsher times, when rebels and betrayers of the sultan's august authority hung exemplarily from bloody hooks or swayed before a silent, cowered people on the sinister 'swing of the brave'.

In a more recent past, I was belatedly informed of the accidental death of

Tabib al Hacharat (the Insect Doctor), to whom Mohamed al Yamani devoted the finest of essays in the magazine *Horizons Maghrebins*. We habitués of Djemaa el Fna were well-acquainted with that little man and his unruly wisps of hair who, in ever rarer public appearances, tottered around the edges of the Square snorting like an asthmatic locomotive beneath the arcades with their cheap cafés and friendly aromas. His life-story, a mixture of truth and legend, rivalled Saruh's: he had likewise chosen the way of vagabond poverty, passed nights in cemeteries and police-stations, spent brief periods in prison - that he nicknamed 'Holland' – for being drunk and disorderly - and, when he grew tired of Morocco, so he said, he wrapped a scarf round his possessions and left for 'America' – that is, the waste land next to the Holiday Inn. His verbal humour, tales of fantasy, wordplay, palindromes, were unconsciously linked to Al Hariri's *Makamat* – lamentably ignored by the ever dozy and dilatory official Hispanic Arabists – and shared a literary territory that - as Shirley Guthrie was quick to see – connects his outlandishness with the 'aesthetic of risk' of Raymond Roussel, the surrealists and OULIPO. His parodies of the television news, recipe for the biggest hotpot in the world, spiced by ritual questions to his audience, are models of inventive wit.

I can't resist a mention of his lines about the therapeutic qualities of products he recommended to his audience: no 'love juices', no 'carrot cream' like the official healers, but grated glass or ambar extract from the devil's backside . . .

'What about coal?'

'Just the job for eyes, for the agate tap in the iris, for the gyrating beam in the ocular lighthouse. Put coal on your ailing eye, let it get to work till it bursts, get a seven inch nail, drive it in the socket and when it's steady in your hand you'll see thirty-seven light years away.

'If you've got fleas in your belly, rats in the liver, a turtle in your brain, cockroaches on the knee, a sandal, a piece of zinc, a twist of gunpowder, I found a sock in the house of one of Daudiyat's wives. Guess where I found it!'

'Where?'

'In a teacher's brain!' (Translation by Mohamed al Yamani).

But the most serious loss, during Ramadan last year, was the surprise closing down of café Matich: though a lot of water has flowed since – heavy rains, flash floods and real – Djemaa el Fna has yet to come to terms with the blow. How do you define the undefinable, the protean nature and all-embracing warmth rejecting any reductive label? Its strategic position, on the busiest corner in the Square, made it the hub of hubs, its real heart. An eagle eye from there encompassed the whole realm and treasured its secrets: quarrels, encounters, greetings, con-tricks, furtive groping or gleeful poking, tale-telling, insults, itinerant hum of the blind, gestures of charity. Jostling of crowds, immediacy of bodies, space in perpetual movement comprising the boundless plot of a film without end. Seedbed of stories, hive of anecdotes, pageant of morality tales crowned by a clothes-peg were the daily diet of the addicted. Gathered there were *gnaua* musicians, schoolmasters, college teachers, stallholders, raunchy roughs, small traders, big-hearted rogues, sellers of loose cigarettes, journalists, photographers, atypical foreigners, the local down-and-outs. All levelled by the straightforward manners of the place. In Matich everything was talked about and nobody was shocked. The ruler of this roost possessed a weighty literary culture and the intermittent attentions he paid his customers only surprised newcomers, enraptured as he was by an Arabic translation of Rimbaud.

It was where I lived the crystallized tension and devastating bitterness of the Gulf War, a harsh, unforgettable forty days and forty nights. The tourists had disappeared from the horizon and even veteran residents, with the exception of a handful of eccentrics, no longer ventured there. An old *gnaui* master listened to news of the disaster, his ear up against his portable radio. The panoramic terraces of the Glacier and Café de France were desperately deserted. A red sun, heralding the massacre, bled at twilight, prophetically stained the Square.

It was also there I spent the most poetic, light-hearted of New Year's Eves. I sat outside the Matich with a group of friends, awaiting, warmly clad, the advent of the new year. Suddenly, as in a dream, an unloaded cart swung round the corner, on its riding seat a young lad hard put to keep himself upright. His glazed eyes dallied on a blonde girl relaxing by one of the tables. Entranced, he slackened his grip on the reins and the cart slowly ground to a standstill. As if in a slow-motion scene from a silent film, our humble charioteer saluted his belle, invited her to climb into his boneshaker. Finally he got off, walked hesitantly over and, with a laboured *madam, madam*, repeated his seigneurial flourish, the majestic invitation to his Rolls or royal carriage, his lordly landau. The solicitous clientele warmed to his endeavour, his old clothes transmuted to finery, the vehicle bearing his ephemeral glory. But someone intervened to end the idyll and escorted him to his place. The youth couldn't break the spell, looked over his shoulder, threw kisses and, seeking consolation from this fiasco, patted the thighs of his mare with a touching tenderness (to a chorus of laughter and encores). Then he tried to clamber onto the driver's seat, managed it with some effort and immediately fell backwards on the empty boards, curled up in a ball (to a fresh round of applause). Various volunteers hoisted him up and, holding the reins, he blew a goodbye kiss to the Scandinavian deity before disappearing at a brisk trot over the dirty, oblivious tarmac, in a melancholy mood of paradise denied. I had not enjoyed such a scene since the happy days of Chaplin's films: such delicacy, oneiric, alive with humour, deliciously romantic.

Once the café closed down, we habitués scattered like a diaspora of insects deprived of their nest. The *gnaua* gather at night on the inhospitable asphalt or meet up in the backroom of an old *fonduk* on Derb Dabachi. The rest of us come to terms as best we can with the demise of that international centre of cultures, reliving episodes and moments from its mythical past splendours, like nostalgic emigrés in the makeshift shelters of exile. But Djemaa el Fna resists the combined onslaught of time and an obtuse, grubby modernity. The *halcas* don't fade, new talents emerge and an audience hungry for stories crowds gleefully round its bards and performers. The space's incredible vitality and digestive capacity glues together what is scattered, temporarily suspends differences of class and hierarchy. The tourist-laden coaches which, like whales, flounder there are immediately wrapped in its fine web, neutralized by its gastric juices. This year the nights of Ramadan assembled tens of thousands in its centre and roadways, around the portable cookers, and raucous bargaining over shoes, clothes, toys and bric-a-brac. In the glow from the oil lamps, I thought I noticed the presence of the author of Gargantua, of Juan Ruiz, Chaucer, Ibn Zayid, Al Hariri, as well as countless goliards and dervishes. The tawdry image of the fool slavering over his mobile phone neither tarnishes nor cheapens the exemplary brilliance of the domain. The dazzling incandescence of the word prolongs its miraculous reign. But sometimes I am worried by the vulnerability of it all and my lips tremble fearfully with a single question: 'For how long?'

ABOUT THE AUTHOR

JUAN GOYTISOLO, born in 1931, has been described as the 'best living Spanish novelist'. He grew up in Barcelona, where his mother was killed by the bombs of Mussolini's air-force during the Spanish Civil War, and attended university there and in Madrid before emigrating to France in 1957 as a result of the repressive authoritarian regime of General Franco. He maintained (and maintains) this self-imposed exile, dividing his time between Paris and Marrakesh. His major novels include *Juegos de Manos* (1954, *The Young Assassins*), *Reivindicacion del Conte Don Julian* (1970, *Count Julian*), *Paisajes despues de la Batalla* (1982, *Landscape After the Battle*) and *La Cuarentena* (1994, *Quarantine*). The essays in this collection appear translated into English, in full for the first time, by Peter Bush. A collected edition of Juan's travel essays is published by Eland (2003) under the title *Cinema Eden*.

A Hadaoui and his Family

from *Hideous Kinky* by Esther Freud

It was a blue cloudless afternoon and we sat at the front of the crowd in the Djemaa El Fna and watched the Gnaoua dancing. They wore embroidered caps fringed with cowrie shells which tinkled like bells when they moved. They played their tall drums and danced in the square on most afternoons.

'Where do they come from?' I asked Mum.

'They are a Senegalese tribe from West Africa. The King of Morocco has always employed them as his own personal drummers.'

'Because they're so beautiful?' I asked, admiring the elegant wrists and ankles of the dancers as their cymbals rang out in time to the men's drumming hands.

'Maybe.'

Khadija, a plump and solemn-faced beggar girl, wriggled through the crowd and squatted next to me.

'Hello Khadija,' my mother said, noticing her, and Khadija smiled a big gap-toothed grin. She touched my arm and pointed through the crowd across the square to where a group of people were beginning to gather. '*Hadaoui*,' she said and began to move towards them, looking over her shoulder to see that I was following.

An old man in faded purple and red robes unfolded a carpet on which he placed variously shaped brass pots. He filled each one with plastic flowers. He talked to the people who stopped to watch, spreading ripples of laughter through the gathering crowd. Once the carpet was unravelled and every last ornament was in place it became clear not all his comments were directed towards the crowd, but some to a tall, much younger man, who threw his words back at him quietly and with a half-smile that made the people sway with laughter.

The old man sat in the centre of his carpet and blew into a pipe that twisted around inside a bowl of water and bubbled and smoked with each breath.

'What's he doing?' I looked at Khadija and pointed.

'*Kif*,' she said, hugging her knees and keeping her eyes fixed on the entertainment.

Bea appeared and sat on the other side of Khadija, 'Where's Mum?'

I looked round to see her standing near the young man who was lifting white doves out of a box and placing them on the carpet. The doves ruffled their wings and strutted about, pleased to be in the open.

'Do you think they're going to do any tricks?'

'Who?' Bea said.

'The doves, of course.'

They didn't. It was the old man who did the tricks. He didn't juggle or dance or swallow flaming swords, but somehow, by talking, mumbling, even praying, he held the crowd, grinning and transfixed, straining for his every word. The younger man seemed sometimes to be his loyal assistant and then, disappearing, would emerge on the side of the crowd, heckling and jibing from amongst them, and, just as tempers began to boil, would disclose himself, much to everyone's delight, by leaping into the open and winking slyly all around. Bea, Khadija and I squatted close to the front, with the hard legs of men pressed against our backs.

After the young man had walked twice round the circle on his hands, and the old man had prayed to Allah on a pretend rug, the people seemed to know it was the end. They threw coins on to the carpet and drifted away. I saw my mother throw a coin, but she stayed standing where she was on the other side of the circle.

The *Hadaoui*'s assistant wandered about, stooping now and then to collect the money, which he placed in a leather pouch. He wore sandals and jeans that had once been white and a thin Moroccan shirt with tiny cotton buttons -that ran halfway down the front. He had wavy black hair and was taller than Akari the Estate Agent and the other Moroccan men I knew. As the people dispersed, Khadija jumped up and ran on to the carpet where the old man still sat, quietly smoking. She took a red plastic flower from its pot and presented it to the man who was collecting coins. He looked at her for a moment. I held my breath. Then he smiled and bent down to accept it. Khadija ran about under my jealous stare, collecting flowers one by one and standing straight and still to present them, while the assistant, sharing her solemnity, accepted them with a ritual nod of his head. I hovered in my place, envying her bare feet as they padded over the carpet, until, unable to resist a moment longer, I slipped off my plastic sandals and skidded across to join her. The man smiled quizzically as I handed him my first flower. He looked over my head and I saw his eye meet my mother's and so identify me as her child and a foreigner despite my caftan and dusty feet.

Khadija and I watched as the doves were collected one by one and replaced in their cardboard box. 'We've got a pet,' I said to her. 'Not a dove. A hen.' I pointed at the cooing boxes. 'At home. Would you like to see?'

Khadija shook her head, but I could tell she didn't understand. 'Mum, Mum,' I shouted as I ran towards her. 'What's Arabic for hen?' But I stopped before I got there because she was deep in conversation with the magic man's assistant. They were talking in a mixture of French and English and laughing. They turned to me as I ran up.

'There you are,' she said. 'I saw you earlier on, helping Bilal.'

Bilal smiled at me. He had the most beautiful smile of all smiles and his dark eyes twinkled in a face smooth and without a trace of anything unfriendly. It was then that I noticed the necklace. It hung around his neck in a string of silver and gold beads.

'Mum,' I said, willing her to bend down so I could whisper in her ear, and when she finally did I pressed my face close to hers and said, 'Is Bilal my Dad?'

She stood up and took my hand and patted it.

'Goodbye,' she said, a little abruptly, 'maybe we'll see you here tomorrow.'

'Oh yes,' Bilal answered. 'Tomorrow. *Inshallah*. God willing.' And he began to roll up the carpet.

The Hadaoui, Bilal and the white doves stayed in Marrakesh for a week, attracting a large crowd every afternoon. Each day Khadija and I waited impatiently for the entertainment to end so we could take up our important role as official helpers to Bilal. The old man remained forever too full of mystery and magic to approach. I kept to the edges of the carpet and avoided meeting his eye.

'When you're old, will you turn into the *Hadaoui*?' I asked Bilal on the afternoon of his last performance.

'I am the *Hadaoui*. Now. You don't believe me?' he said in his funny broken English.

'But you're not magic,' Bea said.

'And you don't have a beard.'

Bilal laughed. 'Maybe children can tell about these things. Today the *Hadaoui* stops here. And from tomorrow I am working as a builder.'

'Here? Staying here?'

'Yes. The *Hadaoui* must have a holiday. So I become builder. Here in Marrakesh.'

I looked over at Mum to see if she was as excited as me that Bilal wasn't to be going away. She was smiling, but she looked as if she might have known all along.

Bilal came to live with us in the Mellah. Every morning he went out early to work on a building site. In the afternoons when it was too hot to work he took us to the square. Best of all he liked to watch the acrobats. There were a troupe of boys, all about seven or eight years old, dressed in red and green silk like little dragons, who did double somersaults from a standing position and tricks so the people gasped and clapped and threw coins into a hat. Bilal instructed us to watch them very carefully. One day over lunch in our cool tiled kitchen Bilal revealed his plan. 'We will have our own show in the Djemaa El Fna!' he declared triumphantly. Bilal was to be Ring Master. Mum was to make the costumes from silk on the sewing-machine we'd brought with us from England, and Bea and I would be the star guests, performing acrobatic tricks. 'People will love to see the English children do the tricks.' Bilal's eyes sparkled. 'We will have a crowd as big as the *Hadaoui* and we will collect many coins.'

'But I can't do any tricks,' I said, frightened of diminishing his enthusiasm, but unable to restrain my anxiety.

'Bea can you do any tricks? At all?'

Bea shook her head. 'I can do a handstand.'

Bilial was undeterred. 'I train you. We start today. Very soon you will be doing this.' He demonstrated with a backward somersault right there in the kitchen.

That afternoon we dressed in shorts and T-shirts and spread a blanket over the paving-stones. 'Soon,' Bilal said, 'you won't be needing any carpet.'

We started with roly-polies. Head over heels. The names made Bilal laugh. Our attempts to perfect this simple trick did not. My version of a roly-poly was a slow tumble which culminated in a star, as I lay flat on my back, my legs and arms stretched in different directions, staring up at the sky. The best part of it, I thought.

'You must end up on your feet.' Bilal frowned. 'Watch me.' From a standing position Bilal took a couple of quick steps, then, tucking in his head, rolled through the air, his bent back barely touching the ground, and he was upright again. 'You see,' he said. 'A flying rolly-polly.'

We kept working at it, Bilal was patient and encouraging. As part of our training he took us regularly to the square, where we sat and watched the acrobats. For me they had taken on a new majesty. They were tiny and fluid and without fear. They cartwheeled through hoops, formed themselves into pyramids and triple-somersaulted off the top, their bodies bending in half as they flew through the air. I imagined Bea and myself dressed in silk, our hair plaited out of the way, dextrous and skilful, taking a bow to the applauding crowd. We would have so many coins to collect that when we sent enough to Bilal's family in the mountains so that he didn't have to work on the building site any more, there would still be some left over. I took hold of Bilal's hand. 'I promise to practise every day, because . . . ' And I felt a rush of excitement as the beginnings of a great plan unravelled in my mind. 'Because I've decided that when I grow up I want to be a tightrope walker. You won't tell anyone, will you?'

Bilal nodded. Bilal was someone I could trust.

That afternoon we walked home through the busy streets. I sat on Bilal's shoulders high up above the crowd and from time to time I asked him to let go of my legs so that I could practise balance.

We began going to the park for our training. Mum thought it would be better to practise acrobatic tricks on grass. As the weeks went by, our bodies didn't turn into the fearless, weightless ones Bilal had hoped they would. Or at least Bea's did a little more than mine, but not enough. We began to spend more and more time playing leapfrog, which anyone could do, or lying on the grass telling stories.

Bilal continued to work on the building site. I realized that in order to be a tightrope walker I didn't necessarily have to be an acrobat. So I kept to my own secret plan and practised balancing whenever I got the chance.

As promised, Bilal took us to visit his family in the mountains. We traveled through a whole day on a bus packed with people and then shared a taxi with a man Bilal knew and was happy to see. We had presents of a large packet of meat and three cones of white sugar for Bilal's mother.

The whole village was waiting to greet us at the end of a narrow track that joined the road. 'They welcome you like a wife,' Bilal whispered as Mum stepped out of the taxi. She was dressed in a swirling blue cloak of material that covered her hair and swathed her body in folds that reached the floor. When she walked she drew up the cloth and let it hang over her shoulder.

Bilal introduced us to his mother. She was a large lady with a throaty voice that billowed out from under her veil. Bilal's father was really an old man and half her size.

The women threw flower petals into the air and sang a low lilting song as we walked back along the path. From time to time they let their fingers brush against my hair. I held tightly on to my mother's hand.

The village was a cluster of low white houses at the foot of a hill that was almost a mountain. We followed Bilal into the dark inside of his family's house. Bilal's family trooped in after us, and we all stood about smiling. Bea nudged Mum and she remembered and handed over the meat and the sugar.

'You see, she likes the presents,' Bilal whispered as his mother nodded, unwrapping and rewrapping her gifts. I had tried to convince him that she might prefer a Tintin book or a clay drum.

That night Mum, Bilal, Bea and I all slept on rugs in the room that was the house, and Bilal's parents, his brothers and sisters, their wives and children all slept outside in the garden. It was a clear warm night and very light from so many stars.

'I wish we could sleep in the garden too,' I said to Bea and she agreed.

'Where's Abdul?' Bea asked next morning over breakfast. We were drinking coffee sweetened with the sugar we had brought. Abdul was Bilal's youngest brother and the same age as Bea. We had tried to teach him hopscotch the evening before.

'Abdul goes to look after the sheep,' Bilal said. 'He is up before the sun.'

'Where?' I asked, looking round for even a single sheep.

'On the other side of the mountain.' Bilal pointed into the hazy distance. 'Over there are all the sheep of the village.'

'Are there other people helping?'

'No, just Abdul.'

So Abdul was a shepherd. I had seen a shepherd that wasn't old and frozen and on the front of a Christmas card. By lunchtime he was back from his day's work. He sat with the sun on his back and ate bread and tajine, his feet covered in dust from the long walk home.

'Bea, would you like to be a shepherd?' I asked her.

'No, not really.'

'What would you like to be then?'

'I don't know. Normal, I think.' She was marking out a new game of hopscotch with the toe of her plastic sandal.

The next morning when I woke, Bea was not there. Mum was sitting on the end of my bed sewing.

'She went into the hills.'

'When?'

'At sunrise. She wanted to see what it was like to be a shepherd.'

I was close to tears. 'But you knew I wanted to go.'

'I did try and wake you.'

I wasn't sure whether or not to believe her. 'Wouldn't I wake up?'

'No,' she said. 'You just started talking in your sleep.'

'Did I?' I cheered a little at this. I liked the idea of talking in my sleep. 'What did I say? Please remember.'

'Something about roofracks, I think,' she said, folding up the dress she was making for Akari the Estate Agent's little girl. He said it could be rent until our money arrived from England. Roofrack. That was a good word. Roofrack. Roofrack. Hideous kinky. Maybe we could teach Abdul to play tag.

It was midday and I sat at the edge of the village and waited for them to come down from the hills. Eventually two specks turned into stripes and then into Bea and Abdul, both barefoot and in shorts. I ran to meet them. As I neared, I stuck out my hand and, touching Bea's shoulder, shouted, 'Roofrack!' Picking up speed, I circled away for the inevitable chase. I ran hard for a few minutes before I realized she wasn't following. I looped back round, keeping a little distance in case it was a trick.

'Aren't you playing?'

'Of course not,' she said. 'I've been working, haven't I?' And she marched on towards the village.

I followed them to where lunch was being served. The whole family ate from one enormous bowl. It was couscous with a sauce of seven vegetables. I tried to copy the exact movement of Bilal's hand as he collected the tiny grains of couscous in the crook of his finger, swept them into a ball with his thumb, and placed it in his mouth without a crumb being spilt or wasted.

'Tomorrow can I go to the mountains with Abdul?' I asked him when the meal was over.

Bilal shook his head. 'No. Because tomorrow we are going to the festival of the marabouts.'

The festival was a little like a market.

'What's a marabout?' I wanted to know.

Mum pointed out a small white building with a domed roof and a bolt on the door.

'Marabouts are holy men, like saints, who live in these little houses.'

'Is he in there now?'

Mum wasn't sure. She asked Bilal.

'Oh yes. He's in there.'

'Will he come out once the festival starts?'

Bilal looked amused. 'No. It is only his spirit we celebrate.'

We walked towards the building. I peered on tiptoe over the white wall surrounding it.

'For many years,' Bilal said, 'he is lying dead inside.'

Mum and I both pulled away.

Bilal's brothers were erecting a large white tent. It was a tent like others that were going up around the edges of the festival. Round and cool inside. The women from each section of the family were laying out rugs and cotton spreads of material to sleep on. They sat and talked from under their veils while their smallest children slept.

'They wanted Mum to wear a veil,' Bea whispered.

'Who did?'

'The mother and the brothers and everyone else.'

'Why didn't she then?'

65

'She said she wouldn't.'

'Are they angry?' I looked over at the women resting, their eyes sharp above a square of black.

'It's hard to tell,' Bea said.

If you stood very close to the veil you could see through the black and tell whether someone was wearing lipstick or not. I wondered if it was a special magic cloth.

'Nylon,' Mum said when I asked her.

When I woke, Ahmed had arrived. Ahmed was Bilal's brother-in-law.

'Ahmed is married to Bilal's sister,' Mum explained.

'No,' Bilal corrected her. 'Ahmed is divorced from my sister.'

Ahmed had two other wives with him and several children. They spread out their belongings near to ours and the youngest wife tried to settle her baby who was crying. As she wrestled with her child, her veil floated up and I saw her face. She was pale and looked a little like Bilal's sister Fatima who was fourteen and wearing a veil for the first time.

The baby kept on crying. Ahmed's other wife took it from her and began to walk around the tent, rocking and soothing it with words.

Bea and I wandered out into the warm night. The circle of white tents had grown, stretching away round the marabout's shrine. Outside each tent fires were burning and meat roasted on twisting sticks. Ahmed, Bilal and Mum sat by our fire. They were smoking a clay pipe. Passing it from one to another in a circle.

Ahmed began to sing. His voice was sad. He sang the Egyptian songs that played in the outdoor cafés in Marrakesh. His voice rose and fell and caught in his throat with such pure sorrow that I was surprised not to see tears running down his face. Bilal joined in on a lower note with a smile on his lips as if to say it wasn't his sad story he was singing.

I crawled on to Mum's lap and basked in the melancholy music and the warmth of the fire. The sour smell from the burning pipe mingled with the roasting meat turning on its spit. It looked like a sheep and I wondered whether or not it was one of Abdul's. If it was, I decided, thinking of Snowy, I would refuse to eat it. Much later that night, when the singing had spread from tent to tent and supper was finally ready, I forgot about my earlier resolutions and, along with Abdul, held out my hands for a kebab.

Mum washed my feet and hands in a bowl of cold water and insisted I change into my nightie. Abdul and his, cousins were sleeping where they'd fallen, wrapped tight in their djellabas.

'Can I have some powder on my feet, please?' I asked, as much to keep Mum in the tent as to feel it, silky smooth between my toes.

She took a tin of Johnson's baby powder out of her bag and sprinkled me a ration. Ahmed's youngest wife, still rocking her tireless baby, watched us darkly from behind her veil. As I patted each toe dry, she laid her baby down and slowly unwrapped its clothes, revealing a damp red ring around its neck. Mum leant over and offered her the tin. She stared uncomprehending, until Mum shook a fine layer of white on to the baby's neck. She smoothed it gently and the crying seemed to quiet a little. The lady held on to Mum's hand. 'Thank you, thank you,' she said in Arabic.

Mum pressed the tin into the woman's hands. 'Sprinkle a little every day,' she said, pointing at the baby.

'What about me?' I hissed at her.

'Shh.'

'But it's our only tin.'

Mum glared.

I put my head under the blanket. 'I want Bilal,' I, wailed. When I refused to come out even to kiss her goodnight she relented a little and promised to ask Linda to bring some powder with her when she came to visit.

'When will that be?' I asked.

Mum tucked me in and sneaked a butterfly kiss that tickled before going out to rejoin the party.

'Who's Linda, anyway?' I asked Bea, when she eventually came to bed.

'You know . . . Linda.' Bea said.

'Linda?'

But Bea said she'd only tell me if I told her a story first and by the time I'd finished 'The Adventures of a Spooky Carpet' she was asleep.

There was everything for sale at the festival. Donkey-loads of water melons, pomegranates, blood oranges – the insides of which you could suck out through a hole in the skin. There was a stall with hundreds of pairs of babouches, the softest most beautiful shoes. They were mostly in yellow or light brown leather but some were black and patterned with stars of silver or gold. There was one pair, red with a zigzag of green, the toes of which curled up like magicians' slippers, that made my eyes burn with wanting them. I was frightened to pick them up or even touch them, and the old man who sat among his slippers gave me no smile of encouragement.

'If you could have any babouches you wanted in the whole world, which ones would you choose?' I asked Mum.

She bent down to finger the leather. 'I was thinking of making you and Bea some sandals . . . ' she said.

My heart fell.

'Out of leather. With rubber soles. They'll be very nice.'

'But they won't be like these.'

'No, they won't be quite like these,' she said, and she drew me away.

By that evening news of Mum's miracles with the baby powder had spread throughout the tent.

'Oh yes, she is the wise woman from the West,' Bilal said proudly, and he put his arm around her.

'There is a lady Ahmed wants you to help,' Bilal told Mum on our last night around the fire. Ahmed had been particularly impressed by the baby-powder cure. 'He has invited us to visit with him.'

The white tent came fluttering down. We said goodbye to Bilal's family who we would see again in a few days, and to Fatima who was my favourite sister and Abdul. We set off in a different direction with Ahmed and his two wives and their children. The baby's rash had almost vanished, but it still screamed unceasingly. No one took the slightest bit of notice.

During our journey on a bus crowded with people who all been at the festival, Ahmed explained through Bilal what he wanted Mum to do. 'There is an aunt of Ahmed,' he said, 'who is sad because she has lost her favourite nephew in a car crash. Since he is dead she will not be happy to live.'

'But what does he want me to do?' Mum asked.

Bilal didn't translate her doubts to Ahmed. 'Just talk with her,' he said, smiling assuredly. 'Just visit and talk with her.'

The old lady lived in a room at the back of Ahmed's house, which was large and airy with tiled floors and slatted shutters covering the windows, filtering in just enough light to see. Ahmed wanted Mum to go to her alone.

I want to come too,' I said. I wouldn't let go of her hand. I couldn't let go. She mustn't go alone into a dark room, with a woman who wanted to die, I thought. She might never come out again.

'Stay with the women,' Mum ordered.

I looked over at the silent veiled wives who waited for me, and my breath caught in my throat. 'Please,' I appealed, my voice wild. 'Bilal, tell her please.'

Mum stood unsure. I could feel her staring at me. 'It's just that they're tired,' she said, and we all walked in silence round to the back of the house.

The old lady was lying in her bed when Ahmed ushered us into the room. Startled by the light, she sat up. Her face was striped with thin lines of dried black blood where she had dragged her nails hard across it. My mother sat on the edge of the bed and rummaged in her bag. She pulled out a large bound book. It was her copy of the *I Ching*. She undid the twist in the velvet pouch Bilal had made for her and poured the three large coins into her hand, warming them in her palm as she always did before she told a fortune. Ahmed's aunt watched her with a glimmer of light in her yellow eyes. Mum handed her the coins. They were Arabic coins with stars on one side and the head of the King on the other.

'I want you to throw the coins for me,' Mum said. Bilal spoke to the aunt softly in Arabic and she scattered the three coins on to the bedspread with a thin worn hand.

Mum made a line in pencil in the back of the book and nodded for her to throw again. The old lady threw the coins six times and Mum made a pattern of six broken and unbroken lines, three on each side of a space.

Mum opened the book. The old lady was sitting a little straighter with her shawl held tightly around her shoulders. Mum began to read. 'Persistence brings good fortune. It will be of advantage to cross the great river. The Superior Man will pass this time in feasting and enjoyment . . . ' Bilal translated in a low murmur as she read and the old lady blinked in concentration with her head slightly on one side. Mum read on and on about lakes and rivers and turning-points until my mind began to wander away from the room.

'Do you think we'll get a chapter of *Bluebeard* tonight?' I whispered.

'Shhh.'

'We haven't had any story for ages.'

The reading was over. There was a silence. Then the old lady smiled and, looking towards Ahmed, commanded him in a startlingly strong voice to bring mint tea and bread. Ahmed hurried out like a small boy. I could hear him shouting out the order as he ran through the house.

Once she had drunk a glass of tea and chewed at the soft inside of a roll, the old lady pushed back the covers and began to climb out of bed. Ahmed smiled a tender smile as her narrow feet touched the floor. She walked slowly over to a painted chest which stood under the window and, opening it, took out a sky-blue caftan. She reached up and held it against my mother's shoulders.

'Thank you,' my mother said, taking it from her.

With the faintest of smiles the old lady climbed back into bed and motioned for us all to go away.

It was mid-morning when we arrived back in Bilal's village. I could see Fatima standing in the doorway of her father's house. I waved and began to run towards her, but instead of coming to meet us she turned and darted inside letting the curtain fall across the door.

'Fatima,' Bilal called after her. 'Fatima,' he ordered, and she reappeared, limping slightly and with a split across her lip.

'What happened to you?' Mum gasped, but Bilal took his sister roughly by the shoulders and began to question her in a voice which shook with anger. Fatima spoke a few tearful words with her head bowed and her eyes on the ground.

'What's happened?'

'It's nothing,' Bilal said. 'Let's get inside.'

The familiar cool of the house had turned so cold it made me shiver. Finally Bilal spoke. 'It is important that Fatima will not make bad her reputation. If she is not good, she will not be married.'

Mum was silent. She looked at him with cold, accusing eyes.

'Fatima has behaved very badly at the festival,' he said.

'Yes?'

'She was seen without her veil – watching the dancing. At night she must stay inside the tent.'

'So she was beaten,' Mum said flatly.

I looked over at Fatima, huddled in the corner, her fingers moving through a bowl of string beans.

'My brothers tied her in the barn and beat her . . .' Bilal looked away, ashamed, then added, 'But now she will be good and then she will be married.'

Fatima lifted the bowl in her arms and hobbled silently to the back door.

Mum watched her go. 'I think maybe it's time to go home,' she said.

'Tomorrow,' Bilal insisted. 'Stay until tomorrow and we will all go back to the Mellah.'

ABOUT THE AUTHOR

ESTHER FREUD was born in London in 1963. She trained as an actress at the Drama Centre, has acted and written for both stage and screen and is co-founder of the women's theatre company 'Norfolk Broads'. *Hideous Kinky* was her debut novel, published in 1992, and looks at a journey of love and adventure in Morocco in the late 1960s through the eyes of a five year old child. It was made into a film, starring Kate Winslet, released in 1998. She was named one of the twenty 'Best of Young British Novelists' by Granta magazine in 1993 and has since written several other books: *Peerless Flats* (1993), *Gaglow* (1997) and *The Wild* (2000). Her latest novel, *The Sea House,* is a love story set on the Suffolk coast.

Travel Writing

The Real Morocco

from *Mauretania: Warrior, Man and Woman*
by Sacheverell Sitwell

Upon old maps of the sixteenth or seventeenth century you can look for the name, Marrakesh, and not find it. This is because the town was called, in various spellings, Morocco, or its equivalent. The town and the kingdom were synonymous, as though the whole character of the one were expressed or concentrated in the other. Fez is easily to be recognized, being then, as now, the Northern capital. Fez has never changed: neither has Marrakesh; but it is to be argued that Marrakesh always was, and still is, the true nature, or genius, of this land. Marrakesh is the real Morocco: Fez, though this can be exaggerated, is the town of the Andalucian Moor. Of such influence there is but little to be seen in Marrakesh. Also, though a place of dust and flies, Marrakesh is gay. It is bigger than Fez, having twice the population, seeming indeed, to be endless in extent compared with the small and defined area occupied by Fez. We have said that Marrakesh is gay. Like Seville, like Venice, like Naples, once upon a time, and, we may imagine, like Isfahan, Marrakesh is a town of music. Its character, that is to say, is exuberant, not mournful. Fez, in its nostalgic beauty, might be portrayed in the lovely slow movement of Debussy's 'Iberia'. That could never call Marrakesh to mind, and this is the difference between them.

But we must delay, for a little, our description of its music. That, it may be, is its final character and should come at the end. For, long before this, we have the wonder of its appeal. No town, unless in high Tibet, could be placed more in a world of its own by the manner in which it must be reached. For the contrast of twentieth century Casablanca lies almost in deliberate foil to Marrakesh. The road that joins the two cities is some hundred and fifty miles in length, the only town passed upon the way being Settat. There, the dusty misery of the street, and the beggars and children deserve a book to themselves. It is as sad and hopeless a place as the mind could imagine, but with a wealth, we cannot doubt it, of dramatic detail and work for a painter or realistic writer. After Settat, for those who have not seen it, the road approximates to desert, but for a fortnight in the spring it is the flowering wilderness, its predominant colour being the marigold. This grows on either side of the road, more richly than in any garden border. Behind it, there are blues and mauves, flower clumps that have their individual beauty, and are not massed and ordered. At other seasons, the road is a monotony filled only with anticipation, or regret, for Marrakesh. But, now, the first snow mountains can be seen. A range of low hills appears, and the interminable road loses its straightness and curves in among them. Upon their other side you are in the Haouz, the great plain of Marrakesh. The whole line of the Atlas Mountains runs from end to end of the sky, its foothills invisible, and the snowy sierra giving above the yellow or tawny plain a peace and coolness to the Oriental scene. For it is, at once and immediately, Oriental. The snow, indeed, is of that Eastern luxury which contradicts, in art and in fable, their squalor and their poverty, hanging the gilded honeycomb and the stalactite in their vaults, planting the fountain and the flowering almond. And now, from fifteen miles away, like a green ocean, there is the oasis and, rising in midst of it, the Koutoubia. The first palmtrees come. A hill with three summits, called the Gueliz, gives Egyptian character. There are flat roofed houses. Marrakesh begins. If the heat of that long straight road, the tufted and fronded palmtrees shooting luxuriantly where their stems are near the ground, and the character of the first mud suburbs, have given an impression of the South, this is true, also, in geographical fact. For the South, like all terms of description, is comparative. Beyond the equator, it is the towns that are furthest North which have the hottest climate and possess what we should term the most Southern character, Elizabethville, for instance, or Urundi, in the Belgian Congo. Taking it from the Cape Province, two thousand miles away, you go North in order to be hot. This contradiction would take effect, from reversal of image and metaphor, were there ever poetry, or great art of the imagination, in South Africa, or, equally, in that part of South America which is beyond the equator. But, so far as the Mediterranean civilization is concerned, Marrakesh is, in very truth, the most Southern town of civilized history. To the South of it there is only Timbuctoo, where, once, there was learning, but never art. Here, in Marrakesh, there are the most Southern fountains, the most Southern gardens. This is the last place of repose and coolness. It is true that this only applies in the epicurean, in the seigneurial sense, affecting only those who live in the palaces of the town, in the hotels, or in the houses of foreign residents. For the vast mass of its population, for all, it may be, except one thousand out of its two hundred thousand inhabitants, the characteristics of Marrakesh must be poverty, great heat, and animation. To the first two of these conditions they must be inured. Persons coming from European countries may think they have never seen poverty until they came here. But, in most of Moslem Africa, such poverty is the universal rule. And, here in Marrakesh, it is relieved by those same baits, or attractions, which, in England, in France, and in America, have drawn people from the country into the towns. Marrakesh is full of tribesmen from the Sous who came to the town, found no work, but remain here. They would not leave, even if they could. This is because of the joys of companionship after the loneliness of the '*bled*'. They have grown used to smoking cigarettes, and to such other of our inventions as motorcars and, even, it may be, to tinned food. It is, then, the animation that attracts them. Poverty and great heat they knew already.

This quality of stir, or excitement, is most typical of the town. It could never be called a sleepy or decaying place. It has no deserted corners. This is not the refuge of a dying population. The effect it gives is one of swarming, pullulating life. Down every alley there are children playing. It has enough beggars to furnish a whole country. Wherever you walk, you are jostled and overtaken; there are persons running, and overladen donkeys brushing past. '*Balec, balec,*' ('Make way, make way,') are the first words that you learn in Marrakesh. There is not the '*dolce far niente*' of the South of Europe. Even the beggars are not silent, but gabble incessantly. It is a town of effort, where there is no effort, now, in Seville, in Grenada, or in Cathedral towns of our own North. Marrakesh has a rude and vigorous life which is irrepressible. This comes of its own turbulent blood, continually refreshed and renewed by tribesmen from the country, pricked to it by starvation. It has a temperature which is torrid without being enervating. There are climates, like that of Istanbul, which bring slothfulness and exhaust the energies. The Turkish indolence, their three centuries of siesta, were born of those milky prospects along the Bosphorus. But Moroccan misrule and anarchy were characterized by violence and by fiery turbulence. At Istanbul, a great empire which had set itself up by military prowess, caught the Byzantine decadence and moved into autumn, shedding its young leaves. But Morocco, which was never great, was too violent even to be prosperous. And of all Morocco, as we have said, Marrakesh is the symbol and was, of old, the name or title.

In all its area there is nothing but dust, no green places or gardens for the poor. The Djemaa el Fna is no resting place. There is never an open square, or a plot dressed back before a rich man's house. High walls are a sign of wealth, but riches are hidden. They dwell by the side of poverty, while beggars lie outside. Thus, the town has no design. There is no rich man's quarter. Rich and poor live side by side. There are no landmarks. It is more easy to know your whereabouts from some corner of a decaying wall, or from the blind man begging there. It may be that the mosques, were they open to Europeans, were they more than but a vision of white arches and straw mats, would correct this labyrinthine notion, for, as it is, the souks are endless, and there are nothing but mean slums. No street leads to anywhere. All are masked and end with walls. The fact that Marrakesh is not so big that you cannot see again, and recognize, the same beggar, or blind child, but adds to this confusion. It is the same poor wretch, but not the same blank wall. The scene has changed, but not the actor.

Almost the only relief from this sameness – for it is not a monotony – comes from the public fountains, though they, too, are centres of talk and busy activity more than places of repose. They are drinking fountains, and not ornamental waters. The first hint of them will come from the water sellers who are to be met with all over the town. Their profession, which is as liquid as that of a pearl diver or coral fisher, has given them generic resemblance as though all were members of one tribe. This is even true, for it is a hereditary guild dating back three or four hundred years, at least, with their own peculiar privileges, and a lore and tradition all their own. They are doubly swarthy of complexion, compared with other Moors, while their goatskin or hogskin of water is a frightening object in itself. It is headless and limbless, boned, as it were, but with the stumps blown out and distended, coated with pitch as was done in the amputations of a hundred years ago upon the battlefields, but with the trunk still furred, its black locks reduced by cold within and heat without to a matted and horrible, a greasy or gory, consistency. As they come, the watersellers ring their strings of brass bells, and there is the tinkling of their brass weights and balances and of their brass cups, a drink from which would spell disease or death to most persons of our Northern temperament. The bright polishing of their brass utensils is that of the canal barge or the Gypsy's caravan, and it is Gypsy or bargee to whom they are akin. Their rags, from heat and damp, have lost all resemblance to clothing. They must wear them, year in, year out, and sleep in them. Where they sleep, in fact, is a mystery; but these watersellers, who are, ever, in damp clothing, and are never dry, in their absence of rheumatism or other ills are worth the attention of the medical profession. As subjects for a painter they are a little too close in spirit to the Neapolitan watercolourists of two generations ago. It would not be possible to paint them; but, in every other respect, they form a part of the fascination of Marrakesh, as they lead us to the fountains.

Of these there are three, Sidi El Hassane, Echrob ou Chouf and El Mouasine. There are others; but all are so far the same that it is better to write of a fountain and forget its name. It is, though, of El Mouasine that we are thinking, for the sound of it, and because it is the finest. Nothing could be more different in form and intention from those monumental waters of the Mediterranean. We mean the Roman fountains, the Fontana di Trevi, or the fountains of the Piazza Navona. Their purpose is but ornament and coolness, the noise of the waters being part of this ordinance of pleasure. The genius of Bernini restored and used the superfluity of Roman waters. They had been contrived for a population of a million souls, but, down the dark ages, poured, unheeded, from the broken arches and from the mossy fountain lip.

Here, in Africa, water is a necessity, being no more of a luxury than is bread or sleep. The certainty of water is like sleep assured, or a pass against starvation. A fountain, therefore, is more of a benefaction than would be a park or garden. It is meant for use, and not for rest and coolness. The form of this fountain is elaborate in the extreme, so that it could be called the chief public monument of Marrakesh. There is, even, a little widening of the street that passes it. The chief feature is a basin, or tank, roofed by a beautiful porch of carved and painted woodwork. This portico has beams of cedar wood and ornaments or frieze of painted stucco in the honeycomb motif. At the side are three more tanks with domed roofs. They are for water for the animals. The main tank is where the watercarriers replenish their black goatskins, a feat always accompanied by much shouting and ferocity of gesture. They stand on the parapet, gesticulating and wasting all the waters, posed against the rayed patterns of the *zellijes*, the tilework. The *zellijes*, for they are a mosaic of cut tiles, are of fine geometric pattern, in convention of stars or flowers, of a complexity which gives a rich effect and immediate southern character. Such a scene, with the exhausted, ill-treated mules and donkeys, next door, drinking from the trough of waters, plays all day and far into the night. It is, after the Djemaa el Fna, the main animation of the town, if we except those quarters which are intended only for music and dissipation. The date of this fountain, El Mouasine, is difficult to determine. The Moorish work can be so easily renewed by craftsmen in the tradition. It is work, probably, of the late sixteenth century, of the Saadian period, but several times restored. In spite of this, the whole effect is of Moorish architecture at its best. There is nothing, it may be, that quite compares with it, nothing in Cairo, nothing in North Africa. We can only call to mind the fountain of Sultan Achmet III, outside the gate of the Seraglio, in Istanbul, a beautiful work of the late seventeenth century, but entirely different in shape and in conception from El Mouasine, taking the form, as it does, of a kiosque or pavilion with leaden overhanging eaves of capricious, pagoda shape, of affinity, it would seem probable, to Mughal work in Ahmedabad or Fatchpur Sikri. Nothing is alien El Mouasine. This is the pure Moorish.

Of architecture, in Marrakesh, there are two main examples. First, because most obvious, is the Medersa Ben Youssef. The Medersas, or sacred colleges, are found in different forms, as Madrasas, or Medresehs, in other Moslem lands, but in Morocco they attain to perfection in detail of carved plaster and of cedar wood. None of the filigree of the Alhambra is more delicate than this. Their fault is that they are all the same. In Fez, there are five or six Medersas. In their way they are the best work in Fez; but when you have seen the Medersa Attarine, you have seen the lot. There is another in Meknes, and one in Sale. This, of Marrakesh, the Medersa Ben Youssef, is as lovely as any of them. It dates from the late sixteenth century and, by many persons, would be guessed as being earlier than that. The stucco panels, which are worked with an incredible dexterity, have, with age, acquired a patina of a faint rose colour. This is balanced by the wonderful silver or grey age of the cedar beams, the carved pattern of which has been altogether worn away upon that side of the building which is most open to the prevailing winds. Some of the ceilings of the corridors have, as well, carved beams of cedar and the scent of this clings to the Medersa, making it a wonderful place of peace and beauty away from the noisome, crowded alleys.

Even more remote and quiet are the Saadian tombs, which were unknown to the world until the French were permitted to restore them, less than twenty years ago. The approach to them, down so many crooked passages, is the proof of how concealed and hidden they must have been. Beyond any question the Saadian tombs are the finest works of art in Morocco. Especially remarkable are the twelve pillars of honey coloured marble, originally of Carrara, with their capitals which are of Byzantine elegance and simplicity. An ingenious author has lately proved that these were the pillars of white marble seen by Montaigne, during his Italian travels, which columns were lying ready to be shipped to the Sultan of Morocco. The great philosopher, who was half-Jewish through his mother, a member of the Portuguese family of Louppes (Lopez), from Bordeaux, may have felt a particular interest in this destination for Barbary, to which so much of the Andalucian learning had fled. The ceiling of the Saadian tombs is of miraculous craftsmanship in inlaid cedar wood, and so are the honeycombed stalactite arches, than which there is nothing more delicate, even in Tlemcen, which is so near to Andalucia and so alive with Andalucian influence. Tilework covers the lower part of the walls, and above are arabesque panels in stucco, astonishing in their variety upon such abstract themes. The whole tomb chamber comes like a revelation of great poetry in this mud-built town, where it might be thought no great architecture could be possible. In date it is the same as the Medersa Ben Youssef, late sixteenth century work.

Marrakesh, of course, had other buildings, long ago destroyed. There remains the Koutoubia, and it belongs to a manlier age. The builder of this was the Almohad, Yakoub El Mansour (1184–1199), who began it at the same time as the Tour Hassane, at Rabat, and the Giralda of Seville. It still dominates the whole town of Marrakesh and, in impressiveness, descends from a period which cannot have been less great and formidable than that which raised the campanile of St Mark's at Venice. In force and vigour the Koutoubia is, at least, the equal of the campanile. We are left to imagine for ourselves what must have been the mosque of the Koutoubia, never, it would seem, completed and, since, ravaged by earthquakes and by wars. Deliberate destruction has been the fate of other buildings. Each new dynasty sought, on purpose, to destroy the monuments of its predecessors. It was in this manner that the Saadian palace of El Badi was torn to the ground by the terrible Alaouite, Moulay Ismall, who wanted all the glory for Meknes. Little is left, then, in the way of old building. The other mosques are later in date and not distinguished in their architecture. Even so, the Koutoubia has set its mark upon the whole city.

Most, if not all, of the private palaces of Marrakesh, are of modern construction. But this does not in the least prevent their being authentic to the last degree, for each new building must be nearly the facsimile of that which it supplanted. There may be six or seven palaces belonging to different chieftains, all with the same interior scheme of courts and fountains. The palace of El Glaoui should be best of all, and his many guests must take back with them an enchanting memory of its delicate arches and its orange trees. This palace, but it would appear to be one out of three or four palaces standing back to back, has only lately been completed, some of it since my first visit to Marrakesh ten years ago. The very arrival for dinner is an excitement in itself, because of the beggars at the door, the tribesmen waiting there, a curved dagger at their waist, and the long, mysterious corridor which forms the entrance. In a hall of white arches El Glaoui is waiting, more modestly dressed than any of his followers, and the way is led across a court of orange trees to an anachronistic cocktail bar, where a bearded and turbaned barman, who is really majordomo, or even confidential adviser, has every known drink upon the shelves behind him. After a suitable interval, and the serving of various preliminaries, or hors d'oeuvres, including a delicious sugared confection made of almonds and with an almond kernel for its heart, dinner is announced.

The dining-room lies across another courtyard. It has the divans, cushions, and brass trays upon carved stands, that are the way of the land, and dinner is eaten with the fingers. An entertainment by the Glaoui has been described before, upon occasions beyond number, but it is necessary to add a personal tribute to the excellence of the food. For the Arab cuisine, when it is upon this scale of perfection, will come as a revelation to gourmets. A typical dinner will begin with soup, followed by pastilla, an Arab dish composed of pastry, made after the fashion of mille feuilles, and containing eggs, aubergine and chicken. It comes in on a round dish of immense size, divided into four or five portions, and dusted in the centre with fine white sugar with which you should touch your handful before eating. The only fault of pastilla is that the portions of chicken, inside it, burn your fingers as you break the flakes of pastry. After this come pigeons stuffed with maize, to which a faint flavour of attar of roses has been given. Next, another and more delicate pastilla. Then, chickens with almonds and pistachios. Every time a new dish comes in, it is rushed in, as if to sacrifice, by servitors, the immense wicker hood to the basket in which it is carried serving to keep it piping hot until the last moment. After chicken comes the mechaoui, the famous Arab way of cooking lamb. It is, indeed, lamb roasted whole, almost as though it were a sucking pig, a dish which is excellent in itself, but it is followed by other and more subtle things. There are young carrots, of a tenderness which cannot be believed, and, after them, a dish of cardoons, the best imaginable, and retaining to a marvellous degree the different quality of their stems and roots in the contrast of that warm, root or heartlike consistency, to the crunching of the stems. Now comes couscous, and, eventually, the tenth course, a choice of two sugared sweets, of fritter form, but coiled, as it were, into snakelike convolutions. And the dinner ends with fruit.

Upon another, previous, occasion, there were ices made of wood strawberries and enough general variety, or difference, to prove the wide scope of the Arab cuisine. It is probably, though, nowhere else to be found so good as in the palace of El Glaoui, at Marrakesh. He is said to own, among other bibliographical treasures, a collection of old manuscripts upon cookery, of Persian or Egyptian origin. This knowledge must help to explain its excellence. Nowhere else, perhaps, this side of China, is the Oriental cuisine of such delicacy. But its interest, to the gourmet, must lie in the development of a technique apart and separate, consisting in dishes that are to be eaten with the fingers and that take, therefore, different shape and consistency. It is another world of invention, which never exercised the faculties of Brillat-Savarin, of Vatel, or of Soyer. The results are as light and digestible, despite their fabulous quantity, as any Western meal. Neither is eating with the fingers, when coldly considered, any more despicable than our eating with universal forks and spoons shared by us with hundreds whom we have never seen. There is, in short, much in this Arab cuisine that should be studied, for it has a multitude of secrets that are lost to us, or that we never knew.

The food of all but a few of the richest families, it may be admitted, would be repugnant, or even impossible, to our tastes. In the souks, and there are not many persons who could endure the souks, day after day, for more than a few days at a time, the most noisome sights of all are the heaps of native butter, scooped away as though with a wooden spoon, and which have, in the course of years, converted the wooden counter on which they stand into a slippery, oily softness. This butter, moreover, has a most unpleasant smell and is nearly always crawling with flies. Scarcely less repellent is the soap, in brown semi-transparent masses that might be mistaken for butter. Soap and butter, in fact, apart from their colour, could change places. Sometimes, the soap is to be seen arriving in a pair of panniers slung on either side of a donkey's back. It must be made in some particular quarter of the town, and the imagination recoils from the thought of this, so horrid must be the profession of those persons who are employed in boiling it. The souks where food is sold are only redeemed by the sugar cones, to be seen nowhere else, now, than in North Africa, though not long ago they were common in the grocer's shop in every English country town, forming, indeed, the staple sign of a grocer. Their shape, of course, is that of the grenadiers' caps of Frederick the Great's army, still worn on gala occasions at Potsdam before the last war. The butchers' shops are in another section of the souks that should be avoided. Worst thought of all is to think of what must be eaten in the Mellah, the Jews' quarter.

But it would be to continue this chapter upon Marxist lines, only to stress the lives of the poor majority of the population. No town, whether it is ancient Rome, or modern London, or New York, derives its character only from the most abject of its inhabitants. If this side of history were the correct way in which to view it, then the greatest, because the most horrible, incident in the history of Marrakesh would be the death, from typhus, of some twenty-five thousand of its inhabitants, so it is said, only two winters ago. We can well imagine how appalling those scenes must have been. How any of the beggars, or the half-starved children, can have survived that pestilence, is a complete mystery. We may think with horror of those cold nights of winter with men, women, and children, dying in every corner of the town. Luckily, owing to the rigorous steps taken by the French authorities, it is most improbable that this can ever occur again. It is a danger that has been attacked, not only locally, but, wiser still, in its cause or origin down in the poverty stricken Sous. It was from the starving south, where harvests had been disastrous for many years in succession, that the poor came to Marrakesh, thinking to find work there, and bringing with them the lice that spread the disease. The only safe way to prevent a recurrence of typhus was to improve conditions in the Sous, and over a great part of the Sud Marocain this has been done by the French authorities. Corn has been distributed free, and expert investigation has been undertaken with a view to improving the harvest by giving better seed, and by starting new irrigation works. Inoculation is less successful than these peaceful measures because of its violence, which is enough to kill off the old or weak.

No one, seeing Marrakesh to-day, could form any notion that it was thus decimated, or worse, only two years ago. There are, as we have said, types of poverty and illness the mere survival of whom would seem to disprove the possibility of any pestilence. But the town, which must always be poor, has regained its gaiety. Any night, and in the early hours of the morning, you have only to open your window in order to hear a continual singing and playing of instruments. In course of time, what sounded only to be monotony, without design, takes on definite and recognizable shape. Certain tunes, or one or two of them, at any rate, haunt your ears, even during daytime, before the music has begun. There are, it would seem, various forms of this music. The real Arab music, as it can be heard more easily in Fez, is, beyond dispute, dull and insipid. There remains the music which has Andalucian influence, more common, also, in Fez and in the North of Morocco, and the Berber music. But it is this latter, the Berber music, which gives the night in Marrakesh its character. There is no hint of Spain in this. Instead, it is something which is quite new to experience, with no trace in it of any music heard before. But that it is music worthy of that name, with beauties and subtleties peculiar to itself, no one will deny who has once caught its flavour.

There are, probably, not many persons competent in this music. It comes from the South, or, more strictly, remains there and does not go abroad. The opportunity occurred of hearing a troupe of singers and dancers who, from the private palace in which they gave their performance, may be presumed to be the best of their kind in Marrakesh. Two musicians accompanied them upon stringed instruments of medieval appearance, like those played in the frescoes of paradise, but this, apart from giving the time, was no contribution to the beauty of the music. The rest of the troupe consisted of four or five young girls, not more than twenty years old. Two of them were artists. One, who was younger, having only just come to Marrakesh, had an extraordinary air of concentration and assurance, when dancing or singing, but, afterwards, if pleasure was expressed, or if spoken to by the host, was contorted and made really ill with shyness. This copied, exactly, the old-fashioned miming in the ballet *Giselle*, when the heroine is approached by the prince. Her stilted rusticity of manner, in that dead Victorian way, set, as it should have been, by the vineyard, or the woodman's hut, under the shadow of the feudal castle, made a most curious contrast with the actual scene. She was a Berber; and just as the Berbers have their feudal castles, so they have their medieval manners and mode of living, of just that dim epoch in which *Giselle* is set, so that our comparison is of true and sensible application. It was, moreover, in the palace of the most powerful of those feudal chieftains that this entertainment took place.

The Berbers, it is now time to remark, more often than not are as fair as Europeans, and fairer, even, than many races of the Mediterranean. The true type of this was the second of this pair of dancers. She wore, like the others, a long silken dress with wide sleeves, and white silk turban. This turban had the touch of Guadaloupe, or St Lucia, of the French Creole of the eighteenth century, but only for a moment from the tight form of the turban, which was tied like a bandana. In front, it showed all the forehead, and by its round arc prepared the round smoothness of her face.

But, now, this dancer becomes no more West Indian but Turkish, of the time of Liotard. This is because of the gouache smoothness of her skin, done with elaborate 'make up' and reddened lips, but leaving the nose, matt, but un-powdered, so that it becomes the personality of her face. It is the life in her, otherwise, completely immobile expression and downcast eyes. But her dress is too medieval to be a Liotard. There is, again, something Persian in her arched eyebrows, though they are thinly pencilled. Her most puzzling appearance and personality, unlike any known before, but compounded of so many hints and half allusions, becomes something quite different when she smiles. This is the living present, the interior of this facade. But, more than anything else, it is the dignity and gravity of these dancers that is remarkable. Their training is most elaborate, to a perfection in little things, as in the curious inflections of their singing and in their studied modesty. This dancer, of whom we are speaking, was so completely Berber that she could not be understood in Arabic. She came from the South, from Tiznit, a town which, as we shall see when we arrive there, is famous for its sheikhat dancing girls; but it is likely that her origin was still further to the South, in Goulimine, a place where the dancers are even better than at Tiznit. She was of a race, then, that is unknown, but who can produce, it is certain, women who would be beautiful in any surroundings and at any time.

It was intriguing to think what her hair could be, without its turban, for a turban hides the hair and, therefore, much of the expression, as did the periwigs of the seventeenth century. Without her turban she might be less smooth and smiling, less of the Creole, less Persian. We have described her person, but how is her music to be described? The instruments are various: guitars, hand drums, an iron ring beaten with an iron file or hammer, or little bells or percussion disks, worn upon the fingers. With these, a music of much subtlety, of minute shade or particle, for much of it is metallic in sound, is set in train. The dances are mostly static; at times, in this instance, a modified version of the 'danse du ventre'; but, mostly, with a rhythmical tapping of the bare feet upon the carpeted floor; or with slow, processional move round the room. Singing, also, is done with downcast eyes and with that odd effect from the glottis, as if the voice had a second gear or speed. We must remember, where the visual side of this dancing is concerned, that the surprise of its appearance comes from the practical invisibility of all women. It is this that makes one wonder, as now, in front of a beautiful woman, as to what her beauty consists in, and what could be its analogies.

She remains in the memory, standing, guitar in hand, that long silken robe, looking like a Persian, like a Liotard, very grave, with eyelids that never flickered for an instant; or, another moment, sitting crosslegged, on a divan, much smaller, with thin wrists, and smiling, her white turban being no little pleasure in itself. Her singing fades more and more in the memory. But the singer and her music can personify Marrakesh to all persons, who, before a living work of art, can forget the dust and flies, the beggars and all the misery of the present. It adds something to Marrakesh that was not there before, either in the memory, or in the imagination, only in the shuttered room, or by the falling waters.

ABOUT THE AUTHOR

SACHEVERELL SITWELL (1897–1988) Sacheverell was the youngest of the celebrated three Sitwell siblings (Osbert and Edith) who played such an important role in the literary culture of Britain throughout the 1920s and 1930s. Sacheverell's output as a writer, poet, traveller, adventurer and a connoisseur of music and architecture was prodigious with over a hundred works to his name. Neil Ritchie's bibliography of his writings itself fills a book of 390 pages. He was one of the cultural trail-blazers of twentieth-century taste, driven by an unerring quest for the beautiful, the odd and the macabre. His training as a poet allowed him to fashion a new style for the appreciation of architecture. His most innovative works (such as *Southern Baroque Art*, 1924, *The Gothic North*, 1929 and *German Baroque Art*, 1927) opened up new horizons of understanding.

Mauretania: Warrior, Man and Woman is brilliant in flashes but fails as a whole. To attempt a comparative analysis of the different nations and cultures within North Africa was an entirely meritable intention but it was too vast an undertaking to be achieved in a February to March tour. Although Sachie had known Tunis, Hammamet and Marrakesh from previous visits he was also too happily immersed within the structure of the ruling colonial regime to be an impartial witness. The 1939 tour was subsidised by the French civil and military authorities who were pleased to show off the newly pacified 'South'. Dressed throughout in immaculate Savile Row suits and accompanied by a distracting train of beautiful women (including Lord Curzon's glamorous youngest daughter), guides and a train of chauffeur-driven cars, they were fêted and feasted where ever they wandered. Fortunately his description of Marrakesh is one of his most famous and assured pieces of travel writing. It may be relevant to his composition that the previous year Sachie had been entranced by a re-reading of Flaubert's *Salammbo* in the ultimate Orientalist fantasy of the d'Erlanger palace of Nejma Ez Zohra that perches beside Sidi Bou Said outside Carthage. Sachie had then written, 'In the terrific August heat all Flaubert's images struck true. Nothing was exaggerated. Such were the real colours . . . '

The Fairy-tale City

from *Lords of the Atlas* by Gavin Maxwell

It is against the setting of Marrakesh that T'hami El Glaoui is remembered best, that incredible city that has changed so little in almost one thousand years of existence. The city was founded in 1062 by the first of the Almoravide dynasty of Sultans, and the very earliest of the mediaeval descriptions of it are but little different from T'hami's Marrakesh between the two world wars.

Marrakesh (always referred to by early European writers as Morocco City) stands on the great fertile plain of Haouz, some seventeen hundred feet above sea level, and forty miles from the foot of the High Atlas, whose mighty peaks tower another twelve thousand feet above it, remote, icy, snow-covered for the greater part of the year, a splendid backcloth for the splendour of the city itself. Some eight miles of now time-worn ramparts enclose the thronging hive of humans, ramparts pierced by ten great gates, each giving its name to a quarter of the city. Dynasty after dynasty of Sultans enriched Marrakesh with the finest architecture of their epoch; it became a royal city, the capital of the South, and many Sultans preferred their palaces there to those of Fez. By its geographical position the town became the great market place not only of the Haouz but of all the lands between the High Atlas and the Sahara, the clearing-house of the camel caravans from all the remote oases of the South with their loads of walnuts and oranges, grain and hides, spices, dates and precious metals. It was the largest slave market in all Morocco; by the time of T'hami's reign the recent disappearance, at least from the public eye, of that weekly auction, was the only external departure from the traditions of the city as they had developed over nearly ten centuries. Marrakesh was much as Europeans visualize the Baghdad of The Thousand and One Nights, but more beautiful than Baghdad ever was, for Baghdad lacked the savage glories of the Atlas as a background to the jewels of palace and garden, orchard and lake, and the glittering green-tiled minarets of the mosques. Over every traveller who visited it Marrakesh cast its strange heady spell – a spell that to many has survived the short French occupation and the partial westernization of the unique and essentially African city. Marrakesh is accessible, it has become perhaps the greatest tourist attraction of all North Africa, but the tourists, however great an impression Marrakesh makes upon them, make little impression upon Marrakesh. In 1904, as Ben Susnan [sic] wrote with a foresight worthy of Jules Verne,

> There are certain cities that cannot be approached for the first time by a sympathetic traveller without a sense of solemnity and reverence that is not far removed from awe. Athens, Rome, Constantinople, Damascus, and Jerusalem may be cited as examples; each in its turn has filled me with great wonder and deep joy. But all those are to be reached nowadays by the railway, that great modern purge of sensibility. In Morocco, on the other hand, the railway is still unknown . . . until the Gordian knot of Morocco's future has been untied or cut. Then, perhaps, as a result of French pacific penetration, flying railway trains loaded with tourists, guide-book in hand, and camera at the ready will pierce to the secret places of the land, and men will speak of 'doing' Morocco, as they 'do' other countries in their rush across the world, seeing all the stereotyped sights and appreciating none. For the present, by Allah's grace, matters are quite otherwise.

Allah's grace did not last long in this respect, and the French penetration was not quite as pacific as Ben Susnan anticipated; nor could he well have known that T'hami El Glaoui would become a scratch golfer and cause a golf course to be laid out for his pleasure at Marrakesh itself. But Marrakesh is still to be approached with awe.

Marrakesh was not only the market place of all the southern riches; since early times it had become a pleasure town for the distant tribespeople who carried them there. The city had a perpetual floating population of some twelve thousand people: wild, pale-skinned Berbers from the mountain villages, black men from the edge of the desert, Arab tribes such as the Rehamna from the plains to the north and the west; they came, they sold their goods, and had money to spend, so that the city became a sort of perpetual fun-fair. Close to the tall Koutoubia mosque, one of the grandest in the country, a great irregularly shaped open space of beaten earth, the Place Dj'mma El F'naa has from very early times been given up entirely to the use of public entertainers, around each of whom would form a dense circle of spectators, its circumference touching that of the next ring, so that the effect in looking down upon the scene from some elevated building is that of a formally-patterned carpet made of some fifteen thousand human beings. The sound of human voices comes up like the muted rumble of some vast engine, an undertone to the perpetual staccato urgency of drums, the wailing of reed pipes, the clang of cymbals, the shrill tinkle of water-sellers' bells, the endless calling of the beggars – 'Allah! Allah! Allah!' The fluid circles form and dissolve and reform around the snake-charmers and sword-swallowers and fire-eaters, all of the Essaoui sect, their hair falling in blue-black cascades over their shoulders; gaudily dressed acrobats from Taroudant forming towers of multicoloured unidentifiable limbs; conjurers and mimers, and storytellers who hold a circle of a hundred solemn-faced children in hypnotized silence; Berber dancers from the mountains, their white-robed lines swaying in rhythmic advance and withdrawal; whirling black Gennaoua dancers from the Sudan, whose little conical caps, tasselled and embroidered with cowrie shells are spun fifty feet into the air as each dancer reaches the climax of his performance; troops of Chleuh boy dancers with painted faces, waggling hips, and clicking castanets, their bare feet flicking through the intricate pattern of the dance while their eyes rove the circle for evening clients; performing monkeys, fortune tellers, clowns - all these and their exotic audiences have been part of the Dj'mma El F'naa for hundreds of years.

Towards evening the din becomes crescendo; the sun sinks and lights the towering snow peaks of the Atlas to orange and pink; the shadows of the thronged spectators in the Dj'mma El F'naa become long black spikes that join group to group like the bars of an iron grille; over their heads drift homing flights of the numberless white egrets that roost nightly on the roofs above the wool market, their breasts lit with the same fiery colours that glow on the mountain snows.

If T'hami El Glaoui had ruled from a less fairy-tale city his myth, which was so great a part of his power, might never have come into being; it would have been less easy to dazzle in, say, the drab setting of Casablanca.

ABOUT THE AUTHOR

GAVIN MAXWELL, was born in 1914. Descendant of Scottish lairds and English marcher lords, he was interested in natural history and zoology from an early age, before coupling this with a thirst for travel. In World War Two he served as an instructor in the Special Operations Executive, charged with training agents who would be sent behind enemy lines on missions of sabotage. It was in this capacity that he got to know the west coast of Scotland, where he returned after the war to buy Soay, a small island off Skye and the location for his first business, a shark fishery, described in his first book *Harpoon at a Venture* (1952). He then tried his hand at freelance journalism, painting and travel writing. He joined up with veteran traveller Wilfrid Thesiger to explore the life and customs of the Iraqi marsh Arabs, a community now all but extinct. His experiences formed the book *A Reed Shaken in the Wind* (1957). After his return from Iraq he moved back to Scotland and his home of Camusfearna, there beginning the study of the otters he had acquired on his journey through the marshes, a study that culminated in the publication of *Ring of Bright Water* (1960). Funded by the phenomenal success of this book, an accompanying film and sequels, his house at Camusfearna became a wildlife preserve with his collection of otters at its heart, but burned down in 1968. Maxwell travelled to Morocco several times over the course of the 1960s, creating a history of the Glaoui Caids who dominated the government of southern Morocco in the first half of the twentieth century. *Lords of the Atlas* is one of the great travel books of the twentieth century, whose influence on British perceptions of Morocco cannot be over-estimated. On pages 235 to 255 Maxwell's biographer, Douglas Botting, examines the creation of *Lord of the Atlas* in detail. Gavin Maxwell died in 1969.

Yusuf-ibn-Tachfin

from *Mogreb-El-Acksa*
by R. B. Cunninghame Graham

Once through the olive groves of Tamasluoqht, the city of Yusuf-ibn-Tachfin [Marrakesh] lay glistening on the plain, almost hull down on the horizon. Above the forests of tall date palms which fringe the town, the tall mosque towers rose, the Kutubieh and the minaret of Sidi Bel Abbas high above the rest. From the green gardens of the Aguedal the enormous stonebuilt pile of the Sultan's palace, all ornamented with fine marbles brought from Italy and Spain, towered like a desert-built Gibraltar over the level plain. Across the sea-like surface of the steppe long trains of camels, mules, and men on foot crawled, looking like streams of ants converging on a giant ant-hill, whilst in the distance the huge wall-like Atlas towering up, walled the flat country in as the volcanoes seem to cut off Mexico from the world outside. The situation of Morocco city much resembles that of Mexico, which has a pseudo-Oriental look, the flat-roofed houses and the palm trees completing the effect.

A hot three hours kicking our tired beasts along, brought us outside the city walls, and passing underneath the gate, which zig-zags like an old Scotch bridge, we emerged into the sandy lanes running between orange gardens, which form a kind of suburb of the town, and where the Soudanese blacks, the men from Draa and the Wad Nun, do mostly congregate. No one would ever think, from the aspects of the lanes unpaved and broken into boles by winter rains, that he was actually inside a city which is supposed to cover almost as much ground as Paris. Still, it took almost three-quarters of an hour to ride from the outside walls to the centre of the town. We passed through narrow lanes where camels jammed us almost to the wall; along the foot-paths beggars sat and showed their sores; dogs, yellow, ulcerous and wild as jackals, skulked between our horses' legs, until at last we came out on an open space under the tower of the Kutubieh, in which square a sort of market was in progress, and a ring of interested spectators sat, crouched, and stood, intent upon a story-teller's tale. I sat a moment listening on my horse, and heard enough to learn the story was after the style of the Arabian nights, but quite unbowdlerised and suitable for Oriental taste.

A certain prince admired a beauteous dame, but an old Sultan (always the wicked baronet of Eastern tales) desired her for his harem, and engaged a certain witch, of whom there were great store throughout his territory, to cast a spell upon the prince, so that the lady should fall into a dislike of him. He, on his part, resorted to a wizard who stirred the ladies of the Sultan's harem up to play strange pranks and turn the palace upside down, let young men in o'nights, stay out themselves too late, and generally comport themselves in a discreditable way. A faithful slave at last made all things right, and after a most realistic love scene the prince and princess were married and lived happy ever after; or, as the story-teller, a sad moralising wag remarked, until the prince should take another wife. Humanity, when crushed together in the heat, either in London ball-rooms or in 'plazas' in Morocco city, sends up a perfume which makes one regret that the cynical contriver of the world endowed us with a nose; so that I waited but a little and rode on, turning to take a good look at the great mosque and tower as I went. Outside the mosque, the name of which in Arabic means 'Mosque of the Books', from the word *kitab*, a book, is not imposing. What it is inside I believe no Christian knows. Had I that moment, dressed as I was, sunburned and dirty, got off and entered it, I might have seen, but the thought did not cross my mind, and afterwards, when known for a European, it might have cost my life. The tower springs straight from the sandy square as the Giralda rises from the level of the street in Seville. One man built both, so runs tradition, and certainly the Kutubieh tower to-day reminds one greatly of the description of the Giralda when San Fernando drove out the Moorish king of Seville, and planted the banner with the Castles of Castille, above the town. The same gilt globes, of which the Spanish speak, are on the Moorish tower, and the same little cupola, which the Christians took away in Seville, replacing it by a renaissance *fleche*, upon which stands the towering figure cast by Bartolormé Morel. The tower, almost three hundred feet in height, is built of dark-red stone, with the alternating raised and sunk patterns (called in Spanish *Ajaracas*), cut deeply or standing boldly out from the solid masonry. At one time tile work filled most of the patterns, or was embroidered round the edges of the windows, but neglect and time have made most of it drop away. Still, just below the parapet runs a band, which from the square appears to be full four feet broad, of the most wonderful black and green iridescent tiles I ever saw. When Fabir, who, tradition says, built it for the Sultan El Mansur, and it stood glorious, adorned with tiles like those which still remain, the gilding fresh upon the great brass balls, even the mosque at Cordoba itself could not have been more glorious, and El Mansur could not have easily foreseen that on his lonely tomb under the palm trees, beside the river at Rabat, that goats would play. Allah, Jehovah, all the Gods are alike unmindful of their worshippers, who made and gave them fame; what more may the great builders of the Crystal Palace and the gasometers at Battersea expect, when they have had their day? Medina, Mellah, Kaiserieh, Sidi Bel Abbas, the tomb of Mulai Abdul Azis, all have been described so many times and by such serious and painstaking writers, who have apparently measured, re-measured, and calculated the cubic capacity of every building in Morocco city, that it would have been a work of supererogation on my part to have laid a measuring tape once more on any of them.

Morocco city struck me, and has always done so, for I have been there twice, as the best example of a purely African city I have seen. Fez has the mixture of Spanish blood in its inhabitants which the expulsed from Malaga, Granada, and from all the *Andalos* brought and disseminated. In the high houses, which make the streets like sewers to walk in, you hear men play the lute, and women sing the Malaguefla Cafla and the Ronderia as in mountain towns in Spain. Quite half the population have fair hair, some pale blue eyes, and their fanaticism is born of ancient persecution by the fanatic Christians of Spain. In every house, in every mosque, in almost every saint's tomb is fine tile work, stone and wood carving, the eaves especially being often as richly decorated as they had been Venetian and not African. The streets are thronged, men move quickly through them and the whole place is redolent of aristocracy, of a great religious class, in fact has all the air of what in Europe we call a capital. Morocco city is purely African, negroes abound; the streets are never full, even in the *kaiserieh* you can make your way about. With the exception of the Kutabieh Tower, and some fine fountains, notably that with the inscription 'Drink and admire' ('*Shrab-u-Schuf*') inscribed upon it, and the fine gate of the Kasbah of the best period of Moorish work, there is no architecture. Sand, sand, and more sand in almost every street, in the vast open spaces, in the long winding narrow lanes, outside the walls up to the city gates; sand in your hair, your clothes, the coats of animals. Streets, streets, and still more streets of houses in decay. Yellow adobe walls, dazzling white roofs and dense metallic semi-tropical vegetation shrouding the heaps of yellowish decaying masonry. No noise, the footfalls of the mules and camels falling into the sand as rain falls into the sea, with a soft swishing sound.

The people African, men from the Draa, the Sus, the Sahara, Wad Nun and the mysterious sandy steppes below Cape Bojador. Arabs quite in the minority, and the fine types and full grey beards of aged Sheikhs one sees so frequently in Fez exchanged for the spare Saharowi type, or the shaved lip and cheeks and pointed chin tufts of the Berber race. For music tom-tom and gimbry, the Moorish flute, ear-piercing and encouraging to horses, who when they hear its shriek step proudly, arching their necks and moving sideways down the streets as if they liked the sound. The songs quite African, the interval so strange, and the rhythm so unlike that of all European music as at first hearing to be almost unintelligible, but which at last grow on one until one likes them and endeavours to repeat their tunes. Hardly an aristocratic family in the place, and few Sherifs, the richer of the population being traders with the Sahara.

A city of vast distances, wearisome perspectives, great desolate squares, of gardens miles in length, a place in which you want a mule to ride about, for to attempt to labour through the sand on foot would be a purgatory. And yet a place which grows upon you, the sound of water ever in your ears, the narrow streets arched over all with grape vines; mouth of the Sahara, city of Yusuf-ibn-Tachfin, town circled in with mountains, plain girt, sun beaten, wind swept, ruinous, wearisome, and mournful in the sad sunlight which enshrouds its mouldering walls.

Fez and Rabat, Safrou, Salee and Mogador with Tetuan, Larache, Dar-el-Baida and the rest may have more trade, more art, more beauty, population, importance, industry, rank, faith, architecture, or what you will, but none of them enter into your soul as does this heap of ruins, this sandheap, desert town, metropolis of the fantastic world which stretches from its walls across the mountains through the oases of the Sahara; and which for aught I know may some day have its railway station, public houses, Salvation Army Barracks, and its people have their eyes opened, as were those of Adam and Eve, and veil their nakedness in mackintoshes

ABOUT THE AUTHOR

ROBERT BONTAINE CUNNINGHAME GRAHAM was born in 1852 of a family of Scottish lairds descended from Robert II. He spent much of his early life on South American cattle ranchs, where he developed a life-long passion for horses. A political radical, Cunninghame Graham served as Liberal MP for North-West Lanarkshire from 1886–92, was a great exponent of Scottish nationalism and spent time in Pentonville prison for his part in the 1887 demonstration in Trafalgar Square.

Mogreb-El-Acksa details Cunninghame Graham's attempts to journey to the city of Taroudant – a journey that openly flouted the Sultan's prohibiton of European travel to the south of Morocco. Through adopting the guise of a Sherif from Fez, and a small, loyal cadre of guides, interpreters and assistants, he trekked across country and the Atlas mountain range, only to be arrested within a few hours of his goal. Robert Cunninghame Graham died in 1936 in Buenos Aires.

Crowds and Chaos

from *The Moors* by Budgett Meakin

It lacks but half an hour to noon: high noon of a Morocco May. It is warm, as one might expect from the time of year, but not unpleasantly so, and the bright streaming light which pervades the scene, with all its colours and contrasts, serves to lessen the heat, in fancy at least. Were the costumes around us of sombre hue, or were the sky filled with cloud, how truly hot it would seem! Yet here, beneath this wayside fig-tree, we can almost discover a breeze. There is room for it, too, on this open space outside the Thursday Gate (Bab el Khamees) of Marrakesh, on the day after which it is named, when the famous market is held.

From early morning country-folk have gathered here -from all the districts round, bringing in produce and live-stock for sale. Many a weary mile have some of them trudged, since long before dawn, women as well as men bowed down beneath burdens more suited to quadrupeds. Some have even arrived over-night, and spent it rolled in their woollen tunics, white or brown, like so many chrysalides, notwithstanding a belated spatter of rain that had over-stepped the wet season. Perhaps that is why the morning seems fresh, and bargaining brisk, as it certainly is, but it requires much heat to turn a Moorish appetite for trade.

So here, too, are some hundreds of townsmen on business bent, though going about it as no European ever would, except in the sunny South. Between them arises a deafening din, loud vociferation interspersed with high-pitched feminine calls and expostulation, in rivalry with which donkeys bray, dogs bark, and horses maintain a lively discussion. Any chance there might be of momentary interval or lull is done away with by the lusty salesmen who perambulate to advertise their wares or publish the latest bid, and shout or sing according to taste, while the peripatetic water-seller jingles his bell and hoarsely exclaims, '*Likhass-hu 'l ma! 'likhass-hu 'l ma!*-for him who wants water! For him who wants water!' as though his life depended on it; or if he has had his skin-full paid for to be given as alms, he cries: '*Sabeel Allah! Sabeel Allah! Mai! Mai! Mai: bi la shai! A'shraboo' ya'l 'atshaneen*- The way of God! The way of God! Water! Water! Water without price! Drink, ye thirsty!' And indeed one would almost like to drink, did one not know whence came the water, for the dust is rising, and the air grows parched as noon draws near.

Overhead the deep blue firmament is cloudless, and yonder rises the Atlas, snow-clad. Against the background of the city walls, red, crenellated, crumbling, everything seems silhouetted, for the crowd is mostly clad in soft wool-white, so that the few in black or brown or colour show up clearly. Pointed hoods, broad hats, red caps, blue head-kerchiefs and turbans intermingled, ever moving, like a sea of full-grown locusts, give an air of bustle to the scene, such as one hardly looks for in the sleepy East. One scarcely knows where to commence its description.

As to massing and grouping, the artist must be consulted, detailed figures and their actions alone come within the scope of the pen, as one by one they detach themselves from that busy throng, it may be only for a 'kodak shot'. From all parts of the Empire representatives are here, white, bronzed and black; of Berber, Arab, Negro, Jewish, stock, but never a Nazarene. There are indeed a few inside the walls, engaged in preaching the Gospel or courting trade – a mere handful, all told, – but so seldom to be met with here that the crowd before us is entirely, typically, native.

The ever-changing scene is a kaleidoscope of Eastern fancy: Ali Baba and the forty thieves, Blue-beard, Aladdin and the Grand Vizier – all in succession pass before us. Possibly, too, under that all-concealing blanket is some fair Shaharah-zadeh – if you can pronounce her name, but do not try to, for in Morocco jealous guardians are not to be trifled with – and who knows but that Al Rasheed and Shah-zenán and Shah-riár are not among the surging crowd? At all events their slaves are here, great, fat, important looking eunuchs, hard-worked porters, all as black as Africa can make them, but right in heart, and thoroughly good-natured. See, here is one of their race who has obtained his freedom or been born to it, dressed as any Moor might be, in flowing gauze-like robes of rain-bow hues. No other can this be than that Othello whom fair Desdemona won, who, having told a traveller's tale, found little difficulty in extending it to make himself a Moor, a lie that lives.

But others take us further back, for with his string of camels here comes Eliezer of Damascus, and behind him Isaac, seated on his ample mule, a barrel-bodied beast that seems to know the weighty character he bears. Surely no more graceful or picturesque costume was ever invented than Isaac wears. Beneath a semi-transparent toga of wool, glimpses of luscious hues are caught, crimson and purple, deep greens and orange – 'sun-of-the-afternoon-tint' they call it, – salmons, and pale, clear blues. Although it is warm, his costume is hardly thin, for over his shoulders is loosely thrown a dark blue selhám or cloak of one piece. His turban is of goodly proportions and glistening white; his slippers are bright lemon yellow.

Side by side with this picture of comfort stands a tattered negro who has had his eyes put out for robbery, a punishment now fortunately rare. His sightless sockets turn appealingly to this and that one as they hasten by, his footsteps guided by a little child. Most are importuned in vain, but here and there one gives, for the Moors believe in alms as steps to Paradise, and no excuse or refusal is taken unless couched in the phrase '*Yajeeb Allah!* May God bring it!' – from which the beggar infers that the speaker at least will give nothing.

'*Ah Muláí Idrees! Ah halawát!* – Oh my lord Idrees, O sweets! – *Ah halawa-á-a-t!*' – It is the voice of an itinerating sweet-seller, whose laden tray of stickiness is hardly freed from hovering swarms of flies by his busy swish, ever and anon descending right or left upon some shaven pate beneath which eyes look longingly, and feet suspiciously approach.

Yonder stalwart form, contrasting strangely with the lighter hues around him, in a thick, stiff robe of goat hair, fringed, shaped like to an extinguisher with tasselled hood to match; jet black except an assegai-shaped patch across the back about the level of the knees – the patch bright-yellow with designs in red or black, – that form is an Atlas Berber, a Shlûh. He represents the original Moor: no mixed blood in him, but a pride of independence dearly bought, and still to some degree maintained. He might be Mephistopheles, to see him stalking there, his bare and bony shanks beneath that curious robe, thrust into leather bags now brown, that once were heel-less yellow slippers. One arm alone is visible, the right, which, holding back the corresponding cloak-flap, is employed in violent gesticulation, for its owner would purchase a mule at half the price asked, and is stoutly swearing that its complicated ailments and defects reduce its value to far less than he is offering. A crumpled, unwashed, cotton bell-sleeve flutters loosely in the breeze, and the garment to which it belongs is seen to be girt at the waist by a leather belt.

Meanwhile a lusty auctioneer endeavours to persuade him to bid for another. Up and down a narrow space amid the crowd he is pacing a distracted barebacked beast, whose head is held back by a cruel bit forcing open its foaming jaws; its flanks made gory by the use of a single-point spur. Hear him crying the bids. '*Wa meeátaïn wa khamseen, thláthá* – and two hundred and fifty-three!' Surely this is famine price, but it will rise, for Morocco auctioneers know well the gain of beginning low, where time is no object. The bids are in metkals or ducats, worth about threepence, and rise by fives, for there is no hurry, though the sun be high. Presently they cease and the auctioneer, dismounting, throws the end of the halter into the hands of the highest bidder, proceeding to parade another animal. But the sale is far from complete, for the apparent purchaser has only gained the right to drive a private bargain with the seller, who, retaining the right to refuse the bid, invariably does so, and stands out for better terms. These having at last been fixed, a visit is paid to the so-called, 'vet', more properly the farrier, who, for a consideration, discovers faults, each of which is an excuse for claiming a reduction in price, while the vendor claims as his right '*hakk Allah*' or 'God's due' in addition to what he has agreed to take. When at last the transaction is ended, the necessary documents exchanged and the market dues paid – after further haggling – it is already past noon, and feeling hungry, we turn to the town.

This, however, is more easily said than done, as we laboriously thread our way through the surging mass, in which each individual behaves as though only his or her business were of the slightest importance, jostling, vociferating, gesticulating and cursing. But in the noise they make the women excel the men. The young and good-looking wrapped in their blankets, so that only the eyes - perhaps one alone – can be seen, the old and faded with a mere pretence at concealing their features – the coquettish letting a corner fall from time to time 'by accident', – they move about like animated sacks, or squatting on the ground beside their wares, drive bargains with the best. Here is a group surrounded by panniers of charcoal, hard by are others with bundles of wood and grass which they cannot lift unaided, but which they have brought in on their shoulders. Others have before them vegetables, pottery, or home-spun and ready-made garments.

'How much? Why, ten metkáls, and cheap at that!'

'Ten metkáls? Art mad? Everywhere else it is sold for five! But I'll give thee six; never mind.'

'Never mind! I like that. Clear out! I'll take nine and a half or nothing.'

'Yes, and thou'dst like to, no doubt. Thou old miser! Think thyself lucky if thou canst get six and a quarter; it's all I'll give.'

'Then what dost thou want with me? Thou knowest it cost me nine, may God curse the liar!'

'God burn thy father! It cost thee five!'

'Well, what if it did? My last price is nine and a quarter.'

'Then get it! In peace!'

Turning on his heel, the possible purchaser directs his attention to the wares of a rival trader, adding as a parting fling: 'Six and a half is all I possess!'

He has scarcely commenced a similar process there, when he hears himself re-called, but hardly deigns to return.

'Hi, Uncle Pilgrim!'

'Yes, my Mother! Well?'

'Look here, take it for eight and three-quarters: I don't mind losing a little by so good-looking a man. Say nine less a fourth?'

'Pooh! That's all rubbish. Thou'dst be glad to get seven, but I'll make it six and three-quarters; come now, thou'dst not be hard!'

'Hard? I should think not, when I make a sacrifice to gratify a fancy. Now – prayers be on the Prophet – acknowledge that thou art prepared to give eight!'

'Not for a moment: seven's the highest price I could dream of.'

'Well, if thou wilt not, thou wilt not: so be it.' Thus the matter drops, both sides requiring the relief of an armistice wherein to take breath, during which their thoughts apparently wander with their tongues to other things, as each engages in conversation with some one else. After a while the customer remembers it is time to move on, and as he turns to go asks languidly,

'Give it me for seven and a half? I can't be bothered bargaining longer.'

'No, eight less a quarter is the furthest I can go.'

'All right then; I'm off.'

So, seeing that he really is off this time, woman exclaims in despair, 'Where's thy money? Take it and leave me to starve!'

'At seven and a half?'

'No, seven and three-quarters.'
'Seven and a half was all I bid.'
'Then pay it and begone!'

But articles in common use, of which there are many sellers, fall to what is
practically a fixed price, so that it is only with some object out of the usual size
or run that the Moor's love of cheapening can be indulged to the full. The
purchaser we have been watching was a stalwart plainsman from the central
provinces, Dukálla, maybe, or Rahámna, Shaweea or Háhá: known by his
coarse white haik or blanket, loosely wrapped about him, draping freely, and
his, slovenly turban, also once white, beneath which his bronzed cheeks and
limbs tell of an out-door life. In contrast to him stands close by a native of the
valley of the Dra'a, across the Atlas to the south, a short, thick-set mulatto with
a rag for turban and a tattered cloak of undyed brown, – quite different in race,
a mixture between the Berber and Negro, - representing an important
province. With him is engaged in deep conversation a neighbour from Sûs, the
province which includes the southern spurs of the Atlas, a fair-skinned Berber,
also in white, a cotton shirt with a red leather satchel, and a camel-hair cord
round his shaven skull; short like the Dra'wi, but keen-eyed and active, sharp
in trade and clever in craft. He and his friend are talking in Berber, –
Tamazeeght they call it – curious-sounding, guttural, sibilant medley, the real
language of Morocco, though its dialects vary considerably from province to
province.

Under a tree in the shade, as we pass along, sit a group of Jews, sombrely clad
in black or blue cloth robes or dark woollen cloaks like some of the Moors but
not for a moment to be confounded with them, even apart from the greasy black
skull-caps and slippers, or the kerchiefs of white-spotted blue which most have
tied over their heads. Their features, their peculiar pronunciation, their cringing
behaviour, all stamp them as down-trodden Hebrews, able though they be to
out-wit their oppressors in money matters. Here they are among the principal
traders: yonder grey-beards in shabby garb, seated on unloaded panniers, are
among the leading merchants of the place, who for a sufficient percentage will
advance you any sum you may have reasonable hopes of returning. Those
others, in Berber cloaks like that worn by the buyer of the mule, but with great
tufts of curly hair below each temple, come from the Atlas, where each one is

tributary to a Berber under whose protection he lives, and without whose permission he dare not travel.

Many others we might stop to notice, had we the time; in most cases we might tell the province, if not the town, whence that came by their dress or their features. So we pass on rapidly, merely spare a glance for the pottery sellers with their primitive, elegant wares displayed around their extemporized tents; then at the dealers in spices, with more elaborate shelters, and a multitude of trays and boxes spread out before them, containing not only the seeds and roots used in cooking, but also those sold as drugs, the gums for incense, the tea and sugar, the scents and the poisons so convenient to jealous wives. For a penny we may buy corrosive sublimate or arsenic enough to put an end to a household – just a little in their tea! Fruit there is too, oranges piled up in abundance and apricots just coming in, sold in cane-work crates.

Less inviting is the butcher's quarter where are hanging carcasses galore on tripods of branches, the soil beneath so saturated that when a breeze blows our way after rain the odour is unbearable. So on we hasten to the city gates where the crush grows greater, the noises are louder, the stenches are stronger and the crowded colours seem brighter, as seething masses pour in and out amid herds of cattle and droves of sheep, here making way for some important-looking dignitary, there anathematising a careless slave on the tail of a bare-backed mule, lashing it with the halter and making his way through with a clatter and cry of '*Bál-ak! bál-ak!! bál-ak!!!* – Mind out! mind out!! mind out!!!'

Like the portals of their houses, the Moors build their city gates with a double turn, presumably in this case to prevent the inrush of enemies, by causing them to lose their impetus. So even in time of peace there is always a crush at the main city gates, the sides of which are torn and worn by the continuous stream of loaded animals. In the crenellated mud-built walls most typical of Moorish towns, deep-red or brown, or in the white-washed, stone-built walls of the coast, the frowning gateway is the one relieving feature, which imparts an air of majesty to what would otherwise be gloomy and uninteresting. Frequently surmounted by a battery, or ornamented by stone-work or tiles, the effect is good in the rudest examples, and here before us is one of the best. Cautiously stepping amid the throng, we follow the passage, first to one side and then to the other, till we emerge in the wider thoroughfare beyond, wide, that is, for

Morocco, where, as in most Oriental countries, streets are only arranged for pedestrians, and where even beasts of burden may block the way. In the gate itself is often an alcove, occupied by an authority administering justice, or it may form the office of the tax-collectors.

The street in which we find ourselves is cobble-paved, if paved at all, with disused mill-stones down the center covering the sewer. At night it needs some local knowledge and care to pick one's way about, for the streets are unlighted, and wayfarers or their servants who need light must carry their own, huge lanterns generally furnished with candles. The street is lined on either side by cupboard-like shops, the floors of which are raised above the ground waist high, the fronts being made to open horizontally in two flaps, one hanging down to the ground with the step affixed, the other propped up to form a sun-shade, from which are often suspended articles for sale. These also line the sides and all but cover the floor, in the centre of which squats the owner, demure and reserved, not seldom asleep, as he composes himself comfortably on his wares. When a customer appears he will be wide awake enough, if there is business to be done, though he may still abstractedly mumble his rosary prayers, as he defends himself against attempts to bargain. To stop and investigate these dark recesses one by one would take weeks: to do so we must seat ourselves on the ledge in front left bare for customers, our feet dangling over the street, and take our time, for nothing is to be done here in a hurry, and the cheapening we heard on the market goes on also in the shops.

As we pass through the city we find that most of the trades have sections to themselves. Just now we were in Grocers' Street, surely this is that of the drapers, and yonder are the silk-plaiters. A deafening din of hammering announces that we are approaching the haunt of the copper-smiths, and round the corner are the shoeing-smiths. For silver-smiths and tin-smiths we must visit the filthy *melláh*, or Jewry. Here, however, are the carpenters, hacking away with hoe-like tools for all sorts of operations, and close by the turners employ toes as well as fingers, spinning the object in hand between two fixed points with a bow drawn back and forth. For apprentices they have mere children, bright lads, though, and full of promise of which their fortune is not likely to permit the fulfilment. In an adjoining street the weavers sit at their primitive looms, in which the shuttles are thrown to and fro by hand, while beside them lads reel off the hand spun threads and fill the spools. Just beyond is the street of the dyers, everything in it splashed with colour, great vats steaming, skins and cloth hung out to dry, and a matted, vine-clad trellis over head to ward off the sun. Many of the busy streets are thus protected, to the great comfort of passers-by who elsewhere are exposed all day to the sun.

Next we light upon the felt-maker, boys combing wool into small square pads which, skilfully laid on one another and soaked with lather, become one piece, some in flat sheets for saddle-cloths and praying rugs; some in moulds for caps, which will be calendered with burrs from bushes outside the walls. Saddlers working in red leather and cloth, shoemakers beating out yellow leather on stones, satchel-makers, belt-makers, all are inspected in turn, not one craft without its special interest and primitive accessories. Then a grateful odour of mint leads us to turn our steps to the cool, well-watered fruit and vegetable market, always a refreshing retreat in summer. Down the centre the mint, which the Moors take in tea, is piled up by the donkey-load, fresh and green, in enormous quantities, while other sweet herbs in abundance add to the pleasant fragrance. Coriander, cummin, parsley, marjoram, verbena, celery and sage scent the air in turn, and one lingers over the delicious oranges which are too tempting to be passed untasted.

Surely this is the place to pause and feast our eyes, too, on the interlacing streams of colour, as they eddy before us, all with a strange unconcern as to time, purchasers and passengers alike in their movements; with an occasional camel, or string of camels, passing through, with long necks swinging from side to side in calm, supercilious observation. The charm of the Arabian Nights is upon us; we have eaten of the lotus, and would fain forget the bustling West. The very Babel of sounds has something subdued and pleasing about it. There is neither scope nor need for shouting such as we heard just now upon the market, though half the people seem to be talking at once, and it is only now and again that a voice rises out of the chorus, some lad who shouts across in not unmusical tones, or the deep bass '*bálak*' of some 'grave and reverend seigneur' or his henchman, as they thread their way with dignity. The sunlight, streaming in patches, tells of the strong glare outside, and renders us more thankful for this pleasant shade, and for the coolness of the freely-sprinkled water. But we must pass on. Though loth to abandon this grateful shelter, we will enter yon handsome portal, so out of repair, for it seems, by the constant going and coming, to be some public building.

So it is, a *fandak*, or public store, with rows of offices and wholesale shops. Packing-cases from Europe litter the central court-yard, and one wonders how the large ones got here. But see, another is arriving, carried by eight stalwart porters, each pair bearing between them a bending pole from which the bulky package is swung by ropes. Poles creaking, men shouting, it is borne in and dumped down, as its bearers 'stand easy' and wipe their brows with their sleeves. In the stores around us sales are being effected of woollens and cottons, goods from Manchester and Birmingham, from Antwerp and Trieste, all with the leisurely disregard of time which is everywhere noticeable. Tea, sugar, candles, prints, satins, silks, muslins, broadcloth, braids and calicoes; tea-pots, tea glasses and tea-urns - all of styles unknown in England although often manufactured there, the last-named being the Russian *samovar*; – knives, looking-glasses, locks, nails, screws and trinkets; a varied, if not an extensive, assortment; all are here, and represent the chief imports from Europe.

Reached by a dirty and broken-down staircase, a sort of verandah surrounds the court-yard, serving as a passage for the upper storey. Here we find a better class of stores, where greater quiet reigns, but few save the important dealers require more than one small store – for their modest display, though they have warehouses elsewhere. Many of these *fandaks* are devoted to some special class of goods, while others are the resort of merchants from some special city. Here, too, Jews have stores and offices, while living in the Jewry, and there was a time when each of the foreign nations trading with Morocco was allotted one of the fandaks, in which the merchants resided under their several consuls.

The name *fandak* is, however, applied equally to any caravanserai or hostelry, the plan of which is always a series of rooms round a court, 'good stabling for man and beast.' In the door-way is a little coffee shop, and here we halt for some refreshment, though coffee is not the cup of Morocco, where tea reigns supreme. This man, however, knows how to make it in Arab style, so we are glad to seize the opportunity. Toasting a spoonful of berries over the fire in a ladle, he replaces this by a tiny, long-handled, lidless copper pot, filled with water, and while it boils, he pounds the fragrant coffee which he next puts into the pot. Letting it boil up a second time, he withdraws it, tapping it on the 'hob' to settle the grounds, and having let it boil and settle again, he pours it out, a vivifying beverage such as we seldom taste at home.

In many of the larger towns there is another class of business centre, a *kaïsarîyah*, or covered mart, surrounded by gateways or bars, and consisting of a somewhat better class of shops in better paved streets, into which beasts of burden are not admitted. These are either the property of the Government or of some mosque, and are fairly well looked after. Those of Marrakesh and Fez are especially fine, and of an afternoon are usually thronged. There sales by auction take place, certain articles on certain days, when the shops are replenished from the stock of home-made goods brought in by country folk. Nowhere throughout the Mohammedan East, – either in Baghdad, Shiráz, Samarkand, Bokhára, Pesháwar, Delhi, Agra, Lahore, Haïdarabád, Muscat, Basrah, Damascus, Constantinople, Cairo or Tunis, – have I seen more picturesque and animated scenes than may be witnessed day by day in Morocco, and thither should the student of the Orient repair, if he would drink in its spirit.

Once again emerging into the narrow, winding streets of constantly varying width, some paved, some littered with garbage amid which mangy curs are poking hungrily, we notice the gateways here and there which shut off the various quarters and most of the many blind alleys at night, to prevent the perambulation of evil-doers. After dark we should all carry lanterns, and shout for the porter at each of the gates; great men send their servants on ahead to have them all ready. In the residential quarter which we are now approaching the shops grow rare, except for small clusters of the poorer sort here and there, and the blank, resounding walls on either side of the way lend an aspect dismal and gloomy in contrast to what seemed just now so gay.

It is only when these walls are broken by the entrance to some mosque, into the tesselated court of which we surreptitiously peep for a moment and then pass on, or a way-side drinking trough – here called by courtesy a 'fountain' – sometimes beautifully decorated, that there is any relief from the window-less, prison-like look of the place. Moorish dwellings are designed for the seclusion of the women, and wherever there is a small window, it is closely barred.

Little decoration is expended outside, save on palace doors. Many of the finest private residences are approached by filthy, dark, serpentine *culs-de-sacs,* across which rooms are built at will, excluding light and air, and rendering them really dangerous at night. There is little of the picturesque about the outside of this class of Moorish dwellings.

ABOUT THE AUTHOR

JAMES EDWARD BUDGETT MEAKIN was born in England in 1866. His father, a keen orientalist, settled in Morocco and founded its first English language newspaper, the *Times of Morocco*, in 1884. Meakin himself moved out to Morocco for health reasons and worked on this paper, first as Deputy Editor then later as Editor. He began to closely study the people of this land and their customs, adopting local dress and learning the local Arabic dialect – in the process producing an English primer on the subject. Though he eventually fixed his permanent home in England, Meakin regularly travelled in Morocco and wrote three well-regarded books on the country, *The Moorish Empire* (1899), *The Land of the Moors* (1901), *The Moors* (1902) – from which this extract is taken – as well as the entry for Morocco in the *Encyclopedia Brittanica* (thirteenth edition). He was also an active social reformer, organising lecture tours and founding the British Institute of Social Services. Budgett Meakin died in 1906.

Marrakesh

George Orwell

As the corpse went past the flies left the restaurant table in a cloud and rushed after it, but they came back a few minutes later.

The little crowd of mourners – all men and boys, no women – threaded their way across the marketplace between the piles of pomegranates and the taxis and the camels, wailing a short chant over and over again. What really appeals to the flies is that the corpses here are never put into coffins, they are merely wrapped in a piece of rag and carried on a rough wooden bier on the shoulders of four friends. When the friends get to the burying-ground they hack an oblong hole a foot or two deep, dump the body in it and fling over it a little of the dried-up, lumpy earth, which is like broken brick. No gravestone, no name, no identifying mark of any kind. The burying-ground is merely a huge waste of hummocky earth, like a derelict building-lot. After a month or two no one can even be certain where his own relatives are buried.

When you walk through a town like this – two hundred thousand inhabit-ants, of whom at least twenty thousand own literally nothing except the rags they stand up in – when you see how the people live, and still more how easily they die, it is always difficult to believe that you are walking among human beings. All colonial empires are in reality founded upon that fact. The people have brown faces – besides, there are so many of them! Are they really the same flesh as yourself. Do they even have names? Or are they merely a kind of undifferentiated brown stuff, about as individual as bees or coral insects? They rise out of the earth, they sweat and starve for a few years, and then they sink back into the nameless mounds of the graveyard and nobody notices that they are gone. And even the graves themselves soon fade back into the soil. Sometimes, out for a walk, as you break your way through the prickly pear, you notice that it is rather bumpy underfoot, and only a certain regularity in the bumps tells you that you are walking over skeletons.

I was feeding one of the gazelles in the public gardens.

Gazelles are almost the only animals that look good to eat when they are still alive, in fact, one can hardly look at their hindquarters without thinking of mint sauce. The gazelle I was feeding seemed to know that this thought was in my mind, for though it took the piece of bread I was holding out it obviously did not like me. It nibbled rapidly at the bread, then lowered its head and tried to butt me, then took another nibble and then butted again. Probably its idea was that if it could drive me away the bread would somehow remain hanging in mid-air.

An Arab navvy working on the path nearby lowered his heavy hoe and sidled slowly towards us. He looked from the gazelle to the bread and from the bread to the gazelle, with a sort of quiet amazement, as though he had never seen anything quite like this before. Finally he said shyly in French:

'*I* could eat some of that bread.'

I tore off a piece and he stowed it gratefully in some secret place under his rags. This man is an employee of the Municipality.

When you go through the Jewish quarters you gather some idea of what the medieval ghettoes were probably like. Under their Moorish rulers the Jews were only allowed to own land in certain restricted areas, and after centuries of this kind of treatment they have ceased to bother about overcrowding. Many of the streets are a good deal less than six feet wide, the houses are completely windowless, and sore-eyed children cluster everywhere in unbelievable numbers, like clouds of flies. Down the centre of the street there is generally running a little river of urine.

In the bazaar huge families of Jews, all dressed in the long black robe and little black skull-cap, are working in dark fly-infested booths that look like caves. A carpenter sits cross-legged at a prehistoric lathe, turning chair-legs at lightning speed. He works the lathe with a bow in his right hand and guides the chisel with his left foot, and thanks to a lifetime of sitting in this position his left leg is warped out of shape. At his side his grandson, aged six, is already starting on the simpler parts of the job.

I was just passing the coppersmiths' booths when somebody noticed that I was lighting a cigarette. Instantly, from the dark holes all round, there was a frenzied rush of Jews, many of them old grandfathers with flowing grey beards, all clamouring for a cigarette. Even a blind man somewhere at the back of one of the booths heard a rumour of cigarettes and came crawling out, groping in the air with his hand. In about a minute I had used up the whole packet. None of these people, I suppose, works less than twelve hours a day, and every one of them looks on a cigarette as a more or less impossible luxury.

As the Jews live in self-contained communities they follow the same trades as the Arabs, except for agriculture. Fruit-sellers, potters, silversmiths, black-smiths, butchers, leatherworkers, tailors, water-carriers, beggars, porters – whichever way you look you see nothing but Jews. As a matter of fact there are thirteen thousand of them, all living in the space of a few acres. A good job Hitler isn't here. Perhaps he is on his way, however. You hear the usual dark rumours about the Jews, not only from the Arabs but from the poorer Europeans.

'Yes, Mon Vieux, they took my job away from me and gave it to a Jew. The Jews! They're the real rulers of this country, you know. They've got all the money. They control the banks, finance – everything.'

'But,' I said, 'isn't it a fact that the average Jew is a labourer working for about a penny an hour?'

'Ah, that's only for show! They're all moneylenders really. They're cunning, the Jews.'

In just the same way, a couple of hundred years ago, poor old women used to be burned for witchcraft when they could not even work enough magic to get themselves a square meal.

All people who work with their hands are partly invisible, and the more important the work they do, the less visible they are. Still, a white skin is always fairly conspicuous. In northern Europe, when you see a labourer ploughing a field, you probably give him a second glance. In a hot country, anywhere south of Gibraltar or east of Suez, the chances are that you don't even see him. I have noticed this again and again. In a tropical landscape one's eye takes in every-thing except the human-beings. It takes in the dried-up soil, the prickly pear, the palm-tree and the distant mountain, but it always misses the peasant hoeing at his patch. He is the same colour as the earth, and a great deal less interesting to look at.

It is only because of this that the starved countries of Asia and Africa are accepted as tourist resorts. No one would think of running cheap trips to the Distressed Areas. But where the human-beings have brown skins their poverty is simply not noticed. What does Morocco mean to a Frenchman? An orange-grove or a job in Government service. Or to an Englishman? Camels, castles, palm trees, Foreign Legionaires, brass trays and bandits. One could probably live here for years without noticing that for nine-tenths of the people the reality of life is an endless, back-breaking struggle to wring a little food out of an eroded soil.

Most of Morocco is so desolate that no wild animal bigger than a hare can live on it. Huge areas which were once covered with forest have turned into a treeless waste where the soil is exactly like broken-up brick. Nevertheless a good deal of it is cultivated, with frightful labour. Everything is done by hand. Long lines of women, bent double like inverted capital L's, work their way slowly across the fields, tearing up the prickly weeds with their hands, and the peasant gathering lucerne for fodder pulls it up stalk by stalk instead of reaping it, thus saving an inch or two on each stalk. The plough is a wretched wooden thing, so frail that one can easily carry it on one's shoulder, and fitted underneath with a rough iron spike which stirs the soil to a depth of about four inches. This is as much as the strength of the animals is equal to. It is usual to plough with a cow and a donkey yoked together. Two donkeys would not be quite strong enough, but on the other hand two cows would cost a little more to feed. The peasants possess no harrows, they merely plough the soil several times over in different directions, finally leaving it in rough furrows, after which the whole field has to be shaped with hoes into small oblong patches, to conserve water. Except for a day or two after the rare rainstorms there is never enough water. Along the edges of the fields channels are hacked out to a depth of thirty or forty feet to get at the tiny trickles which run through the subsoil.

Every afternoon a file of very old women passes down the road outside my house, each carrying a load of firewood. All of them are mummified with age and the sun, and all of them are tiny. It seems to be generally the case in primitive communities that the women, when they get beyond a certain age, shrink to the size of children. One day a poor old creature who could not have been more than four feet tall crept past me under a vast load of wood. I stopped her and put a five-sou piece (a little more than a farthing) into her hand. She answered with a shrill wail, almost a scream, which was partly gratitude but mainly surprise. I suppose that from her point of view, by taking any notice of her, I seemed almost to be violating a law of nature. She accepted her status as an old woman, that is to say as a beast of burden. When a family is travelling it is quite usual to see a father and a grown-up son riding ahead on donkeys, and an old woman following on foot, carrying the baggage.

But what is strange about these people is their invisibility. For several weeks, always at about the same time of day, the file of old women had hobbled past the house with their firewood, and though they had registered themselves on my eyeballs I cannot truly say that I had seen them. Firewood was passing – that was how I saw it. It was only that one day I happened to be walking behind them, and the curious up-and-down motion of a load of wood drew my attention to the human being underneath it. Then for the first time I noticed the poor old earth-coloured bodies, bodies reduced to bones and leathery skin, bent double under the crushing weight. Yet I suppose I had not been five minutes on Moroccan soil before I noticed the overloading of the donkeys and was infuriated by it. There is no question that the donkeys are damnably treated. The Moroccan donkey is hardly bigger than a St Bernard dog, it carries a load which in the British Army would be considered too much for a fifteen-hands mule, and very often its pack-saddle is not taken off its back for weeks together. But what is peculiarly pitiful is that it is the most willing creature on earth, it follows its master like a dog and does not need either bridle or halter. After a dozen years of devoted work it suddenly drops dead, whereupon its master tips it into the ditch and the village dogs have torn its guts out before it is cold.

This kind of thing makes one's blood boil, whereas – on the whole – the plight of the human beings does not. I am not commenting, merely pointing to a fact. People with brown skins are next door to invisible. Anyone can be sorry for the donkey with its galled back, but it is generally owing to some kind of accident if one even notices the old woman under her load of sticks.

As the storks flew northward the negroes were marching southward – a long, dusty column, infantry, screw-gun batteries and then more infantry, four or five thousand men in all, winding up the road with a dumping of boots and a clatter of iron wheels.

They were Senegalese, the blackest negroes in Africa, so black that sometimes it is difficult to see whereabouts on their necks the hair begins. Their splendid bodies were hidden in reach-me-down khaki uniforms, their feet squashed into boots that looked like blocks of wood, and every tin hat seemed to be a couple of sizes too small. It was very hot and the men had marched a long way. They slumped under the weight of their packs and the curiously sensitive black faces were glistening with sweat.

As they went past a tall, very young negro turned and caught my eye. But the look he gave me was not in the least the kind of look you might expect. Not hostile, not contemptuous, not sullen, not even inquisitive. It was the shy, wide-eyed negro look, which actually is a look of profound respect. I saw how it was. This wretched boy, who is a French citizen and has therefore been dragged from the forest to scrub floors and catch syphilis in garrison towns, actually has feelings of reverence before a white skin. He has been taught that the white race are his masters, and he still believes it.

But there is one thought which every white man (and in this connection it doesn't matter twopence if he calls himself a Socialist) thinks when he sets a black army marching past. 'How much longer can we go on kidding these people? How long before they turn their guns in the other direction?'

It was curious, really. Every white man there had this thought stowed somewhere or other in his mind. I had it, so had the other onlookers, so had the officers on their sweating chargers and the white NCOs marching in the ranks. It was a kind of secret which we all knew and were too clever to tell; only the negroes didn't know it. And really it was almost like watching a flock of cattle to see the long column, a mile or two miles of armed men, flowing peacefully up the road, while the great white birds drifted over them in the opposite direction, glittering like scraps of paper.

ABOUT THE AUTHOR

GEORGE ORWELL, born ERIC BLAIR in 1903, was one of the most significant and famous political novelists and literary essayists of the twentieth century. His most celebrated books are *Animal Farm* and *1984*. *Down and Out in Paris and London* and *Homage to Catalonia* – are Orwell's first-hand experiences as a transient in France and England and a volunteer in the Spanish civil war. Orwell was also a prolific and restless essayist and reviewer, gifted with a singularly limpid style.

A man in constant turmoil, caught between the nature of his privileged colonial background (son of an imperial civil servant, educated at Eton, brief stint as a colonial police officer in Burma) and his self-developed individual form of socialism, born of direct familiarity with poverty, snobbery and brutality. This dichotomy in his personality is clear in the essay on Marrakesh reprinted here: intellectually informed sympathy tempered with an instinctive suspicion of Moroccans themselves.

Left permanently weakened by a serious wound received in Spain, Orwell died in London in 1950, after a long struggle with tuberculosis.

The Bazaar

from *In Morocco* by Edith Wharton

Marrakesh is the great market of the south; and the south means not only the Atlas with its feudal chiefs and their wild clansmen, but all that lies beyond of heat and savagery: the Sahara of the veiled Touaregs, Dakka, Timbuctoo, Senegal and the Soudan. Here come the camal caravans from Demnat and Tameslout, from the Moulouya and the Souss, and those from the Atlantic ports and the confines of Algeria. The population of this old city of the southern march has always been even more mixed than that of the northerly Moroccan towns. It is made up of the descendants of all the peoples conquered by a long line of Sultans who brought their trains of captives across the sea from Moorish Spain and across the Sahara from Timbuctoo. Even in the highly cultivated region on the lower slopes of the Atlas there are groups of varied ethnic origin, the descendants of tribes transplanted by long-gone rulers and still preserving many of their original characteristics.

In the bazaars all these people meet and mingle: cattle-dealers, olive-growers, peasants from the Atlas, the Souss and the Draa, Blue Men of the Sahara, blacks from Senegal and the Soudan, coming in to trade with the wool-merchants, tanners, leather-merchants, silk-weavers, armourers, and makers of agricultural implements.

Dark, fierce and fanatical are these narrow souks of Marrakesh. They are mere mud lanes roofed with rushes, as in South Tunisia and Timbuctoo, and the crowds swarming in them are so dense that it is hardly possible, at certain hours, to approach the tiny raised kennels where the merchants sit like idols among their wares. One feels at once that something more than the thought of bargaining – dear as this is to the African heart – animates these incessantly moving throngs. The souks of Marrakesh seem, more than any others, the central organ of a native life that extends far beyond the city walls into secret clefts of the mountains and far-off oases where plots are hatched and holy wars fomented – farther still, to yellow deserts whence Negroes are secretly brought across the Atlas to that inmost recess of the bazaar where the ancient traffic in flesh and blood still surreptitiously goes on.

All these many threads of the native life, woven of greed and lust, of fetishism and fear and blind hate of the stranger, form, in the souks, a thick network in which at times one's feet seem literally to stumble. Fanatics in sheepskins glowering from the guarded thresholds of the mosques, fierce tribesmen with inlaid arms in their belts and the fighters' tufts of wiry hair escaping from camel's-hair turbans, mad Negroes standing stark naked in niches of the walls and pouring down Soudanese incantations upon the fascinated crowd, con-sumptive Jews with pathos and cunning in their large eyes and smiling lips, lusty slave-girls with earthern oil-jars resting against swaying hips, almond-eyed boys leading fat merchants by the hand, and bare-legged Berber women, tattooed and insolently gay, trading their striped blankets, or bags of dried roses and irises, for sugar, tea, or Manchester cottons – from all these hundreds of unknown and unknowable people, bound together by secret affinities, or intriguing against each other with secret hate, there emanated an atmosphere of mystery and menace more stifling than the smell of camels and spices and black bodies and smoking fry which hangs like a fog under the close roofing of the souks.

And suddenly one leaves the crowd and the turbid air for one of those quiet corners that are like back-waters of the bazaars: a small square where a vine stretches across a shop-front and hangs ripe clusters of grapes through the reeds. In the patterning of grape-shadows a very old donkey, tethered to a stone-post, dozes under a pack-saddle that is never taken off; and near by, in a matted niche, sits a very old man in white. This is the chief of the Guild of 'morocco' Workers of Marrakesh, the most accomplished craftsman in Morocco in the preparing and using of the skins to which the city gives its name. Of these sleek moroccos, cream-white or dyed with cochineal or pomegranate skins, are made the rich bags of the Chleuh dancing-boys, the embroidered slippers for the harem, the belts and harnesses that figure so largely in Moroccan trade – and of the finest, in old days, were made the pomegranate-red morocco bindings of European bibliophiles.

From the peaceful corner one passes into the barbaric splendour of a souk hung with innumerable plumy bunches of floss silk – skeins of citron yellow, crimson, grasshopper gren and pure purple. This is the silk-spinners' quarter, and next to it comes that of the dyers, with great seething vats into which the raw silk is plunged, and ropes overhead where the rainbow masses are hung out to dry.

Another turn leads into the street of the metal-workers and armourers, where the sunlight through the thatch flames on round flanks of beaten copper or picks out the silver bosses of ornate powder-flasks and pistols; and near by is the souk of the ploughshares, crowded with peasants in rough Chleuh cloaks who are waiting to have their archaic ploughs repaired, and that of the smiths, in an outer lane of mud huts where Negroes squat in the dust and sinewy naked figures in tattered loin cloths bend over blazing coals. And here ends the maze of the bazaars.

ABOUT THE AUTHOR

EDITH WHARTON was born in New York in 1862 and moved to France in 1910. Having taken up writing in 1897, she published over forty volumes of novels, short stories, verse, essays and travel writing, her most famous work including *The House of Mirth* (1905), and *The Age of Innocence* (1920). Visiting Marrakesh in 1917 she set out to write a contemporary guidebook, producing *In Morocco*. It is a predictable description of architecture and environment though there are flashes of evocative writing, such as this rather breathless account of the bustling bazaars of Marrakesh. She died in 1937.

Ramadan

from Behind Moroccan Walls by Henriette Celarié

I am in luck! – I was able to get back to Marrakesh just at the opening night of Ramadan.

Well before the narrow thread of a moon floats into the sky, I take up my post of observation on the hotel roof. I must not miss one feature of the spectacle that awaits me. My friends had warned me, 'You wait and see – Ramadan is dazzling.'

It is more than that – it is like a fairy-tale vision. There is not a roof below me without its group of festive women. To bedeck themselves, to set their neighbors marveling and make them envy, they have robbed their chests of all their silks, their caskets of every jewel. They may be lacking in what we call a sense of proportion, but so much the better! This first night of Ramadan must be unique among all other nights.

Under a sky of pale limpidity, women and children form glowing groups, bouquets of hardy colors. Rose-corals and purples contrast with sapphire-blue, almond-green with orange-yellow, with nasturtium.

One golden caftan glitters like a second sun; on another, all silvery, marvelous sea-waves seem to break and expand. When the children chase each other from roof to roof they make all the colors of a rainbow that forms and breaks. Elbows on the parapets, faces lifted toward the east, from that distance each woman appears a divine Tanagra figurine. Rockets mount in the air, the cries of 'you-you', the noise of tam-tams.

A radiant dying light is melted over everything. A soft breeze gently balances the long plumes of the palms. On the horizon the high summits of the Atlas take on the appearance of pyramids, of a table spread for some fabulous sacrifice; an incomparable decoration, one of the noblest in the world, for it has both grandeur and simplicity.

Lella Rahama has invited me to take tea with her this afternoon. It required my tomorrow's departure to excuse this breach of tradition. During Ramadan no visits are received in the daytime.

Her son, Si Abd el Aziz, has come to find me at my hotel. Lella Rahama's house is situated not far from the blessed Koutoubia whose shadow casts fortune on all good believers.

At one time this quarter of the city was bustling with activity. About the old tower of prayer and its mosque, two hundred booksellers alone had their stalls and sold their learned manuscripts.

What desolation has passed over the place since! There is a native account for it that one may believe or not. A certain sultan having dared to massacre at their prayers a group of rebels who had taken refuge in the mosque, the indignant counsel of Oulemas ordered, as a means of purifying the place, the demolishing of that part of the temple where the sacrilege took place.

During the succeeding centuries this part of the city has looked like an immense arid field. The curse of God seems indeed to have fallen upon it.

Then came the Europeans. Another curse! Houses of many stories and having 'all the modern conveniences' were erected.

Only a single palace is not out of place in the scene. It is that of the general commanding the region. Its ceilings extend to flat roofs, its walls of purple masonry are flowered over with bougainvillaea. To delight those within, sweet-smelling gardens steep in the sun.

Abd el Aziz and I walk along side by side. However strong the heat may burn, my companion is still in his winter djellaba, and at every step the heels of his babouches click on the hard, dried ground.

An auto passes, another, still another. The dust rises. The color of blood, it mounts in thick clouds and falls back in a rain of hard grains that cut the eyes and irritate the throat. The shining light is darkened. Everything around us disappears – the giant Atlas that upholds the sky on its shoulder, the Koutoubia with its emerald and turquoise tiles.

Asphyxiated, blinded, groaning, I exclaim, 'Allah never made your country for autos, Abd el Aziz . . . He made it for camels and asses.'

But my young guide, who is ambitious to own his own Ford or Citröen, returns stolidly, 'Autos are comfortable.'

Aflame with light the square of Djemaa el F'na opens up before us. Under awnings with hanging flaps like those of the card castles that children build, the native merchants seek an illusory shade. The crowd is fairly silent but tam-tams resound. The air gives off a strong odour of old leather, garlic, sweat and fruit.

Advance is made by precautionary stages. Standing or seated on the ground itself, spectators form large circles around the snake-charmers, the fire-swallowers, and the Chleuh dancers with their pretty gestures that are a bit too pretty.

A couple of giant negroes have joined forces to attract the silly ones. Their brown and white striped djellabas are opened above their ebony chests.

Planted on his big feet and as if rooted from them, the older interrogates his companion in a thundering voice. He puts to him a series of questions that seem to me the most ridiculously childish riddles, but they are of profound interest to the faithful of simple heart, pressed one against the other to listen. They ascribe to them a deeper meaning, connecting them with questions of religion.

'How does a believer with both arms amputated, go about making his ablutions?' demands the black who takes the rôle of schoolmaster.

A moment of silence as if he were plunged in deep thought, then the 'pupil' answers, 'He has someone else make them for him.'

To stand still, if it be only for a moment, to hold motionless under the sun's atrocious burning, is to me a diabolic punishment. The shaded street of banks spreads before us. Abd el Aziz and I turn into it.

He tells me about his family.

'My father died when I was a little fellow. I do not even recall him. I had an older brother of twenty; he was married. His wife died, and he also died last year. He left six orphans, three boys and three girls. My mother is bringing them up. It is hard for an old woman, but Hadra helps her.'

'Who is Hadra?'

'The eldest. She is sixteen.'

'Is she pretty?'

'There is nothing lovelier under the sun of the 'Seven Saints'. A flock of sheep would stop eating to look at her.'

A question mounts to my lips. Perhaps the caïda forbids my asking it. That would never do – if I began to bow to the caïda, I, a traveler and an inquisitive one, would risk passing many an interesting thing without even suspecting it was there.

I ask, avoiding a direct glance at Abd el Aziz in order not to add to the embarrassment I might cause him,

'Abd el Aziz, are you married?'

'Not yet.'

'I understood that the Prophet ordained a believer to marry and found a family as soon as he could?'

Abd el Aziz smiled. 'Is it my fault?'

Intrigued, I went further – and oh certainly this is contrary to the caïda.

'You mean you'd like to marry and cannot?'

'How can I? In Morocco, as everywhere else, things have become so much more difficult!'

Two hay-laden camels suddenly fill up the narrow street. We throw ourselves into the nearest alley to let them pass. Abd el Aziz resumes,

'One must have flouss to marry.'

'You have that, by the grace of God.'

'Yes, but not enough. Listen: Thou wouldst not have me marry a girl who was not of my own class, who was, even, not a bit above me. That is something that a Nazarene does not have to think about when he goes to marry, but which counts above everything with a Moslem.'

'How do you mean?'

'By Allah, I mean the dowry that must be paid to the girl's parents. Not that we buy our wives as you people so readily believe. A Moslem father no more sells his daughter than a Christian buys a husband for his. The dowry deposited by the young man simply serves to repay his fiancée's family for the expense that she puts them to the bride's trousseau, the carpets and mattresses for the new household and a thousand purchases besides.'

More camels and donkeys whose leader bawls out his resounding 'Balek, balek!'

Abd el Aziz is undisturbed in his figuring.

'I've counted the thing up. There's no way out of it but that I must deposit at least thirty thousand francs for a dowry.'

To me it doesn't seem like too much to pay to get a girl of good family, but Allah puts a seal on my lips.

'And that's not all,' proceeds Abd el Aziz. 'There's the question of the necessary gifts . . . At least four or five thousand francs.'

I add up mechanically. 'That comes to thirty-five thousand.'

'Don't think it! It comes to at least forty, for there's the matter of cost for the wedding feast. Forty thousand francs! Where do you expect me to find it?'

I gesture helplessly. I certainly don't know.

Abd el Aziz adds, 'Of course I have property. It is well situated and valuable. I could sell a piece of it. But my property brings in my income, and my wife then would simply be a cause of dispensing it. You surely see why I am not able to marry.'

From the point of view of arithmetic it is impossible to contradict him; Abd el Azizis correct; but every question has several aspects. I begin,

'If you were married, your wife would love you, she would make you happy.'

My young companion throws me an ironical glance. It is quite plain that he judges me naive for my age.

'Do you know how many divorces, how many repudiations, there are each year in Marrakesh?'

'Many, I'm sure of that. You repudiate your unhappy wives as easily, as carelessly, as you leave your babouches at the door when you enter a room.'

'Our unhappy wives! You mean their unhappy husbands! By Allah, you don't know the reasons brought to bear on us.'

'Tell them.'

'It would take me from now to the hour of Moghreb.'

'Tell some of them, then.'

'I will give you a few examples. My friends are almost all married. When they announced their marriage everybody drank to their happiness, for it really seemed they were doing a fine thing. They had aspired to, or rather their mother had aspired for them, to a rich girl of good family connections. But scarcely was the marriage concluded than the girl drew from her social superiority the right to manage everything her own way. No more liberty for the man. If he went out for a moment, if he returned a little late, there were suspicious questions, scenes, clamor – "Where hast thou been? – Where didst thou come from? – Who was with thee?" '

'Your friends should have married women of their own class.'

'That flatters the vanity less. But vanity aside, I'll admit certain unions are profitable.'

There we were exactly at the same point as before. I attempted to reason in a different light.

'A wife should give you children.'

But my argument is valueless. It is a Roumiya's argument. Retorting to it, in two phrases Abd el Aziz has measured the abyss that separates the two civilizations.

'Children? Why should I need to be married to have children? No matter what slave bears them for me, they will be legitimate. With us it is only paternity that counts.'

With this Abd el Aziz stops at the porch of a house in one of the city's oldest streets. Its cedar doorway is flanked on the right by a stone bench. Here the 'master of things' sometimes comes out to take the air, here the porter bears the visitors company who wait their turn to enter, while a slave warns the women to retire to their apartments.

We go first through the passage, then into the patio. It is a large one but with a saddening air, without bright tiles or a fountain.

In one of the inner rooms waits Lella Rahama with her two granddaughters. She makes a high ceremony of receiving me, dressed in a caftan of sober brown. A negress near her, as broad as she is long, gives me her hand with the same familiarity as one of the family. In fact she is one of them – she is Abd el Aziz's dada.

Lella Rahama has me take a seat in *el bahou*. The court opens before us like a green yard. On cither side the doorway the two girls sit face to face.

They have left off all their jewelry to mark that the month we have entered on is a time of penitence. In order to prevent the holes for their heavy ear-rings from closing up in the meantime, they have ingenuously pulled twists of cotton through the openings, whose vivid rose spreads out at the ear lobes into comical-looking loops.

Abd el Aziz was not exaggerating. The eldest of his nieces is so beautiful that at first it is almost disconcerting. Her profile is of flawless purity. Lifting the black fringe of her lids, her glance dazzles you and charms you with its tenderness. When she dips her shy head to her shoulder it is the movement of a turtle dove.

In comparison her sister is all that she is not. Perfect beauty creates a sort of waste around it, and that is perhaps why beautiful women are not more loved by other women.

The third day of Ramadan ends that afternoon. Since four o'clock that morning none of my hosts have eaten or drunk.

Slipping down on one of the mattresses, young Abd el Aziz yawns and draws out his watch every other minute to see how much longer he must wait for the sound of the liberating cannon.

'Allah, Allah!' he sighs, 'these first days are the worst punishment. One's stomach is not accustomed to it. And then there's the lack of sleep. Allah, Allah! I've got such a headache this moment that I'm almost crazy. Everything in me is empty, everything.'

The women, and it is not so astonishing, show more courage. In the patio there is a little girl, a darling of a child, who never stops running back and forth. Each time she passes the door she turns her head our way.

It is not to see if we are admiring her dress, made of a scrap of cotton in a fresh canary-yellow, but because she has fasted today for the first time in her life.

'We permitted it in order to get her accustomed to it,' explains Lella Rahama. 'She is so proud of being treated like a grown-up person that she wants everybody in the world to know it.'

Meanwhile, in a corner of the court, an old woman, a slave, sits folded on her feet. Her great age exempts her from fasting, but soon, she knows, she will be asked to render an account of her life. She wishes to present herself purified, having obtained God's pardon for all her faults.

'I would be ashamed in God's presence,' she tells me, croaking, 'if I had not observed Ramadan. May I be able to keep it up to the time I die!'

Once more Abd el Aziz consults his watch.

'How many minutes now, Abd el Aziz?'

'Sixty-five.'

'If you would occupy yourself with something the time would seem less long.'

'Allah! I haven't got strength enough!'

'The women are showing you an example.'

'They are accustomed to suffering. However, I realize they are more tired than I am. They are the ones Ramadan is hardest on. I went to bed, myself, after the third prayer and slept almost three hours.'

'While your mother and your nieces and the slaves – '

'They went to bed yesterday evening at about six o'clock as usual, but they had to get up at midnight.'

He concluded with a yawn, 'It is obligatory.'

There could be nothing more contagious than to see him yawn. Yawning myself, I ask,

'Why is it obligatory?'

'They have the meals to prepare. Each city has its customs for waking them up. At Rabat a beggar runs through the streets beating a drum, at some of the other places he blows a trumpet. At Fez – but is all this interesting to you?' he asks all at once and, as usual, yawning.

'Very much.'

'Allah, Allah! I see what you are. You are one of these ladies who wants to know everything. All right, my mother will explain it all to you. She is a Fascia and besides – I'm not able to.'

Full length on the cushions, as though he had been laid out, Abd el Aziz yawns and yawns again.

Then she whose name means 'the miserable', Lella Rahama, takes it upon herself to continue the conversation.

'At Fez the believer charged with waking the women is called the dakak.'

'Do you know what that means?' yawns Abd el Aziz.

'No.'

'One who knocks.'

'The position of dakak is hereditary,' goes on Lella Rahama. ' He receives a small sum as remuneration from the Habous and each inhabitant contributes toward paying the dakak of his quarter by handing over fifty centimes with seventeen measures of wheat.'

'The dakak goes from house to house. He has a hammer with which he strikes each door, calling, ' "Oh ye faithful, awake, awake! It is high time to prepare your repasts to keep Ramadan in the peace of God." '

I ask, 'At what hour must the women be waked?'

'At least by five o'clock,' comes from the depths of Abd el Aziz's cushions. 'Ramadan is a time of privation during the day, but of rejoicing during the night. From sunset to sunrise there are continual receptions. Think of all the tagines that must be prepared and all the cakes to bake! For eight hours the women are up, the "mistress of things" as well as the slaves, for the "mistress of things" must give the orders. If she can sleep for an hour or two toward the end of the morning, it is all that she has a right to expect.'

However absorbing the question of Ramadan may be, there is something else that piques Lella Rahama's curiosity. Not once have I entered a harem without someone asking at the very first,

'Art thou married? Hast thou children?'

Even the nuns do not escape this interrogation, 'Why hast thou never married? – Thou art young.'

By a natural ascent this type of conversation leads Lella Rahama to speak of the husband she has lost.

I wonder sometimes if there is a single exception among Moroccan widows? They tell me there is not and I believe it. However, I must say that after twenty years of widowhood this one speaks of her lost lord with the same genuine emotion as if she had just laid him away.

Getting up, she unhooks from the wall a gilt-framed portrait. It is an enlarged photograph of him who was Si Taher.

'Look at him,' she mourns. 'One would have said that he knew he was going to die and that he felt that he must leave a souvenir of himself to me and the children. He had never wanted to have his likeness taken; he decided to do it just a few weeks before he died.

'See how handsome he was and how young! Never had he been sick before. But each man bears his destiny written on his brow. In his hour Allah will summon him home.

'So many people are astonished that I never remarried. When one has such a husband as he, how can one accept another? Where find his equal? Allah never made two like him. He not only had beauty and strength but he had a great heart. He was the best and most generous of men. Since I lost him I have never known a happy day . . .'

Lella Rahama sighed with eyes tear-filled, adding,

'To honor me, to show what confidence he had in me, in his will he named me my children's guardian. Thou sayest, 'Is that not customary?' – Among Nazarenes it is, but not among Moslems. Even if I had wanted to marry again that proof of my husband's esteem and affection would have kept me from it.'

A moment more she stares sadly at the portrait, then as an appeal to one no longer here, her lips murmur,

'My dear, dear lord . . . '

Motioning to Hadra and her sister who are watching her, I try to say,

'These little granddaughters will be your consolation. These children whom Allah has 'dropped in thy lap,' you must cherish them. You must find Hadra a good husband.'

The older woman shook her head.

'Oh my grief! What art thou saying? – Hadra must stay at home! She must help me bring up her brothers and sisters. Her sister will marry, Inch Allah, but Hadra is necessary here. She is a good, devoted girl.'

Abd el Aziz, whom we thought asleep, wakes to yawn and add,

'Hadra was betrothed when her father died. Her fiancee was a friend of mine. I decided that we would give him Zohra, the younger. Because she is so young Zohra can't give the same service in the house as her sister. And besides, she hasn't her qualities.'

Abd el Aziz was expressing himself in French. Lella Rahama did not understand what he was saying, but she guessed that we were speaking of his nieces; she confirmed the decision taken.

'Zohra will be married after Ramadan, if it be God's will. But no husband for Hadra. Allah has written it over her. Allah is the all-wise!'

Hadra makes no response to her grandmother's words; her lids droop, she does not cease her gentle smiling.

But what a laceration must have appeared in her soul when she was told that she must let her sister supplant her, because her role of elder sister demanded it and – what irony – because she was the better of the two.

She had made no protest. She sat with her constant smile, with her sweet virginal air, on the soft woolen carpet beside us – but in the middle of the night, when only the far-off cock was crowing, who could know the silent tears that she let fall . . .

Celibacy imposed by circumstances and by one's own people represents for those of her race the saddest possible fate. Her youth will be passed in devotion to her brothers; when they are grown her beauty will be faded; she will grow old in the household like one already half dead.

One of the slaves had brought in tea. My hosts with big eyes watch me drink a sip of it and crumble my cake. One makes haste eating alone and besides I hurried to shorten the punishment that those who surrounded me were undergoing.

Little by little the day had darkened. One time more Abd el Aziz consults his watch, one time more he yawns. But an unexpected spectacle distracts me.

Across the patio, and coming toward us in the crystal air, was a group of four sumptuous dolls, the most enchanting, the most dazzling that it is possible to imagine. They advanced in a line and sometimes they bumped against each other. Their strange attire was as much in their way as their gigantic and unwieldy head dresses. They glided forward with tiny steps on their shining babouches, hesitating, balancing on their slim hips.

Carried away, I demanded of Abd el Aziz, 'Who are these charming creatures?'

'My mother's daughter's daughters. It is the custom among wealthy Moroccan families that for three days the little girls who have not yet observed Ramadan, are prepared by the g'nafa as if for their marriage. They are fixed up with henna and kohl and everything.'

Arrived at the open door the marvelous dolls stop short, abashed. No one had told them that a Nazarene was making a visit. The smallest, who could not be more than three, sets up a piercing cry.

All Roumiyas are ogresses. She knows it. If they have white skin it is because they eat the flesh of little children – the dada said so. Without waiting to hear anything different, the little thing flees to hide behind the g'nafa whose rotundity affords a screen. With more courage than she could muster, her sisters and cousin gravely advance to kiss their grandmother's hand and their uncle's.

Untiringly I study and admire the charming and magnificent details of their costumes. One wears a caftan of green velvet braided over every inch of its surface. Her little head is crowned with tall black ostrich plumes that undulate graciously with her movements.

Another is dressed in a robe of turquoise blue clouded in silver-pailleted tulle; a kerchief of rose and lilac knotted on her black hair sways a long fringe on her thin little shoulders.

But the most beautiful of the three is the eldest one. Before long she will be observing Ramadan and already she bears herself with the airs of a great lady.

Made of a golden tissue with purplish highlights, her costume puffs out above the hips as if distended by a crinoline; her sleeves, so long that they trail on the ground, are tucked up at the sides like wings. A gold bandeau set with emeralds is twisted around her forehead; covering her ears, failing clear to her shoulders, she wears a hair-net of real pearls and precious stones.

The three little creatures seat themselves side by side on the floor. Their wide petticoats stand out around them like a bell. Thanks to their appearance the whole thing has taken on a tinge of enchantment – the realization of a Persian folk-tale, an unbelievable fairy story.

They hold themselves just so without budging. Their faces are deliciously painted; eyebrows so elongated by kohl that they seem to run into their ears. They are hieratic and vividly alive and I have never seen anything more charming than the expression of fitting gravity imprinted on their round little faces under the arched brows.

The hour of Moghreb approaches, the hour for ascending to the roofs.

Once more the little dolls cross the patio under the g'nafa's care, their little hands holding up their heavy petticoats. Ruby colored, sapphire, emerald, they look like precious birds escaped from some marvelous aviary. Their little shoulders glisten, their little breasts shimmer and one is astonished not to hear them chirp.

They get all tangled up in the narrow staircase whose high steps are difficult for short legs to mount. The porter has already opened the door to the roof with his big iron key.

Armchairs have been arranged beforehand and cushions put in them, many cushions to increase the height of the seats.

With infinite precaution each child is hoisted into the throne erected for her and her petticoats carefully adjusted.

The sun is setting in a nimbus of rays. The emerald's facets catch the light, the orient magnifies the pearls. A little passing breeze shakes the tremulous beauty of the ostrich plumes set in a diadem on a tiny head.

Beyond the Koutoubia a minaret seems to float painted in mauve. Toward the east, in the milky paleness, are other minarets that seem as unreal and as suavely drawn.

Until the end of the day, until the first chill falls from the night sky, these ravishing dolls stay on exhibition. They make no gesture, speak no word – the caïda forbids it – but their eyes shine with a still delight. Lella Rahama who has joined us whispers,

'These little children, we beautify them to make them happy. It is necessary that the rays of their happiness be high enough to mount up to God and rejoice His heart.'

One last time before I go I study the radiant spectacle whose like my eyes had never seen before.

How pretty these babies in their naive joy, and how tender and full of grace is this fierce and disenchanted religion of Islam when it concerns itself with little children . . .

ABOUT THE AUTHOR

HENRIETTE CELARIÉ lived in Marrakesh with her husband, a French officer. Like Leonora Peets, she used her time there to compose sketches of and collect stories from, the female population of the city. The result is a wonderful and diverse volume of which *Ramadan* is the prize. A story that catches the banality, ceremony and celebration of this important religious festival, observed from the angle of the participants.

Men of Leather: the Tanners of Marrakesh

Justin McGuinness

On both sides of the Mediterranean, the names of streets and neighbourhoods still bear the names of long-gone trades and crafts. In Marrakesh, there is a leather workers' souk and a potters' souk, even a souks for rush-weavers and bookbinders. Only one group of craftsmen – whose trade was undoubtedly the hardest – managed to give their name to one of the city's gates. The bastion of Bab Debbagh, the tanners' gate, gave access to the Red City to travellers coming from the East.

Leading their flocks into the covered markets, jellaba-wearing guides say it long and often: each souk was the domain of a different traditional trade. Today, however, things are more than a little mixed in Marrakesh. Tourist gegaws are available everywhere, there are copper lanterns and vivid potteries in every zanka, even a cybernet in souk el Bayyadine, the egg souk near Derb Debbachi. A butcher can easily work alongside a carpet bazaar. The old, carefully constructed hierarchy of trades has largely broken down. However, just behind the ramparts on the eastern side of the Médina are the old city tanneries. Far from restaurants with palm tree patios and other decorative delights, the men of leather are at work, treading and scraping, beating and stretching, creating the raw material for the delicate, supple slippers indispensable for visiting the mosque on the great religious holidays.

The great tannery of Fès features in every tourist brochure. Its tens of vivid vats are a staple Moroccan postcard. ('The tenacious odour', as the Michelin Green Guide puts it, is rather less easy to reproduce). In Marrakesh, there are no terraces to give the visitor a view of the tanners' domain. Nevertheless, visits are often suggested by the faux guides who manage to avoid the watchful Brigade touristique. My first visit to the tanneries was back in the 1990s, during a stay in Marrakesh for the purposes of a vague city-history academic project. Later, in an obscure orientalist research centre, I found a document published in Algiers which told of the tanners in the 1950s. The transformation of skins into leather was clearly a complex affair, here was a real community of artisans whose history was mythically linked to that of the city. I wondered what still might survive of this pre-industrial production process.

Dar Debbagh is not visited in the same way as you tour the Palais Badi and the Saâdian Tombs. On the eastern side of the town, the tanners' quarter is a good way from the crowds of Jamaa el Fna – and trendier districts like Mouassine with their riads and restaurants. While in Fès one gazes down on a sort of honeycomb, the tanners heaving skins in and out of their vats like so many bees in a hive (Goytisolo provides a superb description of this in his novel Makbara), direct contact is the thing in Marrakesh. Even equipped with a delicate nosegay of mint one cannot escape the cruel odours and other emanations. Following their guide, such tourist groups as make it to the tanneries take a perilous route, between the workshops and streams of sticky run-off water, between vats of liquids worthy of some mad scientist and piles of damp, dishevelled fleeces. Tripping up next to a large pool filled with whitening skins, looking for all the world like the insides of some prehistoric beast, a visitor grabs his companion's camera bag, rights himself. Water pours out of stand-pipe, skins are flailed, scattering droplets. Wearing thigh-height rubber boots, young men carry stick-loads of skins along the concrete walkways between the nauseous vats. In a rough shelter, well out of the sun, a white mule awaits its load. A cock pursues its chicken, a comfortable cat, nicely installed on a sack of tannin, pursues its morning toilet. With or without visitors, the tannery has its daily ritual. This is no Chez Ahmed theme experience, peopled with picturesque 'natives' skilled in cavalry charges and carpet-flying.

For a tourist questing after the picturesque, the merkel, the treading of the skins is the most spectacular feature. In a circular concrete vat, up to the top of their wellingtons in gooey liquid and skins, two or three workmen trample away, the aim being to remove the lime with which they have been impregnated to remove the fat and other miscellaneous appendixes. (The smells of the tannery come mainly from this first part of the process, during which skins are soaked in a fine mixture of water, pigeon guano and other waste). It is the debbagh, however, the tannin, which transforms and preserves the skin. Tannin is a vegetable substance, a powder made of ground up bark, roots and fruit. In Marrakesh, it is made from tamarisk fruit (takkout) or even mimosa bark. Gathered on the far side of the High Atlas, takkout is carefully milled into a cinnamon-coloured flour. Then, during soaking in a decoction of debbagh and water, the skin begins the long process of becoming leather. It begins to regain its soul.

The tanners are said to have been the first to settle in Marrakesh at its foundation – and a gate is named for them, the only one to be named for a craft corporation. 'Bab Debbagh, bab deheb' – 'Tanners' Gate, gold gate' the old adage goes, in reference to the tanners' prosperity. One legend runs that seven virgins are buried in the foundations of the gate (sisters of the seven protector saints of Marrakesh), and women who desire a child should offer them candles and henna. Another legend runs that Bab Debbagh is inhabited by Malik Gharub, a genie who dared to lead a revolt against Sidna Suleyman, the Black King, only to be condemned to tan a cowhide and cut out belgha soles for eternity as punishment.

Most important – though surviving in how many memories? – is the tale of Sidi Yacoub, who in a Christian-European context would be the patron saint of the tanners. The legend goes that Yacoub the Master Tanner would shut himself away in his workshop to pray. An apprentice, fascinated by the piety of his master, asked to join him. Yacoub consented. Inside the workshop, Yacoub told the boy to close his eyes. Then he ordered him to open them. The boy found himself in Mecca. He closed his eyes again, and found himself back in the workshop. Yacoub the Maâlem asked the apprentice not reveal this secret. But the boy, playing his reed pipe, spread the news of the miracle by accident. A crowd gathered to ask for the saintly man's benediction – but Sidi Yacoub could not face the crowd. Trying to escape their attentions, he threw himself into the iferd, the black pool at the centre of the tannery, threshold to the limitless world of the Invisible Ones. And so, at Dar Debbagh El Kbira, the big tannery, in homage to his piety, the tanners built a sanctuary for him, around a well where a fig tree had grown – and still grows today.

Until recently, the tanneries used to be regulated by an annual cycle, following the rhythm of the seasons. Work intensified in summer, when the skins can be cleaned in the fermenting water more quickly and dried on the walls and river banks. In the winter, the tanners of country origin would return to their fields to plough and sow. There used to be a sharp distinction between the Arab-run tanneries where only sheep and goat skins were treated, and Chleuh tanneries, specialised in the tougher task of curing cow and camel skins. Today, things are altogether more ethnically mixed.

Though providing a good living, the tannery was also considered a dangerous place – as it was the entrance to the domain of the Other Ones, and a beneficial one, since skins were a symbol of preservation and fertility. For the cultural anthropologist, the processes and places of tanning are no doubt loaded with meaning (Here be the signposts to move from life in nature to society). Bab Debbagh was the key access point to the eastern side of Marrakesh, and there would seem to be a symbolism based on the sun rising in the East and skin being reborn as leather. The tanners, spending their days in pits working the skins, were said to be in contact with the unseen world of the dead; they were also seen as masters of fertility, being strong men, capable of giving a second life to dry, dead skin.

In the old days, the complex process of tanning would start with soaking the skins in a sort of swamp or iferd in the middle of the tannery, filled with a fermenting mixture of pigeon guano and tannery waste. Fermenting would last three days in summer, six in winter. Then the skins would be squeezed out and put to dry. Hair would be scraped off. Then the skins would go into a pit of lime and argan-kernel ash. This would remove any remaining flesh or hair, and prepare the skin to receive the tanning products. The lime bath lasted 15–20 days in summer, up to 30 in winter. Then the skins would be washed energetically, trodden to remove any lime, and any extra bits cut off. Next the skins spent 24 hours in a qasriya, a round pit of more pigeon dung and fresh water. At this stage the skin thins and stretches. (This is a stage to be undertaken with care, because a djinn lives in the pit, and skins can be ruined if left too long). There follows soaking in wheat fibre and salt, for 24 hours, to remove any traces of lime and guano.

There then follow soakings in debbagh, the carefully prepared water and tannin mix, after which the skins have to be prepared to receive the dye. They are scraped with pottery shards, beaten and coated with oil, alum and water. Like the other stages of the process, dying takes place by hand, with the dye traditionally being poured out of a bull's horn, and left to dry in the sun. Finally, the skins are worked again to make them smoother and more supple, stretched between two ropes and worked on smooth pottery surfaces. Skins were sold at auction.

So much for the details of a complex process, learned by observation and experience. There are no manuals to guide the tanner – only practice, and perhaps the metaphors they use to speak of the long process transforming hide to leather – the tanners say that the skin eats, drinks, sleeps and 'is born of the water'. When the skin is treated with lime, it is said to be thirsty, when it is treated with pigeon dung, it is said to receive nafs, a spirit. The merkel (treading) stage prepares the skin to live again, while the takkout of the tanning mixture is also used by women to dye their hair. At this point, the skin receives ruh, 'breath'. Leather is thus born from the world of the dead and the ighariyin, the people of the grotto, and is fertilised in the swampy pool, the domain of the dead – who are also said to have the power to bring rain.

To work in such proximity to 'the Others', courage, confidence and physical force are clearly essential. An apprenticeship might begin around twelve, even younger in some cases. By observation, the trainee tanner learns about the different substances used to remove hair and fat from skins, preparing them to treated in the workshop. Around sixteen, the stronger lads learn to tread the skins. With a knowledge of the washing and softening techniques, an apprentice can become a master-craftsman, a maâlem and aspire to having his own workshop or hanout. But years of practice are required to become a shakkan, an expert in opening the skins.

Eighteen year old Abdelouahid, a straw hat wedged rakishly on his head was well advanced on the long road to becoming a maâlem when I visited the tanneries in early 2001. Following his father into the craft, he had begun young, growing up with the codes and circuits of the tannery – the unit-cost price of takkout, cleaning techniques, wholesale. Simo specialises in dying skins, using milled pomegranate bark, old-style, to produce ziouani, the dazzling lemon-yellow leather beloved by babouche makers. With forty years of experience behind him, Khaled has a hanout next to the mausoleum-mosque of Sidi Yacoub, over on the side of the tannery which gets the afternoon shade. Between piles of finished skins and a beam on which he scrapes away at the skins with a sedriya, a broad metal blade, the tanners' fetish tool, he has all the kit for making tea – and a black and white television set. Brazilian soap operas dubbed into Lebano-classical Arabic and the sports news keep him company. He has developed a niche market, too, specialising in the more delicate task of producing skins tanned with the fleece still on. Often used as prayer carpets, kids fleeces are much in demand among the Mouassine decorators and other artistic souls with a riad to furnish.

But though the process is largely the same as it was in pre-industrial times, the city around the tannery is changing. There are now houses all around and every year someone adds a floor or two. The minaret of Sidi Yacoub, the tanners' patron, is backed by walls of grey breeze-blocks. Because of the drought, the skins are no longer washed outside the walls in the Oued Issil: there is a very practical cistern on spindly concrete legs in the middle of the tannery. The trees which can be seen in old postcards of the tannery – a pomegranate? an olive? – are gone, no doubt succumbing to years of lime abuse. The tanners were great kif smokers: working in such difficult conditions with the foul odours and the presence of spirits was no doubt difficult without a daily pipe of kif. The older tanners have memories of plots of cannabis alongside their workshops. It would seem that acid is now used to speed up certain phases of tanning.

Yet Dar Debbagh remains a very human place. In the early afternoon, the apprentices head homewards, in gales of laughter and horseplay. Some of the older generation go to pray in the Mosque of Sidi Yacoub, open for the afternoon prayer. The visitor, after immersion in pungent pre-industrial process is happy to thread back to Jemaâ el Fna. But what of the tanneries' future? Will property market pressure bring the tanners to cede a few square metres of their terrain? It may be that the city authorities will see the tanners as tourist attraction, re-opening the top of Bab Debbagh to tourists' camcorders. But perhaps the raw process of the tanneries has no place among the spectacles of a world advancing to McDonaldization. Yet, as Juan Goytisolo has so often stressed, on the subject of joyous teeming Jemaâ el Fna and its storytellers, urban heritage is more than mediaeval monuments spruced up by a corporate maecaenas. A city's heritage is surely more problematic. The technical prowess of its people, their daily ways of doing and being, of living and laughing in the world are worthy of consideration.

ABOUT THE AUTHOR

Reading Gavin Maxwell's *Lords of the Atlas* as a child sparked off JUSTIN McGUINNESS's interest in Morocco and the Maghreb. After studying Arabic at Cambridge, he taught at the University of Tunis. As a translator and author of the *Footprint Handbook to Morocco*, he has travelled frequently in the country since the early 1990s. In Marrakesh, he lived in Derb Debbachi in the Médina, Guéliz and El Massira, seeing the whole span of neighbourhoods in a city in full change. Though living conditions in the old town are much better than they were ten years ago, he worries about the loss of ambience with the new 'improved' street lighting and 'urban furniture'. But the old neighbourhoods of Marrakesh will undoubtedly find their own creative ways to resist Disneyfication and massive applications of concrete. Justin McGuinness currently lives in a multi-ethnic enclave in northern Paris – a sort of European antechamber to Africa. As an academic, he lectures in cultural anthropology and urban studies.

Marrakesh

Wyndham Lewis

There is no particularity of the City of Casa to which I need to draw anyone's attention. I stopped there on two or three occasions, spending I suppose ten days within its whitewashed circumference. Most of that time was spent in attempting to undermine the colossal indifference of the French Postal personnel to the welfare of the Public – I was the Public, for the occasion: and I could inform you of course that the large German café in the Avenue du Général d'Amade – upon which I invariably fell back when heavily repulsed at the Post Office – is much the best in Casa. So let us turn, with some relief, from Casa-la-Blanche to the 'City of Morocco'.

Up to a point, *l'un vaut l'autre*. All that can be said, upon the lines laid down in the last chapter, of Casa, can be said – indeed very often has been said – of the Capital of the South, Marrakesh. It stands in a fifty-mile-wide stony tufa steppe, and is in fact nothing but a huge walled oasis, supporting a multitude of palms with the waters that come to it from the wall of the Atlas, at its back. The most populous city in Morocco, larger than Fez or Rabat, Marrakesh is yet a vast rendezvous rather than a capital. It is a walled-in converging point of nomads or of extremely restless peasants. The Brothers Tharaud refer to it as 'this city of the South, which, in spite of a few fine remains, is still nothing more than a great camp of nomads'; or again they refer to it as 'Marrakesh . . . this immense fondouk of asses, mules and camels'.

First of all, from the standard 'Oriental City' of the north of Maghreb el Aksa, you penetrate, once you pass the thirty-second degree of latitude, into a more definitely African World. Dr Leared says: 'There was little to record of my first impressions of Morroco (meaning Marrakesh) except its likeness to the Oriental cities I had visited. Most things, however, wore a more African tinge. The black race was more numerous here . . . '

Everything, indeed, as this writer says, 'wears' a far 'more African tinge'. As you pass from Casa into the South, or the Sous, you find yourself in that part of Morocco that is least affected by the European, in the first place, also (and that is more important) it has come less beneath the influence of the Arab, outside the direct administrative sphere of the cities, and of course the areas are occupied by the Chich tribes. There in the South are to be found the densest Souks, the greatest Kasbahs, and a climate, too, which, approaching more to the tropical, brings in the banana and the date-palm as a natural part of the décor – thereby heightening the 'Isalmic Sensations', with great novelties for the northern eye.

Here in Marrakesh the Saadian Tombs (ramshackle and ruined as that precinct is) are alone suggestive of a more settled society, according to the two Tharauds. They are a little piece of civilisation in the midst of this indifferent Barbarysm or its huge camping-centre of dried mud – Marakeh or 'Morocco'. But, say these two quite readable brothers, 'should you wish to find a sepulchre made after the image of this already Saharan city', you must turn your back upon this little island of orderly beauty, 'go a few hundred yards farther on, following a mud enclosure, and have a look through the planks carelessly knocked together of a miserable patched-up gateway. There, in the shadow of a fine apricot tree – beneath a few bricks assembled without art, and then slapped over with whitewash, which is scaling off in patches – lies Yousseff ben Tachefin, who founded Marrakesh, and led his hordes of veiled Warriors to the conquest of Granada and Cordova'. This is indeed a tomb in keeping with the city. 'Often pious hands have attempted to raise the walls of a koubah above his head: but every time that this happened the illustrious defunct, accustomed to the open spaces of the desert, of life beneath the tent, has kicked away the roof that it was proposed to provide him with, for his last sleep, for he wished for nothing above him, in death as it had been in life, except the roof of the moving leaves!'

So the great Almoravid, the first and greatest of the Saharan princes who galvanised the Berber world with their desert energy, and held it together for a spell, lies buried under an apricot tree, beneath a few bricks in the wild oasis-city he founded almost a millennium ago: and the city is the image of the man and of Berber life as well, in short of Barbary. That is what the Tharauds have to say.

But Marrakesh is far more real than is the tall white city of Casa, fully organised upon the most ample industrial lines, all the resources of Western Civilisation contributing to its quick upbrush. Then, again, Marrakesh is a city after the image of Tachefin: but Casablanca, on the same principle, is not a city after the image of Lyautey, or even of France.

What the Tharaud Brothers say of the *revers de la médaille* – or the hot mud-city of the first nomad-dynasty – may be accepted as fact as far as it goes; the other side of the picture, especially regarding the impressiveness of the Saadian Tombs, is another matter. There are a lot of long plain gravestones – they are like small stone boats, if you like, keel-up: and these tombstones are to be found in a couple of lofty ill-lighted chambers, *à l'Alhambra*. The Tharauds are thinking how all these Sultans died a violent death, one after the other – one at the hands of his Renegade Christian Bodyguard when he was drunk, another through the agency of the same fine body of men when he was sober: another slaughtered by his treacherous uncles, another poisoned by a Barbary fig, at the instigation of a Palace Eunuch, and so on. They are perfectly right, as I have already pointed out, to think like that: a man is a brute merely, who does not. I thought of all that too as I looked at the stone boxes. Only when I hoped to see in them 'a simplicity, a divine proportion', that should remind me of the greatest masterpieces, then I had to confess that where the Tharauds saw so much I saw nothing at all - little more than I see when I pass the monumental stonemasons in the Euston Road, before you get to Great Portland Street Station.

But there is another point upon which I think the Tharaud Brothers, and many others, are gravely mistaken. I refer to the assumptions behind their terms 'civilised' and 'uncivilised', as applied to what we find in Barbary. For me the polished and empty Hispano-Mauresque, the Andalusian Art, is simply dull: it is, as someone has said of it, little more than a dazzling luxury-garment thrown over anything that can pay the price asked for the tiles, fretwork and mosaic – mosque, palace, or Tolba School all getting the same mechanical adornment, the same one stock-outfit. The sheer architecture at the bottom of it is nothing, or next to nothing.

This certainly is 'civilised', in a Parisian way, but it is too narrow a definition. The finest architecture in Morocco is to be found in the High Atlas, according to my view. There the great Kasbahs are splendid works of art, or at least very impressive works of art, however rough sometimes, in a very great tradition. And all the best of these Kasbahs are built by a desert, or semi-desert, tribe, the Ouled Yahya. These people come from just north of Tiznit. (Tiznit is a ksar upon the Saharan slopes of the Western Atlas.)

But there is something else which makes the sort of statement I have quoted from the Tharauds particularly superficial. It is generally believed, according to the latest researches, that the best contemporary architecture in the Maghreb is as a matter of fact the Saharan. Very little is known about the oases in the neighbourhood of Tatta, since only two or three Europeans have ever seen them. But they are said to be particularly finely built. And Gautier (*Les Siècles Obscurs du Maghreb*) insists upon the great superiority of the type of building in the Saharan cities (Figuig and its neighbourhood for instance) to the Kabyle or other 'sedentary' architecture farther north.

If we compare, then, the monuments of the Hispano-Mauresque with the adobe hovels around them in Marrakesh, this very chic Turkish Bath Architecture would no doubt discover itself in the role of the polished gentleman against an African hobo. But that in fact is not quite the contrast, all things taken into account, that a wider inspection would suggest. The Soudenese home-land of the Berber chief, Tachefin (the first Almoravid), was not necessarily quite the savage spot that the Tharauds and the rest assume it to be. On the contrary. There is every indication that the civilisation of the Sahara was of a higher order than that of the Tangitanian Mauretania. The monasteries and famous centres of mystical scholasticism of Senegal and Mauretania were not, evidently, mere deserts full of wild animals and untutored nomads. Mauretania, or what we call loosely the Rio de Oro, has been termed 'the intellectual centre' of Islam in the Berber World. There have at all times been cities and monasteries in those deserts as well as nomadic brigands. So Tachefin should not be regarded exactly as the chief of hordes of veiled brigands. – But I will take up this question again in a moment.

Even if you like the Hispano-Mauresque, however, there is not much to see in Marrakesh. There is the famous Koutoubia, whose silhouette dominates everything; there is the Palace of Ba Ahmed – it is a vulgar descendant of the Alhambra, there is nothing in it that is not coarse and summary in workmanship. But this huge peach-coloured adobe town must not be judged by its few Andalusian remains. It must be judged, on its own merits, as something like an immense human personality.

Marrakesh is indeed 'the mouth of the Sahara', as it is described by Graham. It is a huge, red, windy metropolis of mud and sand. In the centre of it is 'The Place of Destruction' (Djemaa el Fna) which is a small desert in the midst of a city (as 'a square' it is vast) full of the vigorous African crowds – acrobats, potters, Chleuh boy-dancers (like bands of depraved but still strictly-disciplined surpliced acolytes) – many sorcerers and palmists (before whom squats some silent mountaineer, drinking in the words of fate, while the prophetic quack holds fast the tell-tale hand, mesmerising his victim as he whispers to him the secrets of the future) with, at the busy hours, a city of fantastic tents. The tent-making capacities of the natural nomad are here seen to full advantage, in the structures of mats and poles, which take the shapes of a pachydermatous beast, or hollow, carnival giant, sheltering the salesman and artisan – cobblers, lock-smiths, couscous-vendors, herbalists, butchers, letter-writers.

The Djemaa el Fna has often been described: half a century ago it must have been in most respects the same as today, except that the unlovely Post Offices (of a Moorish Operette type) and the slick Paris-Arab pastiche that is considered necessary to indulge in when building a Bank, does not improve the view. The large café in one corner of this Djemaa el Fna affords a select, arcaded meeting-place for officers and Berber notables: the great Caïds, it is said, go up to the roof if they wish to indulge in an extra drink or two, so as not to be observed by their tribesmen: but the 'Islamic Sensation' is necessarily lessened by the presence of this commanding European building. Also much of the dancing that used to occur in 'The Place of Destruction' has been, since the French Occupation, driven underground, or persuaded to remove itself into houses set aside for such strange African licences, which is a pity.

Still the desolation of cracked mud and sand, endless fine upstanding palms, loaded with dates, miles of these plumed plants – everywhere, wall within wall, peach-pink mud-concrete battlements, of which earlier travellers speak, is still perfectly intact. 'This heap of ruins, sand-heap, desert-town' – this 'city of the Mahdis, halt of the Sultans of the South, on their way to capture Fez' – has not capitulated to Europe, it is still the 'Morroco City' of Dr Leared, or, last and worst of all Black Vizirs, of Ba Ahmed. 'Morroco City is purely African', says Mr.Graham; and that is it after all. Those 'handsome Arab types' so beloved of the travelled Briton (of Mr Graham of course) are conspicuous by their absence. There are no magnificoes, in this huge adobe Souk, who hold as heirlooms the monster keys of the houses in Granada unwillingly vacated by their ancestors five hundred years ago. Marrakesh belongs more to the Soudan than to Spain.

ABOUT THE AUTHOR

WYNDHAM LEWIS travelled to Morocco in 1931 in the company of his long-suffering but devoted young wife Froanna. It was a time of chronic uncertainty, the Riff rebellion had just ended and the Wall Street crash had undermined the world economy and with it the whole concept of liberal democracies. They approached the country through the Algerian frontier having first landed in North Africa at the Algerian port of Oran on a Spanish ferry. Though he travelled down through Fez and Casablanca his real objective was Marrakesh and the half conquered lands of the Sous valley and the Berber Anti-Atlas mountains to the south.

It proved a creative trip for Lewis produced a number of drawings, two articles, a study of the Berbers (to be called 'Kasbahs and Souks', though it was never published) and a travel book, *Filibusters in Barbary* that was published in 1932. Wyndham Lewis had read widely before the trip and there are multiple and direct allusions to Cunninghame Graham, the Tharaud brothers and Dr Leared as well as such scholars as Montagne, Budgett Meakin and Gautier.

As a young artist at the Slade Lewis had been strongly influenced by the enthnographic collections at the British Museum and at least part of the motivation for these travels was to directly observe the purity of line and architectural design in traditional Berber culture. In his writings, whether consciously or not, he seems to be almost directly continuing with Cunninghame Graham's travels. He delights in exposing the difference between the high ideals of the French colonial party (who imagined themselves to be following in the footsteps of the Romans in a mission to civilize the world) and the reality on the ground, dominated by the petty crooks, lawyer-politicians and commission men of the Third Republic. His criticsm of such real filibusters (freelance armament suppliers) as Major T. C. Macfie and image makers such as the American director Rex Ingram (whom he saw at work 'faking a Sheik' in Marrakesh) would lead to legal action. Although it is now easy to delight in Wyndham Lewis's company, he clearly alarmed his contemporares – both from the ferocity of his engagement in life and the multiplicity of his talents – as poet, artist, controversialist and writer. Colleagues spoke of the 'messaianic atmosphere' and 'mephistophelian threat' which he brought in his wake. Certainly his behaviour with his earlier girlfriend

Iris Barry, who was left sitting outside the front door with her newborn baby, so that Wyndham could finish fucking the socialite Nancy Cunard, lives up to his reputation as a ferocious and quarrelsome egotist. This baby and its successors were to be given away.

He was born in Nova Scotia in 1882, the child of an American Civil war hero and the British-born Anne Stuary Picket. They brought him back to England aged six though his father, a serial philanderer, soon drifted out of family life so that Wyndham was effectively brought up by his mother and in traditional English boarding schools. He was a lifelong friend of Augustus John and Ezra Pound and a leading figure in the Vorticist school of artists. George Orwell considered that 'he had enough talent to set up dozens of ordinary writers' and T. S. Eliot wrote of him as 'the most formidable personality of our time'. Now it seems that the turbulent deeds of his life, which offers up such a very rich field for biographers, is in danger of overshadowing his art.

Snakes, Rats and Cockroaches

from *The Tangier Diaries* by John Hopkins

September 8th, 1974

Last Saturday I returned home late from one of Bill Willis' rooftop parties in the Marrakesh Medina. As I entered the mud courtyard the car headlights picked up a tiger snake slithering along the wall.

Fearing the snake would climb the Liane de Floride and get into my bedroom, I jumped out of the car, picked up a hoe and chopped it in two.

Next morning I found the gardener Ahmed looking at the carcase and dismally shaking his head. The snake had a useful purpose, he explained. For many years it had lived in the palm trees around the house and kept the rat population under control.

I thought about it no more until Tuesday when something heavy dropped onto my bed in the middle of the night. I switched on a flashlight and glimpsed a rat as it jumped away. All that night rats were running through the house. The windows were open and Le Petite Maison was full of them.

On Wednesday Ahmed and I drove to town and bought big ugly metal traps with teeth. He baited them with fresh bread moistened with a drop of olive oil and placed them on the windowsills.

That night there were loud clankings as the traps claimed their victims. Rats that had not been killed instantly could be heard dragging the traps about. Over the next two nights more than twenty were caught.

My nights became peaceful again, and I thought the crisis had passed. Then last night, groping my way to the bathroom, I shined my light on the walls to discover the place was swarming with cockroaches. They were pouring up through the drain. The rats had lived on cockroaches. I'd found a nest behind the stove and it was littered with cockroach wings. Now the rats had gone, the cockroaches had multiplied by the thousand!

I sprayed the place with bug killer and this morning we carried them away by the bucketful.

ABOUT THE AUTHOR

As a student at Princeton University, and later the University of Madrid, JOHN HOPKINS devoted much of his time to travelling through South America with his friend, Joe McPhillips. After graduating, they crossed the Atlantic and began working their way through Europe and Africa. While on this journey, Hopkins was inspired to become a writer and, in 1962, settled in Morocco, where he would spend the majority of the next seventeen years. Despite this long period of residence, and a conscious effort on his part to understand and immerse himself in the Moroccan way of life, Hopkins retained a Western sensibility, as shown in this extract from his diaries; a Western 'solution' that misinterprets the situation and actually causes more problems.

Historical Perspectives

The Sultan's Munificence

from *The Khalifate of the West* by Donald MacKenzie

When I made my first visit to this city I was surprised at the arbitrary power which the Sultan exercises over his subjects through his governors. The sultan was then present in the city. I sent my soldier to the governor with a letter asking for the use of a house during my stay, thinking they had empty ones. He came back with two soldiers from the governor, asking me to come and choose a house. I replied that I would be quite satisfied with any choice they might make. They went away and soon returned and told me that they selected a nice one for me in the Mohammedan quarter. I went to see it, and found it a dear little house with a small courtyard in the middle, with a small fountain, which was then dry, as the house was empty. So I moved in at once, with all my belongings. As soon as I came in, the same day a strange Jew came in and welcomed me to Morocco City. I did not know him, but he told me he was a Levite. He said that he would send me furniture and bread for my use every day, and also wine from the famous district of Dimnat sealed with the seal of the priest, as an evidence of purity. All this as to be done without any pay. All I had to do, while I remained in the city, was to dine with him every Saturday, which was their Sabbath day. I had no difficulty in making up my mind to accept such a generous offer. He lived in the Jewish quarter, and although, as I afterwards heard, he was a rich man, he was obliged to take off his slippers when coming into the Mohammedan quarter. He sent me the furniture, bread and wine and made me quite comfortable.

I went the first Saturday to dinner, and I found that he lived in a beautiful house. On my arrival the dinner was all laid, with a snow-white cloth over it, and his wife dressed in gorgeous clothes, served the edibles. Another Levite was present when we sat down to dinner. My good friend took his seat, and the cloth was removed. He then took the bread, broke it and blessed it, and, taking the pieces, handed them in turn to each of us. He then took the cup of wine, blessed it and drank a little and handed it over to us. The same ceremony was gone through each time I went. Dining at a Jewish house was quite a new experience to me.

After I had ben in my house a few days an old, respectable Moor came quietly to the house. He was asked in, and he sat down and explained, in a very humble manner, that the house which I occupied was his property, and that the Sultan's governor had turned him out, and all his belongings, at a moment's notice, to make room for me. He even feared worse evils might happen to him. I assured him that I was very sorry to have been the innocent cause of depriving him of his pretty house, but that I would take great care of it. He was then at ease, and often came in to have a chat. I improved his dwelling in some respects by killing a large snake we found in it. I smashed his head with a tent pole, to the great amazement of the neighbours, who flocked in to see it. The Moors leave these reptiles alone, to roam about as they like.

I always remember, with a great sense of pleasure, an incident that took place on the morning I left that house on my way back to Mogador. An unknown female hand came out at a door nearby and handed me a basin of milk to drink. I never saw her face or person, but thanked her all the same.

There are now English missionaries located here, and a Vice-Consul. The population of Morocco City is about 60,000, which is much increased when the Sultan makes one of his periodical visits to his southern capital, or during fair time. A splendid view of the great Atlas chain of mountains can be obtained from the city. Here lived in great affluence, Sidi Boobeker, for many years the agent of the British Government, who rose from a stable boy to be one of the richest men in the country. Mr Gurney and I visited and dined with him at his country house near Morocco City. The house was surrounded by extensive grounds, walled in and watered from the Atlas mountains. He employed over 1,200 people in his garden, as he called it, and the produce from the olives alone made £4,000 a year. Being protected he had no taxes to pay, very much to the annoyance of the Moorish tax-gatherer.

ABOUT THE AUTHOR

DONALD MACKENZIE worked for the British and Foreign Anti-Slavery Society in Morocco, and was a vocal critic of the corruption brought to North Africa by the Europeans. This is somewhat incongruous, given his later involvement in the establishment of Cape Juby, a trading post that became a haven for smugglers and gun-runners and was seen as a first step towards the flooding of a large section of the West Sahara with the aim of producing a shipping route to Timbuktu. He claimed that this post did not come under the Sultan's jurisdiction, and, though the British government admitted its illegality, they would ultimately force the Moroccan Sultan to pay out compensation to Mackenzie.

A Circus for the Sultan

from *Morocco That Was* by Walter Harris

The death of Bou Ahmed naturally brought about changes at Court. Whatever jealousies there may have existed amongst the viziers, and no doubt they were many, they realised that common action was necessary. Each might have, and probably would have, to defend his, own particular position from the others, but collectively they had to defend their united positions from all the world. They must either succeed or fall together, and they determined to succeed.

The Sultan was now about twenty years of age, and might at any moment desire to assert himself; and the self-assertion of young monarchs of autocratic power and no experience is dangerous. The viziers realised that in all probability the disappearance of the strong hand of Bou Ahmed would tempt the young Sultan to become more independent, and it was necessary to come to some arrangement as to how he should be led to think and act. Certainly it must not be in the direction of affairs of State - those the viziers meant to keep to themselves. An occupation must be found for the inexperienced and hitherto secluded monarch.

It was the exact reverse of all the traditions of Morocco; but the situation was an unusual one, for there had never been a Sultan in a similar position. The viziers felt that should influence be brought to bear to keep him in his palace he might rebel against this enforced seclusion, and rid himself, and probably in no gentle manner, of the men who had instituted it. No; it was clear the Sultan must be amused, and his amusements must be so numerous and so varied that his entire attention would be distracted from affairs of State. Morocco itself could not supply the novelties that would be required. Such pleasures and such luxuries as the country could produce were his already - women, horses, jewels, and the whole paraphernalia that goes to make up an oriental potentate's surroundings. For further distractions appeal must be made to Europe. It was not made in vain. It was the beginning of the great debacle, of the reckless extravagance, of the follies and the debts that led to foreign loans, and step by step to the loss of Morocco's independence.

A strong and good adviser might have prolonged the life of an independent Morocco, for although possessed of no great attainments or will-power, Mulai Abdul Aziz was thoughtful, intelligent, and desirous of doing well. It was no easy matter, however, at Marrakesh, the southern capital, where the Court was at this time in residence, to keep the young Sultan amused. Situated 100 miles from the nearest port, which itself was 300 miles down the Atlantic coast, communication with Europe was necessarily very slow, and the Sultan's ever-increasing orders of European goods took long to carry out. Often, too, the heavy Atlantic swell rendered communication impossible between the ships and the shore for weeks together.

The Sultan's caterers were at their last resources. Fireworks were played out. Bicycle tricks had led to bruises and sprains; and even photography had lost its pristine interest. At this critical moment came word of a belated circus at one of the coast towns. It must naturally have been a very poor circus ever to have found itself at that dreary little port, but its advent was welcomed as enthusiastically as if it had been Barnum's entire show. Imperial letters were directed to the local Kaids and Governors, agents rushed wildly to and fro, and eventually the circus, bag and baggage, consisting of a dozen people and three or four horses, started out across the weary plains of Morocco to obey the royal command. It all took time, and meanwhile in Court circles it was the absorbing topic of conversation. One or two serious rebellions among the tribes, and an acute quarrel with the Government of a European Power, passed into temporary oblivion.

Now, the proprietress of this circus was an extremely stout Spanish lady of uncertain age, on whose corpulent body the rough jogging on a mule for more than a hundred miles had left almost as painful an impression as the discomfort, heat, and worry of the journey had upon her temper. She herself took no active part in the performance, and it was on this account, to her intense indignation and wrath, that she was refused admittance to the court of the palace in which the Sultan was to witness the show. His Majesty's orders were that none but the actual performers should be allowed to enter.

So the fat lady and one or two of the employees of the circus remained in an outer courtyard adjoining the enclosure in which the Sultan, seated under a gorgeous tent, was witnessing the performance. A wall some twenty feet in height separated these two courts; and in the outer one; where the fat lady found herself, the Sultan had been building some additions to the palace, and a pile of stone, mortar, and other material reached almost to the top of the wall. The lady was both angry and bored, nor were a herd of gazelle and a few fine specimens of mouflon – Barbary wild sheep – that roamed about the enclosure sufficient to keep her amused.

To have received a royal command to come all that way to the Moorish capital, and then to be deprived of the glory of seeing her own circus performing before a real Sultan, was more than she could bear, and she straightway began to climb the great heap of building material that lay piled against the wall. It was hard work, nor was her figure suited for such mountain-climbing; but she was to receive assistance from a source undreamed of. Affected, no doubt, by her slow progress in a sport of which he himself was so proficient, the old ram mouflon lightly bounded after her. Balancing himself for a moment on his hind-legs, he lunged forward and butted the fat lady so successfully from below that her ascent was materially assisted. In a series of repeated bounds, owing to no voluntary action on her own part, she found herself pantingly grasping the top of the thick wall.

Meanwhile the performance of the circus was progressing to the Sultan's satisfaction. Suddenly, however, an expression of wrathful consternation be-came visible in his face, and, speechless, he pointed at the wall. There, far above, was the agonised and purple visage of the fat lady, peering down at the Sultan and his Court. In a moment the officers of the suite were shouting and gesticulating to her to retire. But the only reply they received was a sudden vision of a considerable portion of her immense body, as a playful mouflon, himself invisible, gave her another hoist up. At last all her body was on the wall, to which she clung for dear life with arms and legs, as she lay extended on its summit. It was at this moment that the mouflon appeared. With a majestic bound he leaped on to the summit, stood for a moment poised on his hind-legs, then suddenly dropped, and with a terrific prod from his wide horns, butted the fat lady at least a yard along the wall. He was evidently intent upon taking her round the entire circuit of the courtyard.

For a few moments there was turmoil. The Sultan sat silent and amazed, while the Cabinet Ministers all shouted to the lady to disappear, which she was certainly most anxious to do. The slaves, more wisely, pelted the mouflon with stones, and drove him from his point of vantage. Then slowly the lady disappeared-the fat legs first, then the heaving mass of body, and finally even the purple face was seen no more.

ABOUT THE AUTHOR

WALTER HARRIS was born in London in 1866 and attended Harrow, where his extravagant story-telling earned him the nickname 'the liar'. Some of his later writing, colourful and anecdotal in nature, seems to justify this tag, but most of his work has independent corroboration and to a large degree his life was the exciting adventure he described. This adventure began early. After a brief stint at Caius, Cambridge Walter Harris wandered through Asia, Russia, Arabia and Europe before settling in Tangier in 1886 where he became the Times correspondent for Morocco. Harris spent time learning the local language and customs and establishing a web of contacts. This all paid off for him when, from about 1903 onwards, Morocco became prominent on the world stage as a sparring ground for Germany and France. He did more than just file newspaper stories, undertaking espionage for British and French governments. *Morocco That Was*, deals with the Morocco and the lives of its sultans of this period. Harris perhaps over emphasises the decadence of the court in this time, but simultaneously conveys the great friendship he made with many diverse Moroccans from the Sultans themselves to Muhummad Er-Raisuli, the bandit who held Harris captive for some months. Walter Harris died in 1933.

The City of the Seven Saints

from *Saints and Sorcerers* by Nina Epton

Despite the rigid, snow-crested barrier of the Atlas, Marrakesh belongs to the Saharans, by whom the city was founded in the tenth century. Long before they started to build their rose-red palaces, they had been content to pitch their tents beneath the date-palms and the debonair atmosphere of a nomad's camp has not been completely dispelled by sophisticated generations of Arab architecture and French hoteliers.

Marrakesh has always been concerned with the things of the spirit as well as with unorthodox explorations into the occult. Warrior-saints have descended from the mountains again and again, burning with missionary and imperialistic zeal. Necromancy arrived with the shackled slaves from the south. The peoples of the Sahara, the vast Sahara rippling in rose dunes beyond the frozen unfurled waves of the Atlas, are responsive to mystiques and hospitable to those who journey long and far to reach them. Names jut out like rocks viewed dimly beneath the turgid waters of memory: Abdallah ben Yassinem, for instance, the Sufi Malekite who came from Kairouan to preach to the veiled Sanhadjas of the western desert and who founded a *ribat* – a fortified camp of warrior- monks, the crusaders of Islam. He called his people Al Mrabtime, which the Spaniards and everybody else after them distorted into 'Almoravids'. They marched on camelback to the Draa and the Tafilelt, proscribing flutes and other musical instruments, burning the houses in which they found liquor.

Abdallah was killed in combat near Rabat. His successor north of the Atlas, Youssef ben Tachfine, was the real founder of the Almoravid dynasty . . . ben Tachfine, who raised Marrakesh in the year 1002 after he had pitched his tents in the burning plain where he made his decision to conquer the whole of Morocco. He acted upon the advice of his Berber wife Zeineb bint Isschak la Nafzaouia, an experienced woman who had already had two illustrious husbands: a prince of Arhinat and Abou Beker ben Omar, Youssef's elder cousin.

A quarter of a century after he had founded Marrakesh (in 1086) Youssef ben Tachfine flew to the rescue of the sorely pressed Muslim princes of Spain, the successors of the Ommeyads, and crushed Alfonso VI's army near Badajoz. And there he stayed. Youssef ben Tachfine remained virtuous and frugal until his death at the age of ninety, always clothed in coarse woollen garments and expressing himself in the uncouth Berber tongue, but his descendants soon degenerated. In 1121 his grandson's lax conduct was loudly condemned in Marrakesh by a fierce Berber rival, Ibn Toumert of the western Atlas, who had roamed from Cordoba to Baghdad and from Tripoli to Tlemcen.

In the beautiful Atlas valley of the N'fis, he founded a *ribat* of unitarians – violently opposed to the anthropomorphism of the Almoravids, called the 'El Mouahidiyine', better known to us as the Almohades. They took their name from the *taouhid* or doctrine of divine unity, which Ibn Toumert placed at the head of his precepts. The Almohades vanquished the Almoravids and like them were vanquished by Andalusia. For the second time in the history of Morocco a Berber dynasty, born in a *ribat*, was stayed in its impetuous course by the subtle corruption of gracious city life in Arab Andalusia. And yet these rulers, aided by mystics such as Moulay Abderradem ben Medrich (the great saint, the 'western pole' who is said to have introduced Sufi doctrines into Morocco) and his disciple Abou Lhassen ech Chadili (1175–1258) took Islam to the remotest tribes and paved the way for the unity of Morocco.

Moroccan saints began to assert themselves and to criticize the Sultans openly and in public. It was in the *zaouias*, not the universities, that leaders like Sidi Moussa of the Anti-Atlas and Sidi Said ben Abd el Moumin were recruited to establish order and combat the infidel Spaniard and Portuguese, who reached the gates of Marrakesh in 1515.

It often happened, however, that the saints became jealous of one another's influence and prestige; this led to unsaintly deeds of a violent, Renaissance nature. The great mystic reformer Jazouli (who also hailed from the anti-Atlas) died, poisoned in his retreat of Afourhal near Mogador, between 1465 and 1470, after having roused the envy both of the Merinid sovereigns and of rival marabouts. One of his disciples, Es-Sayyef, sought to avenge him and raised an army of fanatics for this purpose, but he was strangled by Jazouli's wife and daughter, whom he had forced to become his wives.

The marabouts began to acquire more and more temporal power. By the end of the sixteenth century, after the reign of the Saadians, many of them were heads of tiny, turbulent Berber states. Their influence over the tribes lasted well into the present century. The Saadian princes, who fought a holy war against the Portuguese along the Atlantic coast of Morocco, self-conscious of their Arab blood and kinship with Ali, the Prophet's son-in-law, disdained the unsophisticated Berbers. But these eagles of the Atlas, led by heads of *zaouias*, conquered them in the end. Few of the Saadian princes died in their beds. We would hardly remember them, were it not for the artists who fashioned their tombs in Marrakesh.

Every tourist knows that guidebook 'stars' for Marrakesh include the Koutoubbia tower, the tombs of the Saadian princes, and the gardens of the Hotel Mamounia. Pre-independence guidebooks as well as travel books never failed to omit the Djema el Fna square, whose snake charmers and medicine men provided the richest local colour in the whole of Morocco. The purists now in power have transformed the Djema el Fna into a car park. This, they feel, is more modern, and independent Morocco must at all costs be modern. Even at the cost of all that distinguishes her from the rest of our standardized contemporary world. The more tourist-conscious Moroccans, however, are in favour of a compromise: 'We shall bring some of the old characters back', they promise their disappointed European friends, 'but we must have them cleaned up and organized.' (Fatal, ominous word! Doubtless we shall soon be hearing about a Snakecharmer's Trade Union. The Chleuh dancers will be 'purified' and all traces of inversion abolished by official decree . . .)

Although the now famous tombs of the Saadian princes are close to the Djema el Fna, the French only 'discovered' them in 1917 when they were spotted, quite by accident, upon an aviation map. The local French Director of Fine Arts was taken to see them at dead of night because he had to walk through a mosque in order to reach the site, and all mosques in Morocco are closed to infidels.

It was only by a stroke of good fortune that the tombs had remained intact. The palace of the Saadians, the 'wonder of wonders, El Bedi', had been razed to the ground by Moulay Ismail upon one of his 'yellow' days, but he did not dare to desecrate the tombs. Jealous of their beauty, he screened them off by a wall and blocked the main door leading to the sanctuary. One reaches them now through a narrow passage ending in a small, untidy courtyard filled with nettles and a solitary palm tree. Those who know how abandon and splendour live happily side by side in Morocco will not be deceived by this mean approach to one of the country's greatest marvels.

You step straight from the weed-filled courtyard into a lofty sepulchral hall of marble and delicate plaster embroidery that prove, more convincingly than all Morocco's history books and chronicles put together, that the Saadian princes were aesthetes comparable to those of India and Persia.

In the first pavilion lie three long marble tombs surrounded by slender columns, from which arcades rise to a gold and multicoloured ceiling. In the second necropolis the cedar ceiling is supported by twelve unadorned marble pillars; their calm purity enhances the polychrome walls behind them, the honeycombed corners transparent as alabaster, the silent harmony of Arabic characters weaving in and out of stucco designs. It would take many hours of contemplation to absorb all the detail and perhaps, in the end, we would find the decorative fare too rich, too overwhelming. Less overwhelming, however, than Indian temples, because of the flat surfaces and the absence of human form. These geometrical designs, like eastern music, are satisfyingly impersonal and formless. They flow unceasingly without ever coming to a predictable end . . . such, at least, is the effect of a pattern that seems to grope after eternity and makes us forget the limitations of time and space, as well as the density of human forms.

The tombs at the foot of all this glory bring us back to the distinguished assortment of people for whom the necropolis was planned. Their size varies between long tombs that appear to have been made for giants, and miniature tombs small enough to hold newborn babes. The first to be buried here was the famous 'pole', the saint El Jazouli. After him came Sherif Abou Abdallah Elkaim, who chased the Portuguese from their fortresses in the Sous; Sherif Aboulabbas and his children, who were murdered by a governor of Marrakesh; Sherif Eccheikh, assassinated by the Turks; Sherif Moulay Abdallah, the alchemist; Sherif El Mansour, the 'Golden One', poisoned by one of his sons at the bidding of a female slave; Sherif Abou Abdelmalek, who caused so much scandal because of his excessive love of alcohol and was ultimately stabbed to death during one of his drunken bouts by his bodyguard of renegade Christians; Elaoulid, a great lover of music, was strangled, again by his renegade Christian domestics. Moulay Elahbas was put to death by his uncles of the Chebana tribe . . . But the obituary phrases that flow above and around the tombs take no account of these sordid crimes and hatreds. Pompous and conventional, they extol the dead in hollow hyperbole. The peace they never knew in their lifetimes enfolds them, ironically, in death.

Few tourists on their way to an expensive meal at the Mamounia by the handsome French-built Mauchamp hospital, realize that this was the site of a murder perpetrated in 1907 in extraordinary circumstances. Students of the secret arts will recognize the name at once, however, because Dr. Emile Mauchamp is the author of one of the best documented books on Moroccan magic to be published since Doutté's classic on the subject, apart from Westermarck's well-known *Ritual and Belief in Morocco.*

Mauchamp was a free-thinker, and he hated superstition to the point of fanaticism. He appears to have been determined to implant western hygiene in the inhabitants of Marrakesh and to show up the charlatanism of their numerous magicians, thereby incurring the wrath of the most powerful of all the southern magicians at that time: Sheikh Ma el Aïnin, who ordered his men to enter Marrakesh and bring about the death of the sacrilegious infidel. Paradoxically enough, Mauchamp was believed to be a powerful magician practising a western and highly dangerous form of voodoo upon his un-suspecting patients! Mauchamp's French biographer points out that this rumour was deliberately spread among the Moors by the German Consul at Marrakesh at a time when Germany was casting covetous eyes upon Morocco. (This was five years before the 1912 treaty by which Morocco became a French Protectorate).

Little by little, every one of Dr. Mauchamp's activities became suspect. One day a strange pole appeared in his garden. It was intended for a clothes line, but the excitable natives of the *souks* were sure that it was to be used for sinister purposes. A few of them had heard vaguely about a fearful western invention called the wireless through which strange, disembodied voices could be heard, especially at night. The pole must be connected with this; the magician-doctor was about to introduce the wireless to Marrakeeh and perhaps capture their voices and with them, their souls . . .

When Dr Mauchamp came out of his house that morning, followed by his interpreter, a hostile crowd formed round him. The crowd grew and began to murmur angrily. The frightened interpreter fled, leaving the doctor helpless, because he had never taken the trouble to learn the language of the people among whom he worked. Confronted by an ignorant, exasperated mob, he could not even explain himself. Ma el Aïnin's men were in that mob. They judged that this was the opportune moment to put their master's orders into execution. The crowd was on their side . . . no representatives of authority were in sight. One of them forced the uncomprehending doctor into a doorway and stabbed him. Others eagerly followed their example. Ma el Ainin's men withdrew discreetly to carry the news to the snow-capped Atlas. The mountain sorcerer had vanquished his alien rival and enemy.

There was an interesting political sequel to this incident: the French Government seized the opportunity to march into Oujda, on the confines of Algeria, declaring that they would continue to occupy the town until adequate compensation was paid to them for Dr. Mauchamp's assassination. They remained there until 1955 – that is, until Morocco once more became an independent State.

Many more magicians-Moorish and European-have flourished in Marrakesh since those days. A French water-diviner, the Abbé Lambert, caused a stir some thirty years ago by discovering water upon a site given to a German doctor by the Pasha, which had been reputed to be as dry as the Sahara. Then, within the last decade came a French wine merchant who was better known for his bone-setting and healing powers than for his wines. None of the local magicians appear to have objected to him. This may of course have something to do with the decline of their own powers and reputation.

One of the outstanding personalities who believed implicitly in magic lore was El Thami Glaoui, Pasha of Marrakesh, uncrowned king of southern Morocco until the return from exile of the present Sultan. He was probably the last picturesque figure in the tradition of the Saadian princes. There is no scope for such autocratic despots in the new political set-up. The Moors must be relieved. I only met one, and he was a French-educated, military man, who looked a little sentimental when I spoke of the Glaoui's rotting palaces, and it was he who lent me a jeep to visit his ex-'capital': the *kasbah* of Telouet, half-way up the N'Tichka pass.

I left Marrakesh at dawn, after a night at the Hôtel du Parc that overlooks the cars and cabs of the Djema del Fna. I had been lured to this obscure hotel by its misleading name and by the shy, sad little arch of an entrance at the back of the square. As a rule such entrances lead to better things. Perhaps, I had thought, to more undiscovered tombs or to an interesting piece of abandoned palace? Alas, no . . .

The outward appearance of my Hôtel du Parc was unfortunately a true reflection of the drab interior. The 'Parc' was but a baked patch of earth planted with a dozen lanky shrubs whose struggle for survival was a painful spectacle. A large board at the far end of this patch indicated the location of the only water-closet in the establishment: dark, bolt-less and uncomfortable.

A row of eight dreary rooms looked out on to the 'Parc' and a high wall behind it, upon which plants with immense mottled leaves rested like lazy turtles.

My room was high enough for spiders to live to a shrivelled old age undisturbed by brooms. The door was immensely tall and narrow. It was obvious at once that the key would never fit into the worm-eaten keyhole. Two ridiculously small windows only a little above floor level and fitted with rusty grilles flanked the door like dwarf sentinels. The three of them were provided with the forlorn, fungus-green shutters that I always associate with provincial France, and that film directors never fail to make use of when they wish to portray sordid continental love scenes. They would have loved the interior of my room. There was the bleak, black iron bedstead, the thin soiled cover, the hard pillows, the lumpy mattress, the naked electric light bulb, the cracked washbasin – no plug, of course – one bad-tempered tap and its placid twin opposite, silent and immovable.

I still had time to change my hotel and take a taxi out to the palm groves beyond the rose-red walls of Marrakesh where all the travel agency-recommended hotels are situated and all 'nice' people go, but I was both too lazy to make the effort and too fascinated by the Hôtel du Parc's advanced state of decay. These sunken places give one a sense of utter isolation and detachment. They make me personally feel deliciously insecure. And this, I believe, is good for the soul. On a less abstract level, I did not wish to offend the Hôtel du Parc's amiable management, who had been so delighted to direct me to a Moorish restaurant where I consumed with enjoyment a tasty *kouskous* at the tenth of the price of a European meal in the palm groves.

The night watchman roused me (and no doubt everybody else in that single row of rooms) at five o'clock in the morning; soon after, the hollow-eyed boy who slept in his *burnous* in a corner of the passage brought me a glass of black coffee. In the Djema el Fna, dawn buses and their drivers were beginning to spit and groan. Muffled passengers appeared on the faintly pink horizon, breathing heavily as they dragged their corpse-like bundles after them.

Was there nothing to eat? I enquired plaintively. The hollow-eyed boy shook his head and gazed at me thoughtfully as I sat shivering in the reception cubicle. Then, as if suddenly inspired, he conjured a bicycle from the shadows where he slept and darted off across the square. He was away for quite ten minutes, but when he returned he gleefully presented me with a sticky trophy of large *beignets,* still dripping with fat from the frying pan, which constitute the main item of a Moorish proletarian breakfast. Then he sat and watched me while I struggled through them with much licking of fingers between bites.

Dawn and sunset are the two most striking moments of the day in regal, ragged Marrakesh. Sunset is almost exclusively regal, when everything is so saturated with gold that the palm trees reel under the impact and lean drunkenly against the glowing ramparts. There is gold dust in the air and the magic powder transforms and beautifies every profile that passes, every fold of every *burnous,* every twitching donkey's velvet-lined ears. All things that appear commonplace during the rest of the day become extraordinary at sunset. A canter through the palm groves among singing *bulbuls* at this time in an old-fashioned cab becomes an unforgettable experience, however banal the suggestion may sound when conveyed through trim print. It is just this absence of trimness, the straggly nature of Marrakesh, that makes the city so attractive. That is why the conventional authorities who wish to tidy up the Djema el Fna can only succeed in destroying the wanton soul of this southern capital. They may suppress the cabs one of these days. They will certainly do so as soon as some distinguished visitor tells them that these venerable vehicles are 'old-fashioned'. Then yet another leisurely pleasure will have gone for ever.

Hurry, then, if you wish to enjoy Marrakesh and its sunsets from a cab. Tarry when you get there for an aperitif in the gardens of the Mamounia on the way back from your ride. The gardens are all that remain of the palace that used to be, but they have kept all their trailing, languorous splendours, all their languid memories of princely day-dreams. Infectious, voluptuous day-dreams . . .

In the dawn, Marrakesh is a magnificent window on an incandescent world; beyond the miles and miles of ramparts lies a nomad's land, a plain stretching to the foothills of the Atlas with here and there the broken silver thread of a *oued*, and a clump of black-plumed palms silhouetted against the sky like upturned ostriches, their heads for ever in the sand.

My dawn was cold, and many of the people on their way to the souks were crouched over fires by the wayside under the palms, or in the shelter of a *koubba*. Few words were spoken, The great snow waves of the mighty Atlas loomed before us, dangerously unfurled, quickening to rosy life. There are few isolated peaks in this range. The Atlas rise like a natural dam, a wall of snow to shield Marrakesh from the sandstorms of the Sahara.

'*T'es pas fatiguée?*' my Moorish driver enquired considerately after we had veered round scores of hairpin bends. He had informed me at the outset that there are a hundred and seventy-five bends on the road up the N'Tichka. It is a treeless road, except for the sudden luxuriant plunges of vegetation beside the river beds where red, flat-roofed villages peep above pink oleanders and golden-leaved pomegranates. Palm trees fringed the rivers for quite a long way up the pass. Then the *kasbahs* began to appear: Berber fortresses fashioned out of red mud and river water, with slit-small windows from where the inmates used to watch for their enemies from the next village or valley. It is not thirty years since all the tribes were pacified, and there is no guarantee that they will remain for ever peaceful in an independent Morocco.

The Glaoui were the heads of the comparatively unimportant Glaoua tribe, but thanks to a combination of ruthlessness and political acumen the two brothers El Madani and El Thami Glaoui ended by running practically the whole of the Atlas. They supported the French and were paid handsomely in return. High-walled Glaoui *kasbahs* were built at every strategic point. The Glaoui palace at Marrakesh was renowned for its banquets and its dancing girls and boys – slender Chleuhs whose effeminate gestures and perverse eyes were so appreciated by the feudal pashas, for homosexuality in Morocco – as one author has described it – used to be 'almost a national institution'.

El Thami Glaoui, with his falcon face and long, artistic fingers, his western sympathies and his tangled roots in the past, built a golf course in the sand, entertained distinguished foreign visitors and kept a Jewish magician at his side . . . his dark, enigmatic side. Few people knew about this closely-guarded, secret aspect of his life. For some years – almost two decades – he reigned supreme. He was known as the 'Lord of the Atlas'; the 'King of the South', and he revelled in it. He could be cruel but, like many other cruel individuals he was intensely refined in his tastes, and a connoisseur of Berber music and poetry.

At the close of his life, a few months before his death, he went to prostrate himself at the feet of the Sultan whom he had opposed and helped to send into exile. A tired old man of eighty, he knelt humbly before his forty-year-old sovereign to beg forgiveness for his past disloyalties. Was it just that he wished to redeem his reputation and assure the future of his descendants in newly independent Morocco, now that French support was of no more avail? Or was it that his conscience was troubling him now that his end was near? Had his Jewish magician dared to foretell that he had only a few more months to live? One can only guess. But the gesture and the medieval *mise en scene* were noble and moving, in graceful accordance with old Moroccan and Muslim tradition, a page out of an Arabian Nights' code of chivalry. The Sultan gravely granted his royal pardon, and the aged pasha returned, satisfied, to Marrakesh to die. He has left sons, but none of them have the grandeur of El Thami Glaoui. Grandeur is not an attribute of this age.

The Glaoui *kasbahs* of the Atlas were empty. No official decision had yet been taken about the various properties, which had been left in the casual hands of caretakers. Most of the kasbahs were already beginning to crumble; these imposing structures are far from solid. Decay comes quickly in Morocco where so many things – life itself – is fluid and impermanent.

I reached Telouet at the end of the day, after a long detour. Telouet is situated a few miles off the main road in rugged, hilly country. The immense kasbah with its whitewashed towers and many wings stands haughtily aloof from the rest of what can only be described as a poor mountain village. The air was sharp and we shivered in the cold yellow gleam of an almost extinguished sun.

We drove through a high-walled passage: in the old days of less than ten years ago it would have been lined with domestics when visitors were expected. Now it was deserted and filled with tossing weeds. We had to bang long and loudly on the iron-studded gate before weary footsteps approached on the other side and an invisible hand pulled back a long succession of rusty, reluctant bolts.

The gates finally creaked open and we drove into a sloping courtyard, where we left the jeep. A straggling group of caretakers and their relatives and cronies sauntered up to us and offered to show us round the apartments. Before doing so, I had to submit to the usual glass of mint tea. We drank this in one of the vast salons on the ground floor in which El Thami Glaoui used to receive his guests. The silks and velvets had begun to fade; damp and fungus spread over the ornate ceilings, and were already effacing the painted panels of the slim doors.

The caretakers exchanged local gossip with my driver while I sat on the cushioned divan recalling the glitter of ten years before, when the Glaoui was in his prime and I had been entertained to a sumptuous *diffa*. His ghostly presence filtered slowly into the room with the last dying rays of the sun. It blew through the cracks in the door with a whiff of perfume. It was not the odour of sanctity, but a sophisticated Arabian perfume well suited to the fastidious aristocrat who had appreciated the luxuries of his own country as well as those of our world: weapons and automobiles, wars and kasbahs. His heavy eyes, his shrewd smile, his gentle yet talon-like hands, seemed to follow me sadly when I rose to wander round the colonnaded patios that melted one into the other in a dream-like proximity.

His world, and ours . . . and the best of both. He would only consent to wear the *burnous* woven by the women of his own tribe. In his youth he took part in mountain battles and he threw himself with equal passion into Berber rondos of improvised songs. Since his death, the prudish Moroccan authorities have frowned upon the Berber *haouash*. 'It was a pretext for prostitution', they say. Nevertheless, the *haouash* still goes on under the Atlas moon, as it must until the firmament ceases to revolve, for it is a planetary dance; a 'Creation dance' childishly simple, grave and impressive. All the magic of their race is in this Berber *haouash*, and those of Telouet were organized, as they should be, on a vast scale.

The Berbers call themselves the 'Sons of Shadow' and the 'Daughters of the Night', and their astral choreography is at its best when it is performed under the stars. The rhythm is slow and intoxicating, the movements few. The oscillating torsos, the tight row of men and women wedged shoulder to shoulder, the gradual sinking half-way to the ground, and then up again abruptly as the hands beat time and the nasal voices ring out in the night round the tremendous bale-fires . . . how the Glaoui loved this ancient ritual of his people! To what pagan divinity was this dance first dedicated? To whom was it first revealed? These are questions which must remain for ever unanswered. The turning dervishes were more articulate, for it is written in one of their prayers:

> By revolving as rapidly as lightning we must become intoxicated with Thy love . . . Let us remain silent and humble before Thy divine majesty. Let us turn in unsullied clothes before Thy throne. Let us imitate those luminous bodies . . . let us turn day and night at the foot of the celestial throne. Let us likewise imitate those of Thy movements which are regulated by our perseverance in serving and adoring Thee. Let us revolve like the sun and the moon. Let us turn like the planets. Let us turn like the stars in the heavens. Let us turn like the waves of the sea in their continual unfurling. Let us turn like the circle which has neither a beginning nor an end! Lastly, let us open wide our arms to prove to Thee our ardent desire to return to Thee and then let us cross them as a sign of our eternal bondage . . .

This strange, remote litany came to my mind as we embarked upon the ever-mysterious itinerary of a Moorish *kasbah* with its carefully calculated effects of light and shade, its deliberately dark passages and sudden patio-oases, where carefully-measured patches of heaven are a planned part of the décor. The furniture had been removed from most of the rooms, but on the first floor I came across an intimate little salon that had somehow been overlooked. The frail arcaded grille in the window screened off the barren plateau of Telouet and the white-nosed Atlas beyond – too harsh a view for its alcove delicacy. A dying sun shone faintly upon the brass-topped tables and the purple velvet pouffes that still exhaled the provocative scent of women. This was a room which must often have served as a prelude to love. Now that all passion was spent, the sepulchral cold and stillness were intolerable.

It was not only cold, but also a little sinister. The *kasbah* of Telouet always was sinister, even in its inhabited days. One of the Tharaud brothers visited the Glaoui there nearly thirty years ago, and he too shivered in the same glacial, doomed atmosphere.

He arrived in winter in the company of the Glaoui. The bowed domestics approached to kiss the master's knee and he, with a protective gesture worthy of a monarch or a bishop, gravely laid his hand upon the heads nearest to him. M. Tharaud followed a black slave carrying enormous keys who unlocked countless doors before him and then locked them again behind him, along a labyrinth of passages in places open to the sky, so that at times they walked upon rugs and at other times upon steps felted with snow. A furious wind blew under the doors and through the chinks in the painted ceilings.

'How lost I felt in this corner of the immense château!' exclaimed Tharaud, 'lost in some eastern fairy tale which had itself become stranded amid the snow-clad mountains.' And then the door opened, the wind blew out several tall green candles unsteadily poised upon the tables, and the Glaoui entered, preceded by several slaves carrying large lanterns. 'With his impressive stature, his sharp profile, his feverish black eyes, the *burnous* hanging close to his sides under which a slit of white *kaftan* could be seen and yellow *babouches* lightly powdered with snow, he looked like an immense bird brought in by the tempest.'

Together they walked back along the maze of steps and passages, until they reached the largest of the inner courtyards where an immense bonfire was burning, continually fed with uprooted *thuja* trees, the lumps of earth still clinging to their roots. Round this fire a hundred women in white with brilliant silk headscarves were beating their hands, swaying gently right and left 'like the grains of an enormous rosary moved by an invisible, magic finger-a spectacle of astonishing unity and harmony, a form of collective beauty quite unknown to us in Europe.'

'What is going to become of all this?' I asked one of the caretakers. He shrugged his shoulders and smiled sadly.

'We are waiting. Nobody knows. But Sidi [the Sultan] has promised that the Glaoui's property will be respected.' I glanced at the crumbling, honeycombed walls. (Crumbling . . . how often one is obliged to use this word about Morocco!) 'Nothing lasts long here,' my driver observed fatalistically as he followed my eyes.

Nothing lasts long. Neither war nor peace, neither hatred nor friendship, neither Glaoui nor Sultan . . .

ABOUT THE AUTHOR

NINA EPTON was born of Scottish and Spanish parents and educated in France before going on to run French Canadian programming for the BBC world service. She wrote many books on travel and several biographies. *Saints and Sorcerers* should not be read for historical accuracy but for its romantic aura and emphasis on the coexistence of superstition and religion.

The Mob

from *Lords of the Atlas* by Gavin Maxwell

The Aftermath – Marrakesh in 1956

I was only a child when these things happened, but I remember them well, though I don't like to remember them or to think that I laughed to see a man burnt alive. It was a short time after the Glaoui's death, and I was a child of about nine, living with my parents in Marrakesh as we always had. I had just eaten the midday meal, and I was playing in a street of our quarter with other children of about my age when someone came running and calling out, 'Come and see the fun! They've broken open the Glaoui's garage at the Dar El Glaoui and they're smashing his cars!' We ran with him and we found a great crowd round the garage and men smashing a big black car – I think it was a Delahaye. Then they set fire to it and everyone watched it burn, talking and shouting excitedly. Suddenly someone in the crowd yelled out, 'Let's have vengeance on the other traitors!' Others repeated it, and in a moment or two a wild yelling crowd had formed in the Riad El Arrouss beside the Dar El Glaoui, all shouting, 'Death to the traitors!' They began running towards the house of a man who had been one of the Glaod's judges – his name was Kittani, but I don't think he was any close relation of Abd El Hay Kittani, a very cruel man who had punished the young people who were against the Glaoui by making them sit naked upon bottles that had been broken half-way up, and then confining them chained in dungeons with just enough food to live. I ran with the crowd, and when they reached his door and beat upon it he opened it himself. He held the Koran open in his left hand, and at his right were his small sons. He began to speak at once, asking for mercy and for pity, but immediately one of the foremost of the crowd shouted 'No pity for traitors!' and struck him a great blow on the head with a cudgel. He fell, unconscious, and they seized him and put him on a *kourrissa*, the hand-cart on which people push goods about, and rushed him outside the city walls at Bab

Doukkala. All the young people were stoning him, and stripping him of his clothes. They put him upon a rubbish dump, poured petrol over him, and set him alight. I remember the smell and the way his skin blistered and burst. We were laughing, all of us, and that is something I am ashamed, bitterly, to remember.

The crowd went back into the town, this time led by a jeep manned by four quite young boys with masks over their faces. They made for the house of one of El Glaoui's intimates, a man called Bou Raghba [pronounced *Bourgba*] who was hated by all his neighbours. I ran behind them, laughing and excited as we all were. I suppose there's no point in saying I was just a child, because the adults were behaving in the same way. We were showing of what stuff human beings are really made, without the disguises and pretences behind which we hide.

When we reached Bou Raghba's house it was barred and shuttered and Bou Raghba himself began to fire upon us with a sub-machine-gun from an upper window. In the first burst of fire he killed two of the boys who had been driving the jeep, and wounded many of the crowd, including us children. Then the leader of the mob decided to attack the house by following the roof-tops from the next street. They did this, and threw down incendiary bombs; this stopped him shooting, and while he was suffocating in the fumes they broke down the door, and a man who was an old soldier of France, and who had been wounded by Bou Raghba's first shots, went in first and shot at Bou Raghba with a rifle. Then he was dragged out as Kittani had been. They stripped him quite naked and hauled him through the streets – I remember how his shaven head looked like a jelly, because the skull had been dashed to pieces. We all thought it was funny – why? Then they burned him too, on the same rubbish dump.

Another party of rioters seized the *Chef de Quartier* of Bab Doukkala, a man named Mghinia. I remember him particularly because my mother had ticked off one of his children for fighting me in the street, and as a result he had sent a deputation of his guard to intimidate us. My father had to pay them blackmail money and because of this we went hungry for a long time. My mother said that Allah would curse this man for what he had done, and when he was burnt alive that day she said that Allah had answered her prayers. When the rioters reached the burning place he held out his *shaccara* (the leather bag all Berbers carry) and took from it a huge sum of money. He said, 'I know I am about to die, but in Allah's name give this money to my children.' The crowd yelled 'No mercy!' and pushed him on to the fire, throwing petrol over him at the same time. I remember how, as he burnt, the hand holding the purse of money raised itself, clenched, above the flames, and remained visible long after the man must have been dead.

I think nothing worse ever took place in Marrakesh, even in the terrible old days. Nothing could be worse. My father, who could remember the dynastic wars and horrors of the days of Moulay Hafid, said, 'No man has the right to burn another and thus deprive him of resurrection – it is the privilege of none but Allah himself.' It is said that when the Sultan Mohammed V heard of these happenings he did not eat for seven days.

Although no police intervened in the course of these horrors, the new Pasha of Marrakesh, El Skalli, placed his guards round the corpses that smouldered all night, so that the women of the city could not take pieces of them for use in black magic, for the relics of these burned enemies were thought to be potent. Indeed El Skalli did more, for he took to himself the orphaned children of Bou Raghba, and I remember that as he put his arms around them he said, 'This terrible happening, this shame, can never be wiped out in any of our lifetimes.'

You have made me remember these things – remember the real story behind what is still called 'The Place of Burning', and have made me ashamed for remembering. We Moroccans are a violent and a cruel people – but is not all humanity the same before they begin to think? Please do not disclose my name. I was a child, following a mob.

[This extract is taken from an appendix to Gavin Maxwell's *Lords of the Atlas*: an interview with an anonymous Marrakeshi who participated in the riots against the Glaoui that followed Morocco's return to independence in 1955.]

The Seven Saints of Marrakesh

Katri Skala

The seven sufi saints, also known as the sleepers, lie deep within protected vaults among mazed streets, through tree-lined cemeteries, often at the centre of a courtyard. Inaccessible to non-Muslim, these holiest of holy shrines, offer to its piligrim visitors a direct communion with the sublime. Often decorated with the seductive curves of the arabesque and plunged in a chiaroscuro of flickering candlclight, the tombs offer up stories of asceticism, patience, charity and study. The sleepers are expected to awake one day and resume their roles as mystics, interlocutors and spiritual leaders. Until then, devout men and women stream to the sepulchres, sometimes to meditate, sometimes to chant, and always to seek union with the Divine.

Who are these saints? The legends of the seven are sung in a poem by Sheikh Al Youssi:

In Marrakesh appear lofty stars, imposing mountains and sharp swords. Abou Youssef, man of the cave, is the reflection of every man's gaze; the learned son of the Abou Imran Aayad is known to all, Abou El Abbas, so generous he knew no boundaries. Ben Sliman El-Jazouli, celebrated for his many skills, the saint who comes to the aid of whomsoever calls. Tebaa is a sea of generosity and correctness; Ghezouaini the shining dawn, Abou el Kassem Assouheili, Imam of learning and mercy. Vast is the sea of their knowledge and in any circumstance, visit the tombs of these saints, the Lord will help and protect you.

The shrine of Sidi Youssef is set in a nest of dark, narrow streets. A woman at the door sells white candles. The saint's tomb is covered in green cloth with verses from the Koran illuminated in gold thread. A young man in a floating silk djeballa instructs the visitor to descend into a cave beneath the tomb. In this barren hole, Sidi Youssef spent many days fasting and praying. Day became night and night day as the saint plunged into a mystical trance, reciting the Koran, battling hunger and pain. And in so doing he fulfilled the Prophet's Hadith 'Die before you die'. Thus he was able to fully experience for himself the pain of the hungry and the sorrow of the sick. He lived with the lepers and visited the ailing throughout the city, bringing them the blessings of God on High. They say he never laughed; only on the threshold of death did a large smile cover his face.

The approach to the shrine of Cadi Aayad, in the cemetery of Bab Ailen, is lined with tombs still much venerated by the people of Marrakesh. Women stand in shaded alleys and sell small padlocks; when affixed to the railing they allow the pilgrim to shed his misfortune, and to pass it to the saint, whose purpose is to soothe the suffering of others. If you have time, one of the women may invite you to sit with her while she tells you the story of Cadi Aayad's greatness.

Cadi Aayad's father was the renowned Imam de Ceuta. The child was raised in an atmosphere of devoutness and discipline. He excelled in the art of exegesis and Islamic law. He became famous for his rigorous orthodoxy and studied with the great scholar Averroes. He renovated many places of religious worship, and built a great college. He was made Cadi of Grenada, however, very quickly fell victim to palace intrigue, and with the rise of the Almohad Empire became an exile first in Tadla then Marrakesh where he lived out his life at Bab Ailen, dispensing justice in acccordance with the Malekite code of Islamic law.

Sidi Bel Abbes is the patron saint of Marrakesh, and is invoked by the young and old alike, at times of great joy and of great pain. The direct approach to this *zaouia* is through an arch lined with merchants selling beautiful pieces of jewellery, and the non-Muslim can just about catch glimpses of the great pyramidal shrine at the centre of the complex. Orphaned at an early age, Sidi Bel Abbes was put into a Medersa by his uncle. His reading of the Koran generated an abiding and profound insight: Justice demands the sharing of all goods. He lived for a while at the foot of the Gueliz, and when the Caliph Abdel Moumen came to visit the hermit, he was told that 'everything you want your people to do for you, you should do for your people'. Abdel Moumen's successor, Abou Yousssef Yacoub invited the saint to Marrakesh and paid him to teach. Bel Abbes used the money to clothe and feed needy students. He became a well-known figure in the streets, chastising the unbelievers, giving alms to the poor, railing against injustice. Once he came upon a man whose clothes were so ragged you could see his naked flesh. So he undressed on the spot and gave the man his clothes. And one night, so the story goes, he felt so cold, in spite of numerous covers, that he could not stop shivering. So he got up and knocked on his neighbours' door, only to find them without any covers at all. So he gave them his own, returned to his bed, and was warm.

He attracted the attention of Averroes, who became his friend and defined his philosophy in three tenets: generosity (joud), being (woujoud) and charity (sadqua). Legend has it that when Averroes body was exhumed to be taken to Cordoba, Sidi Bel Abbes was buried in his vacant tomb. He left behind him an impressive zaouia, centred on the shrine where hordes of the poor and the blind gather to this day to be fed and schooled, and where the takings of blind beggars are distributed equally throughout the city to all those who see badly.

'Death, death, always death'. Such was the inscription scrawled on the wall of Sidi El Jazouli's room at the Medersa of the Saffarine's where he had locked himself away for a prolonged retreat. His religious study revolved around this powerful preoccupation, and he is known for being one of the great mystics of Morocco. His teachings are summed up in a famous book *Dalil el Khayrat*, around which have grown many legends, not least that no matter which edition you pick up, it will always smell of musk. El Jazouli also became a leading figure in the struggle against Portugal, and his body was used as a totem in these battles, until finally the Sultan Moulay Ahmd Arej ordered that it be enshrined in Marrakesh to end once and for all the intrigues of the saint's zaouia. It too has an impressive green pyramid roof which can be seen by the non-Muslim from a neighboring street.

In order to reach the holy sepulchre of Sidi Abdelaziz Tebaa, you have to climb over a steel chain wound across the road. It is arranged in the sign of an upside-down cross and the word 'Attaslim' (peace) is spelled out for all visitors to read. It is said that once inside the courtyard, you may be surprised by the spectacle of many young women who chant and dance till they fall, literally, to the ground in a deep trance; and are then carried into the mausoleum and laid in piles at the feet of the catafalque. In addition, they say, to this tableaux of ecstatic women, stands an older woman by a brazier, her face tattooed, her hands warm, ready to pass over the head of any ailing newborn, for it is said, she has the power of healing and can cure any illness brought on by the evil eye.

Among these female figures, stands the tomb of Sidi Abdelazz Tebaa. Come late in life to a religious way – he was a silk merchant – he became known for his excellence in exegesis and the Hadiths. A man of bounty and goodness, the following words, written on his tomb, give hope to those who visit 'Rejoice, you who come as pilgrims to this place! Be satisfied, your goal has been achieved. The brightness of the tomb of Aziz shines on those who visit and predicts happiness. You who come into this sanctuary, God will make you prosper. Rejoice, the goodness of your master will be lavished on you'.

The great Berber ascetic Sidi Ben Abella El Ghazouani was a student first in Fez then Grenada, before returning to Marrakesh to study alongside Sidi Abdelaziz Tebaa. He then rejoined his tribe, and soon his reputation was giving such offense to the Sultan Wattasid Sidi Mahamed Chekh that he was imprisoned. However, when news reached the Sultan of supernatural happenings in the prison, El Ghazouani, was released and despatched to Fez to create a zaouia there. However, he could not be kept away from Marrakesh, and after forecasting the end of the ruling Beni Wattas reign, he established a zaouia in Marrakesh which was dedicated to absolute prayer and the demands of the ascetic life.

The seventh shrine is that of Sidi Souhail, the poet-saint. Set within a large cemetery lined with tombs and an olive grove it sits on a small hill near Bab Robb. The mauseoleum is dominated by a handsome high-stretching coupola. At one end of the courtyard, a young child in white recites verses from the Koran, as glacial Alpine water runs from a fountain. Students who have lost their memory come to here to regain it.

Sidi Souhail was born in a village near Malaga. He became a great sage and followed the King Yacoub El Mansour to Marrakesh where he lived out his days. He wrote two masterpieces: one on the names of the prophets mentioned in the Koran, the other on the life of Sidna Mohamed. Unlike the other patrons, Sidi Souhail came to lead the life of a religious man217 as a result of a passionate love for a woman.

As a young man in Andalucia, Sidi Souhail saw a young woman one day out on horseback. She was covered head to toe in white and black cloth. He was immediately smitten but she turned him away. He followed her everyday to a clearing. He played ballads and recited from the Koran. He was unable to sleep and wrote poems into the night. Still, the cloaked woman rebuffed his advances.

Until one day, unable to bear it any longer, she removed the black veil from her face and revealed to him her leprous features. He took her in his arms 'Nothing has changed for me', he said ' I will love you forever'. He took her back to his house, and looked after her until her death.

ABOUT THE AUTHOR

KATRI SKALA is managing editor of Pretext, a twice-yearly literary journal published by Pen&inc. She has compiled a free translation from various sources; *Les Septs Dormants de Marrakesh* (Dar Kortoba, 1994) by Mustapha Akmisse, *Morocco* (Cadogan Guides, 1989)) by Barnaby Rogerson, *Islam – The Way of Submission* (The Aquarian Press, 1987) by Solomon Nigosian, *Regard sur le Temps des Soufis* (Editions EDDIF, 1995) by Ibn al Zayyat al Tadili.

The City in the 1960s
Anthony Gladstone-Thompson

August 1965

Marrakesh, exemplar of cults, journeys, markets, rebellions, first camp, then capital: expectantly trailing such notions I reach the city after a torrid, three-hundred-mile drive from Fez, and park near the Café Renaissance in Guéliz. Expensive Oulmès water (*'source déclarée d'intêret publique'*). The atmosphere in the *ville moderne* seems attenuated, provincial: ruled-off boulevards, orange trees in sunken pits, understated buildings with splayed corners, veiled locals outnumbered by European women, dark glasses pushed back in their hair.

Guéliz's architect, Landais, may too have first come here across plains scorched grey by summer, and pondered how the approaching city could face down such climatic power. For his trim villas, he ordained a paint finish pinker than the vastly older, sunburnt walls a mile to the south; but he valued the character of old Marrakesh, the olive and orange trees, the palms, the fields of mint, orchards and gardens, and decently emulated the Saadian tradition when he raised in the desert a French suburb.

On to Place de la Liberté, pausing for a gap in the procession of bicycles. The ramparts stretch before me, visible for more than a mile in each direction, a series of fortifications encircling the medina like the Atlas Mountains in miniature. I follow the walls as far as Bab El Jedid, turn through the gateway and drive past the Mamounia Hotel towards Place Jemaa El Fna. I park in Rue Bab Agnaou: the Grand Hôtel Tazi has caught my eye, and they have a room. The hotel boasts a 'solarium', but has no restaurant.

Place Jemaa El Fna

I make my way to the famous square by a roundabout route to inspect the Koutoubia. The low-built city hugs the plain, but this minaret, albeit set in an untended garden patrolled by a bored policeman, would with the greatest propriety lift itself to heaven. Thence to the crowded terrace of the Café de France, overlooking a thronged Jemaa El Fna. The man with whom I'm obliged to share a table turns out to be a most knowledgeable English resident called Quentin.

'You should really have approached Marrakesh from the south, as traders from beyond the Sahara have done for eight centuries. Marrakesh was the finest oasis city known to them, worthy of the huge distances they'd travelled and the mountains so laboriously crossed.' Quentin ordered red Martinis. 'When I arrived fifteen years ago, thousands of camels still came every year, bearing merchandise. The Berliet lorry has largely done for them, but you still encounter an astonishing variety of races. Look at the Gnaoua down there: a black brotherhood, descendants of Sudanese slaves who've kept their ethnic purity. Their dancing's a religious expression as much as an entertainment.'

The dozen white-robed Gnaoua rely on huge castanets to clap out their mesmerizing music, accompanied by a single drum player; they stamp, gyrate and turn somersaults, their red cap tassels continuously whirling as they toss their heads. When they briefly fall silent, the air is filled with other music: men sing to the melancholy rasp of home-made stringed instruments, snake-charmers are abetted by drummers, flautists and lute players, and individuals wander about banging tuneless drums or working through outlandish scales on double-reed pipes.

I take a sidelong glance at Quentin: he is in his forties, stout, with thining hair; his features in repose brim with severe and precise intelligence. He doesn't smoke, and as if in compensation his fingers constantly stray to his temple and fiddle with a strand of hair.

'Ready for a closer look?'

After paying we emerge into the bustle outside, stepping over two near-naked infants sleeping in the care of a ten-year-old, who thrusts her cupped hand towards me.

Jemaa El Fna is more crowded than it appears from the terrace. Tourists are outnumbered by Moroccans, Berbers in brown burnouses, black-capped Jews and off-duty army conscripts in neat uniforms. They have gathered in large circles round the performers. Craning over their heads I see a fire-eater; he preens himself and utters some incantation as he marshals his tins of spirit and a black candle before swallowing the inflammable liquid.

As beggars pluck my sleeve, three men clown through a routine, the audience cheering their knockabout antics. Further on, youthful tumblers in brilliant pantaloons execute cartwheels and jump on each other's shoulders to form a three-storey pyramid. Long-haired snake-charmers, mystical adepts who appear to be both master and servant of their reptiles, flirtatiously coax the inactive serpents. There are story-tellers, whose voices and gestures, by turns cajoling, bombastic, pathos-filled and accusatory, appeal particularly to the very old and very young.

'They're the most skilled of the entertainers,' Quentin says. 'Their themes are love, death, conquest: the more melodramatic the better. Once a story's been declaimed, it's taken up by another teller and passed on to an ever-growing audience: a verbal chain letter, registering new shifts of emphasis each time it's retold.' On the fringes of the square, letter-writers and fortune-tellers sit cross-legged with their clients; a solitary greybeard listens intently to his supplicant before handing him a minute philtre and a folded charm. 'A *taleb* – student of the magic arts,' Quentin explains. 'The most experienced have the power to resolve unrequited passion by summoning the object of your dreams, or to reunite you with a lost love.'

'Moroccans seem very suggestible to occult practices, genies and the like.'

'The plural's "jinn". They're taken seriously: even intellectuals look over their shoulders in case a genie is following. Although they're mostly invisible, they sometimes take the form of animals. There's no doubt they dominate the lives of many people. Magic is the residue of all the civilizations that have clashed and melded in Morocco.'

As we pass two men lounging round a table, one springs into action and wins a fifty-dirham note off his confederate in a trick shuffling upturned beakers, tempting us to try their luck. Quentin ambles good-naturedly on, heading for a row of stalls. Here are barbers, metalsmiths, dentists and photographers, all operating with primitive but well-burnished equipment. At an apothecary's stall I inspect the array of jars and woven platters displaying desiccated adders, frogs and birds' wings, as well as baskets of dried leaves. The shopkeeper panders to my interest with cackles of laughter.

'He's recommending those wrinkled roots. They're a Berber remedy for the pox.'

Other stalls dispense food. Youths buy quarters of flat Moroccan loaves crammed with olives, chickpeas or salad; those with more money eat red-brown *Merguez* sausages, snails, sizzling pieces of fish. A bicyclist calls out his order; greaseproof paper is twisted into a cone and piled with some savoury, pinkish treat scooped from the bubbling pan.

'Fancy going native, and partaking?' asks Quentin, eyes twinkling.

'Those prawns? I think I won't.'

'A wise decision: they're actually locusts.'

Dar Er-Rbia

Instead, Quentin invites me to dinner at his medina hideaway, the 'House of Spring' on account of its greenery. We leave Jemaa El Fna and turn into an alley suitable only for two-wheeled traffic. Mobylettes have been adapted as delivery vans, their tortured motors resounding infernally in the confined space; they weave among the pedestrians, each showing a reckless disregard for the other but never actually colliding. Soon the road is no wider than a corridor, with featureless walls and the occasional low archway giving on to gloomy, even narrower alleys. Emaciated cats stare at the intruders. Quentin greets male passers-by, though neither party breaks his step. Finally he stops before a large, studded door set in a blank, ill maintained wall, and pulls on a metal handle, jangling a bell deep within.

'You forgot the front-door key?'

'I never take it. It's eight inches long.'

We are admitted by Quentin's manservant, Hamid, who is dressed in a shabby but well-pressed uniform, the relic of some past employment in a hotel. I enter an obviously authentic medina house built round a garden perhaps forty feet square with an octagonal, parapeted pool at its centre. The *riad's* raised flower-beds are so densely planted with fruit trees and shrubs that the paths offer the best sightlines. Quentin quotes a Sufi proverb: 'The earth does not return the stones thrown at it, but only offers us flowers.' Sun-burst mosaic tiling white, turquoise, red and black reaches to waist height on the surrounding walls.

'What a contrast with the dilapidated, windowless outside walls.'

'Like the heart, the house looks inwards,' Quentin ripostes.

The ground and upper floors are arcaded, with horseshoe arches soaring upwards to support each facade. The interconnecting reception rooms give on to the courtyard on three sides; the fourth side is open, creating a shaded patio. Tucked into a corner, stairs lead to the first-floor gallery, running uninterrupted round the house and serving the bedrooms with their cornflower-blue shutters. A wooden staircase continues up to the flat roof, but Quentin warns that appearing in daylight would upset any women on adjacent rooftops, traditionally considered their preserve as they gossip across the alleyways.

However, at dusk he takes me up. The sky is a Wagnerian celebration: indigo with pinpricks of starlight, deep sapphire, cerulean, its colours are funnelled down through the horizon in the wake of the setting sun. The vivid sounds of the medina are borne towards me: dramatic cries instantly stilled, metallic clashes, the whine of an engine and the distant hum of Jemaa El Fna, its location given away by smoke from the food stalls. To the south the crescent moon hangs over distant battlements, riven with dark gashes as if partly ruined, and over majestic ramparts enclosing the King's Palace. Beyond, a minaret to rival the Koutoubia rises stark and luminous against the backdrop of night. The fairy-tale buildings seem to float above the feathery tops of the palm trees in the stark but serene radiance.

The dining-room is separated from the kitchen corridor by an intricately carved, pierced screen. 'It's a carpentry of knots. The turners in the nearby souk achieve the lattice by assembling dozens of two-inch lengths of aromatic cedarwood.'

Hamid proffers the food on outsize metal dishes, Quentin addressing him in a mixture of French and Arabic as he pours wine.

'This Cabernet should slake our throats after Jemaa El Fna's dust and fumes.'

'Why have they allowed such an animated arena to become a car park?'

Quentin corrects me. 'It's a place where people park their cars, which is not the same thing. It hasn't been tarted up for tourists; instead, its functions have evolved in line with what the locals require. A Moroccan who can afford a Peugeot will always prefer it to a donkey, and will not indulge tourists as a figure in the landscape by riding one.'

Hamid removes the remains of the pastry *briouats* stuffed with cinnamon-flavoured chicken, before bearing in a tajine under its two-foot-high conical cover.

'Jemaa, El Fna is not about cars or architecture,' Quentin goes on. 'What counts are the folk who assemble there, and the dignity they radiate whatever their status. One often notices how mean-spirited the poorer sort of French *colons* look compared with Moroccans.'

'Weren't the British ever interested in Morocco? I know we once occupied Tangier.'

'At a certain point in the history of colonialism, the English and French stopped competing, and divided what remained of the earth's surface between them. In return for our taking much of the dark continent, the French were given a free hand in North Africa. We were happy to let them have it. As Lord Salisbury said, "The Gallic cockerel has acquired a great deal of sand; let him scratch about as he pleases." '

'You have a rosier view yourself?'

'Even Moroccans describe Marrakesh as an African sandheap. But you're right, of course. The Red City is my *raison d'être*, my heart's Orient: a perennial caravanserai where desert, mountain and oasis finally come together.'

The Souks

I wake early in my hotel, a car door slamming or the muezzin's call to prayer, yet already the air is alive with the secular litanies of the meeting place two hundred yards away. The daily rituals in Rue Bab Agnaou, too, are making themselves heard: the screech and thump of shutters coiling into their housing, the tap of draughts in a just-opened café, the slop of water cleansing the pavement.

The souks are a jostling bedlam of trades and donkey-carts intensified by the smell of leather, charcoal, cumin and piquant olives: a medieval world of narrow, raucous streets, seething, organic and brooking no resistance. I covet a brass tray. Sundays, Quentin decreed, are as good a day as any for Allah to deliver a moneyed westerner into the merchants' hands. Despite my studied indifference, I am lured into the first shop in Souk Smarine, a warren of well-stocked rooms.

'Welcome, my friend! I'll make a good price for you.'

I examine various trays before asking the price of a handsome, two-foot-wide example.

'Four thousand francs. You have come to the right place: brassware is more expensive elsewhere, and it is often mere plate. Look at this piece.' The man scratches a shiny yellow sweet dish kept at hand for the purpose, revealing the nickel beneath, 'I'm not fussy about solid brass. My budget's two thousand.'

The man grasps my sleeve as if imparting a state secret. 'You should know this tray was engraved by a craftsman who worked on the King's Palace.'

'Then I must settle for something cheaper.'

'Given Monsieur's obvious connoisseurship, it would be wrong for me to suggest an inferior product. I will accept three thousand five hundred.'

'Two thousand five hundred.'

'Business is poor these days. I suppose I can let it go for three thousand two hundred and fifty.' He begins wrapping the tray in newspaper.

'Three thousand – my final offer.'

I leave the shop with my package, wondering who has triumphed.

The Saadian Tombs, April 1967

The highlight this weekend is Podgorny's visit. Quentin is unimpressed by Russian politicians, and offers instead to take me to see the Saadian Tombs.

We pass through a gateway with a second beyond it. 'Bab Agnaou and Bab Er Robb, where criminals' salted heads were exposed to view.' Quentin laughs. 'A French visitor in 1900 reported seeing several heads, which had gone by the following day. The guide mistook his client's relief for disappointment. "Don't worry, M'sieur: plenty more coming." Perhaps they'll lay on some for Podgorny.'

By the Kasbah Mosque, Quentin enters a narrow passage. Ducking through an opening m the thickness of the wall, we find themselves in a tranquil garden. The high walls surrounding it shelter grey doves.

'That wasn't a very ceremonial entrance.'

'The original approach was through the Mosque itself. We owe the Tombs' survival to the religious scruples of the first Alaouite sultan, who demolished everything else of the preceding Saadian dynasty, but restricted his ravages here to blocking up the entrance.'

The miniature necropolis consists of two lofty mausoleums, their arched sides open, revealing nobly proportioned, colonnaded chambers and alcoves. Every cedarwood ceiling is domed or vaulted with a profusion of stalactite carving, the honeycomb forms as light as sugar icing, while the walls with their decoration of *Zellige* mosaics and lace-like plasterwork honour the Saadian craftsmen's faith and skill.

'Have you identified the sepulchre of Ahmad El Mansour?'

I reply that they all look similar.

'They are indeed alike, all hundred or so, in their perfection and purity. Ahmad's is in the chamber with the twelve marble columns.' The tombs do not boast their occupants' greatness by size or splendour. Each marble slab rises in a series of moulded, ogival steps to a height of about twenty inches, the sides carved with arabesques. Those belonging to royal children are pitifully short.

We are almost alone among the graves. Ahmad and the Shereefian dynasts who followed him slumber in marmoreal splendour, beneath the chaste, long-necked pillars and alveolate plasterwork; 'Death found them, in spite of their strongholds and wealth.'

'You don't need a guidebook with me,' Quentin chided. 'Although many of the occupants are unknown, I remember a few: Esh Sheikh, El Alibas, Moulay Zidan – the tomb under the cedarwood cupola, where the gilding has fused to the wood. Montaigne saw all these marble columns in Carrara on the eve of their shipment to Morocco. No European set eyes on them again until the Tombs were rediscovered during an aerial survey in 1917.'

The Menara

On our return we find Jemaa El Fna impassable. The road surrounding it, normally seething with mopeds and dun-coloured taxis, has been cordoned off, the crowd held back by self-important policemen. We work our way round into Square de Foucauld. To the wail of sirens, ungainly limousines now sweep past.

'Podgorny – and he's brought his own Zils,' Quentin exclaims. 'Let's follow them.'

We catch up with the Minister's party engaged in a round of hand-shaking outside the Mamounia. As the VIPs are conducted inside, Quentin attaches himself to the rear. The doormen are deceived by his imposing presence, and we follow the Russians until they disappear into the lift.

'Let's avail ourselves of the all-marble Gents, then have a drink.'

Women with jackets draped over their shoulders pose vacantly in the hotel corridors. We sit on white slatted chairs in the garden; tall palms rise from an island in the swimming pool. It takes so long to get served that Quentin feels he is entitled to pocket an inscribed ashtray.

'No visit to the Mamounia is complete without a souvenir,' he confesses.

He has a lunch appointment elsewhere, and leaves me consuming a pricey sandwich. Afterwards I walk to the Menara Gardens, passing through Bab El Jedid, whose ancient, ironbound gates cannot have moved for generations. Close to, the ramparts are disfigured with crevices, and the surface rendering has worn away; nevertheless they are twenty-five feet high and run for seven miles round the city.

During the long walk I am hailed by drivers of empty *calèches,* one prods his reluctant horse into turning round, and drives alongside. The carriage's upholstery looks inviting, but I wag my finger to refuse the man's blandishments.

The gardens are enclosed within minor ramparts of their own, a strip of sloping ground, dotted with olive trees, hiding what lies beyond. I breast the rise, and find myself beside a square, ornamental lake; recalling school athletics fields, I judge it half a mile round. Moroccans stroll beside the shimmering expanse, fingering strings of beads in the sunshine. I follow the lakeside path, admiring the much-photographed pavilion, with its green-tiled roof and balcony overlooking the waters; when I reach it, however, I am confronted by a closed door in the curtain wall extending to the water's edge, and have to turn round.

Wilfred Thesiger, Easter 1968

I recognize Thesiger (he only uses his surname) from his dust-jacket photograph in my copy of *Arabian Sands*. Wearing a substantial three-piece suit in the Tazi Hotel foyer, he would stand out anyway. I engage him in conversation: the smart attire is because he is lunching with Field Marshall Auchinleck, who has a villa in Hivernage near the Menara.

He invites me to dinner at a Guéliz brasserie the following evening, and afterwards we stroll in Jemaa El Fna eating yoghurt from a late-night stall. Although *Arabian Sands* describes Thesiger as always travelling on foot or by camel, he prefers to rent a Gibraltar registered Peugeot 404 for Morocco, especially when accompanied by his mother. He is very generous with his time towards those who share his Arabist sentiments. In this context he recalls two young English enthusiasts, invited to visit him in Chelsea, who arrived dressed in full Saudi-Arab costume. He is also very amusing on the subject of Gavin Maxwell, whose *Lords of the Atlas* is this season's splendid if risque read. At one point the author relates that in the last days of the Protectorate a Casablancan diner found a severed penis in his soup, and I dare to ask Thesiger if this could really be true. 'With Maxwell, it would have to be that particular bone,' Thesiger observes.

The Folklore Festival, May 1968
I ask Quentin to obtain tickets for the Festival; in return I promise to drive him up to Setti Fatima in the Atlas, which he claims never to have visited. Quentin is surprisingly solemn. 'Don't tempt providence with over-concrete plans. In Marrakesh events unfurl as fate decrees; history has foundered and pet beliefs been laid low in its red earth.'

Our way lit by mounted tribesmen holding flaming torches, we enter El Badi's rampart enclosed precinct, whose walls I first glimpsed from Quentin's rooftop. Close to, they radiate the overpowering conviction that Morocco was fashioned within them: the summoning of tribes, the audience and proclamation – history in the very mouths of men. Thence into the vast courtyard, designed for state ceremonies in Ahmad El Mansour's reign.

We climb to our seats facing the open space for the performers: no stage as such. More cavaliers lined up by a rectangular pool. Beyond, flanking a reservoir stretching into the darkness, a floating walkway of alleys criss-crosses gardens so deeply sunken that the tops of the orange trees are barely visible. I study the programme notes, which grandiloquently interpret each dance's symbolism – French less painful to read than the English translation.

The spectacle begins with Andalus music, played with the ancient instruments one sees in frescoes of paradise; next, acrobats from Amizmiz, and the black Gnaoua, their skullcaps embroidered with cowrie shells, banging their *garagab* castanets. Then stylistic, cat-like prancing of pairs of men in a slow-moving sabre dance from the Draa Valley, their swords held upright and clashing when least expected.

'Now there's a classic *ahouash*, the creation dance. It's performed after dark in recognition of the Berbers' sobriquet, "Sons of shadow and daughters of night." '

A man with a violin marshals musicians and dancers into two lines, men alternating with women, who wear black and green striped woollen cloaks and necklaces threaded with amber. To a rhythm of three beats followed by a pause, the *derbouka* drummers move one pace forward, then back, then sideways. The mixed dancers, wedged shoulder to shoulder, clap in time while swaying where they stand, gradually sinking to the ground and then rising abruptly. Now the master of ceremonies skips backwards and forwards between the lines, which rotate about him like the spokes of a wheel. To my ears the unrelenting music has no structure; I seize on scraps of tune only to lose them immediately. At length, overwhelmed by its vividness and brilliance, its imperative to celebrate, I catch its flavour as the phrases skirmish and circle endlessly.

The finale is an unforgettable *guedra* – blue-robed nomads from Goulimine, striking drums first with their fingertips then their palms, surround a remarkable Berber girl, whose stunning headdress, shot with white and silver, frames her face to a perfect round. Although kneeling, she gyrates her hips and breasts as well as her arms and hands, sinuous, sensual movements in time to the ever-faster beat. Her veil slips and her downcast eyes appear to close, as she becomes entranced by the music and succumbs to ecstasy.

Afterwards the horsemen fire their *moukhala* guns into the air. Tremendous applause, though the performers do not bow or acknowledge it.

The Aguedal Gardens, June 1969
The *calèche's* scarlet leather is cracked, but I and a girlfriend settle back in the open carriage. After Place des Ferblantiers we skirt the Mellah and the Royal Palace, cross the Mechouar and enter the Aguedal Gardens: an age-old, laborious Eden irrigated by underground conduits from the distant Ourika, full of orange groves, pomegranate and fig trees, cypresses, neglected kiosks and fountains.

We leave the *calèche* to await our return and walk for what seems miles. At the furthest point from the medina we come on the largest of the artificial pools with its summer pavilion. Its now dilapidated, box-like interior once shaded royal boating parties, and it still serves as a focus for those embarking on the circuit of the lake. We climb to the roof; crossing to the parapet overlooking the pool, we kick up eddies of dust charged with gold. Orchards, lakes, ramparts, mountains: whichever way we turn, I am humbled by a panorama so sharply coloured, so cartoon-clear as to invite disbelief. Surely this garden of joy with its fifty thousand fruit trees is the equal of Paradise, whence from his seat its founder, Ahmad the Golden, must be looking down on his creation today.

Quentin says a sultan drowned in the pool; also, that it was once drained and became a squatters' settlement, with buildings and a market.

Envoi, March 1970
I collect the car from Jemaa, El Fna as the afternoon circus is getting underway; the clash of the Gnaoua's castanets has all the tourists stopping their ears. With my life at a crossroads and sensing I might not return to Marrakesh for some time, I too feel they are rebuffing me and my preconceptions, as Quentin once warned. Thus the drums of Jemaa El Fna drown out their listeners' complacency, and void our puny, mortal exchanges.

Now the car turns away from the jostle of low buildings; it rounds square de Foucauld where the shoeshine boys vainly take on the dust of the city and, hemmed in by bicycles passes through Bab Nkob. In my absence swallows will wheel through the sapphire dusk and Jemaa El Fna's rituals unfold without missing the merest beat in their tempo. The city has enticed, parried and briefly revealed itself before discarding me; there is nothing I can give, Marrakesh seeks nothing from me and no head turns.

ABOUT THE AUTHOR

ANTHONY GLADSTONE-THOMPSON lives in London. He is a traveller and writer long devoted to Morocco. His Recollections, printed here, speak of his first visit to Marrakesh, and indeed Morocco, in 1964. He went on to teach in Casablanca from 1966–73 where he met his French wife Janine who was born in Morocco.

Explorers & Envoys

The Harem

from *A Tour to Morocco* by William Lempriere

From the unsuccessful efforts which I had made for the purpose of procuring my dispatches, I had begun to reconcile myself to the idea of remaining a prisoner at Morocco, when, to my great surprise, at the expiration of a month from the time of the prince's departure, his Moorish majesty sent to me in particular haste to repair to the palace.

Upon receiving this message, my best hopes were excited. I naturally expected an immediate emancipation, as it is necessary that every stranger should see the emperor previous to his departure; and I flew to the palace with all the alacrity which such an expectation was certain to inspire. What then was my astonishment, when, upon my arrival at the palace, a messenger brought orders from the emperor, the purport of which was that I should immediately examine one of his sultanas who was indisposed, and in the afternoon return with proper medicines, and at the same time report my opinion on her case to his majesty.

It is difficult to say whether disappointment or surprise were the predominant emotion in my mind on receiving this order. After the prejudices which from his dislike to the English, and his ignorance of the effects of internal medicines, the emperor was known to have entertained against me, and after having detained me at Morocco for such a length of time, with no apparent view but that of manifesting his contempt of me as an Englishman, it appeared unaccountable that he should give orders for my admission in to the *harem*, where, in addition to the former objections, there were also some still stronger in the eyes of the Moors; as the admission of one of our sex into that sacred depository of female charms was almost unprecedented, and I believe totally so with respect to the *harem* of the emperor.

Whatever might be the motives with his imperial majesty for the violation of Moorish decorum in this instance, I did not conceive that I had much reason to rejoice at this event. I had already experienced too much ingratitude from the prince, as well as too much ungenerous treatment from the emperor, to encourage me to undertake any future engagement of the kind in this country; and the difficulties and prejudices which from experience I knew I had to encounter, when employed in my professional line by the Moors, united to the uncertainty of removing the lady's complaint, rendered it altogether not very safe to administer my advice under such disadvantageous circumstances; and even that curiosity which would most naturally be excited in most persons on such an occasion, was not sufficient to reconcile me to this new employment.

Unfortunately in this dilemma I had very little time allowed me to determine, since the messenger was waiting to conduct me to the gate of the *harem*. My embarrassment, however, continued only for a short period; for I soon recollected that it was in vain to oppose the emperor's order. I therefore deferred giving a decisive answer till I had seen my patient, and made myself fully acquainted with the nature of her complaint.

The public and usual entrance to the *harem* is through a very large arched door-way, guarded on the outside by ten body guards, which leads to a lofty hall, where the captain or *alcaide*, with a guard of seventeen eunuchs are posted. No person is admitted into this hall, but those who are known to have business in the *harem*.

The emperor's order being delivered on the outside of the door to the *alcaide*, I was immediately, with my interpreter, conducted into the *harem*, by one of the Negro eunuchs. Upon entering the court into which the women's apartments open, I discovered a motley group of concubines, domestics, and Negro slaves, who were variously employed. Those of the first description had formed themselves into circles seated on the ground in the open court, and were apparently engaged in conversation. The domestics and slaves were partly employed in needlework, and partly in preparing their *cuscoosoo*. My appearance in the court, however, soon attracted their attention, and a considerable number of them, upon observing me, unacquainted with the means by which I had been admitted into the *harem*, retreated with the utmost precipitancy into their apartments; while others more courageous approached, and enquired of my black attendant who I was, and by whose orders he had brought me thither.

The moment it was known that I was of the medical profession, parties of ten were detached to inform those who had fled that I was sent in by order of the emperor, to attend Lalla Zara, my intended patient's name, and requesting of them to come back and look at the Christian. '*Seranio Tibib!*' Christian Doctor! resounded from one end of the *Harem* to the other; and in the course of few minutes I was so completely surrounded by women and children, that I was unable to move a single step.

Every one of them appeared solicitous to find out some complaint on which she might consult me, and those who had not ingenuity enough to invent one, obliged me to feel their pulse; and were highly displeased if I did not evince my excellence in my profession by the discovery of some ailment or other. All of them seemed so urgent to be attended to at the same time, that which I was feeling the pulse of one, others were behind, pulling my coat and intreating me to examine their complaints, while a third party were upbraiding me for not paying them the same attention. Their ideas of delicacy did not at all correspond with those of our European ladies, for they exhibited the beauties of their limbs and form with a degree of freedom that in any other country would have been thought indecent; and their conversation was equally unrestrained.

This apparent laxity of conduct in the Moorish ladies does not proceed from a depravity in principle. As the female sex in this country are not entrusted with the guardianship of their own honour, there is no virtue in reserve. A depraved education even serves to corrupt instead of to restrain them. They are not regarded as rational or moral agents; they are only considered as beings created entirely to be subservient to the pleasure of man. To excite the passions and to do and say every thing which may inflame a licentious imagination, became therefore necessary accomplishments in the female sex, and their manners and conduct naturally assume a cast totally different from those of women in a more refined and more liberal state of society. In those instances to which I refer, they were not conscious of trespassing the limits of decency; and in others they manifested a singular attention to what they conceived to be decorum. When I requested to see the tongues of some patients who described of feverish symptoms, they refused to comply, considering it as inconsistent with their modesty and virtue; some of them indeed laughed at the singularity of the request, and attributed it either to an impertinent curiosity, or an inclination to impose on their understandings.

As the number of my patients continued to increase rather than to diminish, there appeared but little prospect of an introduction to the sultana Lalla Zara, whom I was first directed to attend, in any reasonable time. The eunuch, however, wearied out with waiting, exerted all the vigour of authority which his natural effeminacy would admit of in obliging them to disperse, and which was so far effectual at least as to allow me room to pass, thought this female crowd still followed me till I had nearly reached the lady's apartment.

From the first court through which I had been introduced I passed through two or three similar, till I at length arrived at the chamber of my intended patient. I was here detained a little time in the court, till my patient and her apartment were ready to receive me. Upon my entrance I found the lady sitting cross-legged on a mattress placed on the floor, and covered with fine linen, with twelve white and Negro attendants, seated on the floor also, in different parts of the chamber. A round cushion was placed for me next to the lady on which I was desired to be seated. I should have remarked that, contrary to my expectations, I found that none of the emperor's women disguised their faces in the manner which I had experienced in the prince's *harem*, but I saw them all with the same familiarity as if I had been introduced into the house of an European.

Lalla Zara (Lalla signifies lady or mistress, but is only applied in this country to the sultanas), who was of Moorish parents, was about eight years ago remarkable for her beauty and accomplishments; on which account she was then in every respect the favourite wife of the late emperor. So dangerous a pre-eminence could not be enjoyed, without exciting the jealousy of those females whose charms were less conspicuous; and who, besides the mortification of having a less share of beauty, experienced also the disgrace of being deserted by their lord.

Determined to effect her ruin, they conspired to mix some poison (most probably arsenic) in her food, and conducted the detestable plot with so much art and address, that it was not perceived till the deletrious drug had begun its baleful operations. She was seized with most violent spasms, and a continual vomiting; and had she not been possessed of an uncommonly strong constitution, she must immediately have fallen victim to the machinations of her rivals. After a severe struggle, however, between life and death, the effects of the poison in some degree abated; but it left the unhappy lady in a state of dreadful debility and irritation, and particularly in the stomach, from which it was not perhaps in the power of medicine to extricate her. Her beauty too, the fatal cause of her misfortune, was completely destroyed, and her enemies, though disappointed in their aim of destroying her life, yet enjoyed the malignant triumph of seeing those charms which had excited their uneasiness reduced below the standard of ordinary women.

When I saw her, she had such a weakness of digestion, that every species of food which she took, after remaining a few hours on her stomach, was returned perfectly crude and undigested. As she did not receive proper nourishment, her body had wasted away to a shadow, and her frame was in so weak a state, as not to allow her to walk without assistance. Her complexion was entirely altered. Her skin, from being naturally clear and fair, as I was informed, was changed to a sickly brown, which, joined to a ruined set of teeth, and a ghastly countenance, had effaced every trace of that beauty, which she before might have possessed. Upon my first entering her apartment, though from my profession accustomed to behold objects of distress and misery, yet I was so forcibly struck with her unhappy situation and wretched appearance, that I was obliged to exert all the fortitude of which I was master, to avoid the discovery of my feelings.

Lalla Zara was at this time about six-and-thirty years of age, and though in so weak a state, had two beautiful young children; the first was in its sixth year, and the youngest, which was then under the care of a wet-nurse, was very little more than a twelve month old. I was quite astonished to observe such strong and apparently healthy children, the offspring of a mother whose constitution was so dreadfully impaired. It was certainly, however, a very fortunate circumstance for Lalla Zara that she had these children; since by the Mahometan law a man cannot divorce a wife provided she bear him children; so that though the emperor took very little notice of this poor lady, yet he was, for the above reason, obliged to maintain both her self and her offspring.

From the wretched situation in which I have described this unfortunate female, it is easy to conceive that her spirits must revive at the most distant prospect of procuring relief in her disagreeable complaint. Such, indeed, was the case. She received me with all that satisfaction which hope, united with some degree of confidence, most naturally inspires.

Under these circumstances the predicament in which I found myself was, I must admit, most truly embarrassing. It was one of those unpleasant situations, in which duty and interest are completely in opposition to each other, or rather when the sympathetic feelings stand opposed to personal safety. Humanity pointed out to me that it was my duty to relieve her if possible; on the other hand, self-preservation no less strongly dictated, that it was absolutely necessary to my safety and happiness to embrace the first opportunity of leaving a country where I existed in the most critical and most disagreeable situation. Both these sentiments for some time pressed equally on my mind, and left me at a loss how to determine. I at length, however, fixed on a middle plan of conduct, which appeared likely to effect the safety of the lady, without endangering my own. This was, to give a proper course of medicines a fair trial for a fortnight; and then, if the least prospect of amendment should appear in consequence of them I could leave her more, with such directions as might enable her to use them without medical attendance.

ABOUT THE AUTHOR

WILLIAM LEMPRIERE was a member of the army medical service, attached to the Gibraltar garrison in September 1789, when Sidi Mahommed – (Mahommed III), Emperor of Morocco – made a request for a doctor to attend on his son – Muley Absolom – who was suffering from cataracts. So began the journey that would become the subject of Lempriere's tour, a book providing a unique insight into Morocco of the late eighteenth century from the perspective of a British traveller.

Lempriere's professional capacity and imperial commission gave him unparalleled access to the workings of the royal household as well and led him on an extensive trip through the interior of the country, from Taroudant to Mogador and over the mountains to Marrakesh. On the other hand, he was a far-from willing 'guest' of the Sultan for much of his time in this city, and a great deal of his account deals (rather repetitively) with his attempts to gain a release from the emperor's service, finally effected in February 1790. Nonetheless, such a narrative was groundbreaking in its time and presents an interesting counterpoint to the sight-seeing stories of other, more conventional tourists.

After returning from Morocco, Lempriere was assigned to the Jamaica regiment of light dragoons and spent five years in the Caribbean. He eventually left the army at the rank of Inspector General of Hospitals. He died in Bath in 1834.

A Gift from the Sultan

from *The Travels of Ali Bey* by Ali Bey

I had in my garden four antelopes that were become very tame. The play of these animals, when they are at liberty, is really attractive; they jump and canter in an astonishing manner. My gardeners were always at war with them, because they eat or destroyed the plants; but I took them under my protection, as the garden was large enough to make their consumption either of no importance, or hardly perceptible. As they were as tame as storks, they always came about me at dinner and supper; and these seven companions became my best friends.

As I wished to keep the circuit of my dominion free from all bloodshed, I gave strict orders not to fire off a gun, or to kill any animal, by any means whatsoever. My intention was to give the birds a sacred asylum; and I can say, that the warbling of these many various kinds made a real earthly paradise of my Semelalia [an estate given to Ali Bey by the Sultan]; so much so, that when I walked within the limits of my territory, though without the walls, whole bands of partridges came about me; and the rabbits ran almost over my feet. I did my utmost to attract and tame all those animals; and they answered my friendly intentions more cordially than many men, who call themselves civilized.

The birds were so tame that they came to eat the crumbs which I threw to them; they frequented my rooms and I slept with my curtains crowned with birds, enjoying their freedom in a country of slavery. I could, however, never succeed in taming a stubborn chackal which had been given me. I had a small house built for him on purpose, and had him taken from his chain, in order to give him liberty in his new house; but he undermined the lower part of the wall and escaped, with as much skill or reason (I don't know which) as any sensible being could have exercised. It is true my chackal was encouraged by the call of his companions, who came in whole bands howling every night in the vicinity of Semelalia; and as a set of dogs of all kinds answered them from within by barking, I had two nocturnal concerts, which often were increased by the braying of our asses and the crowing of our cocks and guinea fowls. This cacophony, far from being disagreeable, gave me pleasure, because every thing in it was natural.

One might fancy that the immunity of my residence became known to a class which is called unreasonable by man, for the antelopes came in bands of hundreds to the walls of Semelalia to play their tricks, and seemed to ask for admittance.

I formed a fine collection of plants, insects, and fossils, at Semelalia. Among the insects I have some *aranea galleopedes*, of a very scarce kind, with regard to their size. The first of them I saw frightened me very much, as it was passing over my chest when I was sitting on my canopy. Among the fossils, the collection of porphyrs and of rolled pebbles from the Atlas is valuable.

As I had foretold that an eclipse of the moon would take place in the night of the 15 January 1805, several Pashas and other men of rank assembled at my house to observe it; but unfortunately the weather was so thick, chiefly during the night, and it rained so hard, with continual gusts of wind, that it was impossible to discover the least thing.

The Sultan never makes a long stay at a place and a few days after the eclipse, we had the news that he would soon arrive at Morocco. This caused much satisfaction to the inhabitants, and particularly to me, as I was waiting for him to take my leave, in order to begin my pilgrimage to Mecca.

The Sultan arrived in fact on the day which had been announced; I went to a pretty good distance to meet him. He was on his litter, which was placed between two mules. As soon as he saw me, he ordered it to stop, and conversed with me, assuring me of his particular affection. Mulei Abdsulem, who was with him, was as kind as a brother to me. During his absence, we had been corresponding together; and at the time I was ill, and unable to write, they sent messengers from Fez with an order to have news concerning my health. As they now saw me recovered, and able to mount on horseback, they did not know how to express their satisfaction; and during their stay, our relations continued on the most perfect intimacy.

Some days afterwards, I was strangely surprised, when I heard *that the Sultan had sent me two women*. As I had fixed my resolution in this respect, and determined not to give way till my return from my pilgrimage to the sacred

Caaba, I refused the present. But as the women had once been dismissed from the Sultan's harem, and could not be admitted into it again, the good-natured Muley Abdsulem took them to his house, afraid of speaking on this subject either to the sultan or to me. The whole court was curious to know how this matter of state would finish. Every one was whispering into another's ears, without daring to make any reflection. In the meanwhile, I continued going to court, as if nothing had happened. Muley Abdsulem at last found his silence too oppressive to him, and hinted something to me about the matter. I promised to discuss it next day. Our meeting took place in presence of the principal Fakih, or doctor of law of the Sultan's, who was a very respectable man. The attack began, and I was obliged to refute the arguments of my two antagonists. Our discussion lasted several hours. Muley Abdsulem finding himself engaged between the Sultan and myself, was very much embarrassed, and tears ran from his poor blind eyes. I was much more affected with the dangerous situation to which this respectable Prince had been exposing himself on my account, than with any thing that could result to myself from it and, therefore, I took him by the hand and said; 'Well Muley Abdsulem, as I am sensible of the interest you bear me, and convinced that you know the bottom of my heart, even my most secret thoughts, pray tell me how I am to act; I shall abide by your advice; but consider well.' He took my hand to his heart, and, after a few moments silence, he said, almost stammering; 'Then let the women be taken again to your house.' I replied, 'I consent to it; but I must tell you, Muley Abdsulem, that I shall not see them. The day of my departure for Mecca is approaching, and not seeing them, it shall be at their choice to stay or to follow me; in the latter case they may rely on my protection.'

This declaration put Muley Abdsulem at his ease. He could not command himself; and the transition from the extreme depression of his mind to the greatest joy, worked so strongly on him, that he embraced me most heartily; his face became bright and tears of joy rolled from his eyes. We agreed that these women should come back to my house that very night, but without noise or ceremony. Upon this I went home. These women, being a present of the Sultan, were a white one called Mohanna, and a black one called Tigmu.

I ordered private apartments to be got ready for them in my town house, and had them neatly furnished, provided with the necessary objects, as coffee, sugar, tea, &c.; and also with a trunk containing various kinds of stuffs and other trifles, some trinkets, and a purse with some gold pieces.

It was near ten o'clock that evening, when my steward came to tell me that the women were arrived. 'Let them be taken to their apartments,' said I, and continued my conversation with my secretary, my fakih, and two other friends. The governess of Muley Abdsulem's harem and half a dozen of his women had been conducting my two ladies.

There was a supper served to the women and another to the men. After supper I asked for the governess of Mulei Abdsulem's harem and she came to me wrapt up as usually. I gave her a keepsake; and in handing to her the key of the trunk, I made her the following discourse:

'Give this key to Mohanna, and tell her that I value her; but that some circumstances prevent me from seeing her. Every thing in her room and in the box, to which this is the key, belongs to her. I recommend to her Tigmu. I am going to Semelalia; however, my head servant, Scherif *Muley Hamet*, is to stay here and to take care that she be served by two male and two female servants; and any thing she want will be furnished her by Muley Hhamet.'

I dismissed the governess, who was quite astonished at my declaration. Though it was midnight I mounted my horse, and parted with my friends and servants, who accompanied us with lanterns to Semelalia, where I settled. Muley Abdsulem's women staid at my house till next morning.

If the Court of Morocco was astonished at my refusal of these ladies, it was not less surprized at the manner in which I had received them. The thing could not be kept a secret, on account of the servants and others that had been witness to the transactions. It therefore became publick in less than four-and-twenty hours; and every one in the town was informed of the most trifling circumstance relating to it.

I continued frequenting the Sultan's and Muley Abdsulem's society as if nothing had happened; for decorum requires that Mahometans never speak of women.

At length I decided that I should set off for Mecca, and had, upon this subject, several discussions with the Sultan, with Muley Abdsulem, and with my friends, who all united to dissuade me from the journey. They observed that even the Sultan had never made it; that their religion did not require it to be made personally; and that I might hire a pilgrim, who, making it in my name, would confer on me the same merit as if I had performed it myself. All these objections, and others useless to mention, did not alter my determination.

The Sultan, who from the bottom of his heart wished to make me stay, came to me one day, accompanied by his brother Muley Abdsulem, by his cousin Mulei Abdelmelek, and by the first people of the Court. The Sultan arrived at about nine in the morning, and staid with me till half past four in the evening. During this time my journey became several times the topick of the conversation, but I was not to be persuaded. I had a repast served to my guests on their arrival, and again before their departure. The Sultan gave me a proof of his attachment and unbounded confidence, in partaking of both meals; he took coffee, tea, and lemonade at various times; he wrote and signed his dispatches of the day on my writing desk, and treated me like a brother; and, going away, six of his servants handed me two very rich carpets, of which he made me a present. Soon after the officers of the Court had accompanied the Sultan home, they returned almost all a second time to my house, in order to pay me their compliments, to renew their advice against my intended journey, and to suggest me the most flattering insinuations on my future fortunes in case I did stay; but all their endeavours were in vain, and I fixed my journey to take place thirteen days afterwards.

The day on which I took leave of the Sultan, he renewed his entreaties for me to stay; he represented to me the fatigues and dangers of so long a journey, and at last, embracing me, we parted with tears in our eyes. My leave from Muley Abdsulem was really affecting; and to my last breath I shall bear in my heart the image of this beloved Prince.

The Sultan made me a present of a very magnificent tent, lined with red cloth and adorned with silk fringes. Before he sent it to me, he had it put up in his presence and twelve fakihs said prayers in it, in order to draw down on me the blessings of heaven, and every possible success on my journey. He added to this present some leather bags to contain the necessary provision of water for the journey, which is a matter of great importance.

Upon this I sent word to Mohanna to wrap herself up, as I wished to speak to her. As soon as she was dressed, I went to her in presence of all of my people; and I said to her: 'Mohanna, I am going to the East, and shall not forsake you if you wish to follow me; but if you prefer to stay here, you are at liberty, for you know this is the first time I have spoken to you.'

She answered modestly, 'I shall follow my Lord.'

I replied, 'Consider well; your decision admits no retraction.'

Mohanna said, 'Yes my Lord, I shall follow you to all the parts of the world where you are going, and to death.'

Upon this I said to all those who were present, 'You hear Mohanna's declaration, and are witnesses to her resolution.' And turning to her, I said, 'You are a good creature; you are attached to me, and I shall always protect you; prepare yourself to accompany me. Good bye.'

I ordered a kind of litter to be made for Mohanna. It is called Darbucco, and could be shut on all sides; it is placed on a mule or camel and only used by ladies of high rank in this country. Poor Tigmu did not require so many ceremonies, she might wrap herself with her haik or bournous. Both ladies had a tent assigned to them which protected them against any one's indiscretion. Thus I prepared for my journey from Morocco, leaving behind me, with the necessary instructions as administrator of my estates, Sidi Omar Buseta, who was Pasha of the same town.

ABOUT THE AUTHOR

ALI BEY EL ABASSI alias DOMINGO BADIA Y LEBLICH was born in Catalonia in the late 1760s. His life is full of enigma; time spent studying science and Arabic at Valencia was followed by a reported meeting with London's African Association in 1802 to discuss an expedition to Central Africa, entering via the South Atlas Mountains. In 1803 he turned up in Tangier, in the guise of a descendant of the Abbasid Caliphs from Aleppo, a disguise so convincing that he was warmly welcomed by Mulai Sulaiman who sent him two wives (an event recounted in this extract). This hospitality was perhaps not all that it seemed as Ali Bey himself recounts difficulties that dogged his footsteps as a result of his time in Morocco. He went on to provide the first accurate report of Mecca by a European.

Ali Bey appears to have been an agent either of the French or the Spanish – after his return to Europe he had several meetings with Napoleon before settling in Paris as 'General Badia'. In 1818 he died in Damascus, poisoned, according to some French reports, by the British.

In Moroccan Disguise

from *Travels in the Atlas and Southern Morocco*
by Joseph Thomson

The one great obstacle to our realising the everyday life of the Moor, was the sad fact that we were bachelors. The Moor can in no way imagine life on earth, still less in heaven, without the solacing presence of women. They are his sole companions and friends at home, his dolls or toys, his entertainers, servants, everything that any one can well be to him. Without them he can undertake no journey, and he cherishes them as the apple of his eye. Not that it follows that he cares for them in our sense of the term. On the contrary, he may even go so far as to hate individuals among them; but he nevertheless cannot bear the thought of others getting a glimpse of the living treasure which has become distasteful to himself.

Failing this prime essential of a Moorish existence, we had to fall back for a little variety in our monotonous existence on such public entertainers as could be hired. Of these, none amused us more than the itinerant half-Negro half-Arab musicians from Sus and the desert. These generally go about in pairs, got up in the most fantastic fashion, with rags, skins, bands of cowries, and iron bells about their legs and ankles. One performs with a drum, the other with a curious species of iron double cymbals. Their antics are of the most absurd description, and sometimes irresistibly comic. Their appearance, and performance, however, had an added interest to me in bringing vividly to my memory entertainments of a similar character in the Sudan, where I had first formed the idea of visiting Morocco. At other times we brought in a troupe of Jewish singers and dancers, who had the reputation of being the best of their kind in Southern Morocco. That may have been so; but if it were, it said very little for the singer's and dancer's art in these parts. The women in frightfully shrill voices screamed out Arab and Jewish songs, accompanied by violin-grinding and tambourines. One man danced in the Moorish fashion, and that was all.

By dint of such arts as one may employ in Morocco, we obtained a coveted invitation to the house of a Moor. Needless to say he was one of lax morals, though otherwise of firm religious principle; that is to say, he would, for a consideration, hand over the key of the house in which was his wife and daughter to another, though he would have thought twice about eating forbidden meats. In our case, we wanted to see the interior of an inhabited Moorish house, and if possible get a photo of some Moorish women, one of the most difficult things to obtain in these parts.

Of course we had to go in disguise, as the idea of allowing a Christian into a Mohammedan household would have been too horrifying a scandal, even for the gentleman in question, and, if discovered, would have been followed by very serious consequences to both parties.

Under the guidance of our Gibraltarian friend Bonich, we started on our adventure some time after mid-day, when the excessive heat had driven every one within doors. We did what we could to adopt the Moorish stride of a man of substance, and with apparent success, for no one took any notice of us. I soon, however, had something else to think of than what people were thinking of us, for the slippers I had on began to chafe my sockless feet, and take, with the assistance of the fine gritty sand which got plentifully inside, the skin from my toes and instep. If my feet had been rubbed continuously with sandpaper, as they were indeed with sanded leather, I could not have been more painfully flayed. Under these circumstances dignified easy motion was out of the question, while the skinning of the toes made the necessary pressure to retain possession of the slippers extremely difficult. My walk became an awkward shuffle, and more than once my slippers came off. But for the fact that there was hardly a soul in the broiling streets, we would have been detected and probably followed. At last we turned to the right and entered a blind alley, at the end of which was a door where Bonich knocked. A woman's voice replied; the next moment the door was opened, and with guilty haste we slipped inside, turning round as we did so to see that we were not observed.

We now found ourselves in a dark passage, with an unveiled woman beside us. Of course, in a well regulated household no woman would have opened the door, and the announced approach of a male visitor would have been followed by the flight of the women to their own sanctums. We were first conducted into a small garden enclosed by walls and shaded by an overarching vine and a large fig-tree. In this deliciously cool retreat mattresses and cushions were laid for our comfort, and with no small delight I divested myself of the most cumbersome of my Moorish garments, and especially of my slippers. The woman who had let us in, seeing the pitiful condition of my feet, hastened to bring water to wash them. The master of the house now arrived, a villainous looking fellow of fluent speech, plentifully garnished with the name of Allah and phrases from the Koran. While we exchanged the courtesies of life with this detestable fellow, his two wives, one of about thirty and the other about thirty-five, waited on us. They brought us first fruit and melons, then bread and honey, followed by a *tajen* of stewed beef in rancid butter. A little of each course went a long way in satisfying our appetite; no more, in fact, than politeness demanded.

The mid-day meal over, the master of the house, retired to say his prayers, and his daughter arrived resplendent in her best clothes. She wore a *kaftan* of rich yellow brocade, partially veiled by an upper garment of fine muslin. Her dress was drawn in at the waist by an embroidered belt. Her black hair, covered with a brilliant crimson silk handkerchief, was gathered into two plaits tied together at the ends and hanging down the back. Heavy silver wristlets encircled her arms, and strings of beads her neck. The adornment of her person was completed with henna tints on her hands and feet, black-painted eyelashes and eyebrows, and tattooed dots and squares on the middle line of her brow and chin and on her arms. Her face was broad across the cheekbones, which were prominent, and her mouth was somewhat large, displaying a magnificent set of white teeth. Her great attraction, however, were her almond-shaped eyes of the most brilliant black. These were wide apart, and had glossy, luxuriant eyelashes. Upon the whole, however, she could not be termed handsome or pretty, though her figure, as far as we could judge, seemed well-made, and certainly the feet and hands of this Moorish damsel of fifteen or sixteen were all that could be desired in size and shape

When on this subject of women, I may take occasion to remark that, as far as we got opportunities for judging – and these were strictly limited – the Moorish ladies were not remarkable for their beauty. We were apt to acquire erroneous notions on this point from only seeing their eyes, and these were frequently quite fascinating; but more than once, on seeing our unconcealed admiration, and no Moor being nigh, our expectations of seeing a beautiful face to match were belied on the *haik* being coquettishly drawn aside, and withered features and general ugliness displayed. Of course we only got glimpses of the faces of the older women, and those of the very poor and the loose. Beauty naturally gravitated into the harems of the wealthy, from which it never came out except by night, so that we had no means of acquiring correct notions on the subject. My observations, however, such as they are, make me believe that young women from fourteen to twenty-five years of age are exceedingly well-proportioned, and sometimes very beautiful. After that age, figure and beauty alike disappear with great rapidity.

The dress of the women is almost identical in make with that of the men, even to the trousers. They employ, however, much more expensive materials – gorgeous brocades, silks, &c., generally covered by a gauzy stuff. The wealthy have exceedingly heavy *hazams,* or waistbands, worked in silk in the most beautiful manner, and varying in price from eight to two hundred dollars. The *haik,* in which they are shrouded when they go out of doors, is nothing more nor less than a very large woollen blanket, heavier than any used in England. At Saffi and Mogador no face-cloth is used, and absolutely nothing but one eye is shown. In Morocco generally, a face-cloth of light open material is worn, and the *haik is* drawn round by the chin and held there by the hand. At Amsmiz the *haik is* held by both hands in such a way as to form a narrow slit quite a foot long. This must be the most troublesome of all the ways of wearing the cumbersome garment. The shoes of the women are distinguished from those of the men by being red in colour, and frequently daintily embroidered.

This habit of always having to think of hiding the face has aroused the curious feeling among them that it is more indecent to show it to a stranger than any other part of the body. In the hot weather it was no uncommon thing, to see women going along the streets with their faces jealously veiled, and their breasts more or less exposed.

Though the women we now saw before us were by no means shy, and could make use of their charms with all the consummate skill of a Frenchwoman, we soon got tired of trying to keep up conversation. We hastened thereupon to take some photos of them, no easy task, for they thought it a terrible sin to have their portraits taken.

This done, we would willingly have bolted; but that was impossible, for we had to await the arrival of a servant to smuggle away the apparatus, and – I blush to mention it – to bring me a pair of socks, without which I could not venture to trust my feet in Moorish slippers again. While we waited, we explored one or two of the rooms of the house, only to find it absolutely devoid of all furniture other than rugs, mattresses, and cushions. The walls were plainly whitewashed. Everything was clean and neat.

Needless to say, my socks drew the attention of passers-by and revealed our identity; but we did not now care, as we were on our way to our own quarters.

In pursuance of our design to 'do' Morocco as thoroughly as possible, we resolved to have 'a wash and brush up' in the native fashion. The *hammum* in Morocco, as in all Mohammedan countries, is an institution. Every quarter of Maraksh has one or more of them.

There was one great obstacle to our carrying out our wishes. The *hammum* was sacred to the faithful, and no Christian had ever been known to desecrate the hallowed precincts. That of course was the more reason for going; for what *else* did *we* travel but to do and see things that other people had not done and seen. Our hope lay in this, that after the *Acha*, or supper-prayers at nine o'clock, the baths are reserved for families, and those who can afford to take them for the night and bring with them their own servants, &c.

We accordingly dispatched our most intelligent and fluent liar of a servant with *carte-blanche* to exercise his special talents to secure the *hammum* for our use, of course strictly hiding our identity with anything infidel. To our delight he succeeded in arranging the matter. Needless to say, it was necessary to go in disguise to the *hammum* as when visiting our Moorish friend.

After the call to prayers had resounded over the city, we started off, accompanied by most of our men, all in a great funk, and very reluctant to go, no one more so than Assor, who, to the fear of detection, added all the imaginary horrors of a thorough washing, an operation of which he had had no practical experience in his whole lifetime.

We had barely left our quarters before we had nearly spoiled all. Each, in his absurd eagerness to see that the other looked the Moor, broke more than once into audible English speech, till energetic tugs from the men brought him once more to his senses. These latter did their best to surround us and ward off inspection, but the narrowness of the streets and the numbers of people still moving about made that next to impossible. At one place an unmistakable reference to Christians was made. All that we could do was to take no notice and hurry on, quite unaware whether we were being followed or not. It seemed not, however, as we reached the door of the *hammum* without obstruction or disturbance. Here we were again nearly caught ; for thinking that the baths were deserted, we were about to bolt inside the moment the door was opened, when we found ourselves face to face with several bathers carrying lanterns. Instinctively we turned our backs, and our men crowded around us and kept up a continuous gabble till the enemy passed out. There had clearly been mismanagement somewhere, for we soon discovered that some people were still left in the *hammum*. To escape these, we were huddled into a small cellar, used apparently as a refuse bin, and there, in complete darkness, and hardly daring to breathe, we were kept for several minutes, till it was quite certain every one had left.

We were now ushered through a badly-formed passage and into a filthy vaulted chamber with square pillars. We had only a couple of candles to light up the place. What we did contrive to see, hardly realised our idea of an Oriental bath, with its couches and luxurious fittings. Few European cellars would compete with the black and repulsive chamber which served as an undressing and cooling room. It was not even whitewashed, and a damp, mouldy, flea-populated straw mat was all there was to represent the soft cushions and comfortable divans we had looked forward to. A singularly horrible smell assailed our nostrils too, instead of sweet perfume and incense, so that every-thing was in harmony. Though disappointed, we were in too high spirits to be very much put out. As we tried to pierce the gloom, and remarked the dimly-seen flitting naked figures of our tawny or copper-coloured attendants, and heard their half-suppressed whispers, we concluded that this was some-thing to be seen *once* in one's life.

While we compared our own appearance with that of our men, and noted our general surroundings, we began to picture ourselves as white captives in a Moorish dungeon, and about to be put to the torture, which might consist in being boiled, to judge from the steam which filled the room. Assor looked very much as if he felt the awfulness of his position, and indeed it was a terrible ordeal he had to face, a whole lifetime's washing at once. How terrible too for the operator, we thought! Encouraging each other with jokes, as of men who knew how to die, we half pushed, half dragged the interpreter to his fate, the Moors grinning with delight at the prospect of scrubbing him. From the black hole we had undressed in we groped our way, with the aid of a single candle, into a second warmer chamber full of steam, our men following with wooden pails.

This was more gloomy, more dungeon-like than the other even, and poor Assor groaned aloud. After encouraging him with an account of what was still in store for him, we penetrated to another and the warmest chamber, full of steam like the others. This inner sanctum was an oblong vaulted room which had never been plastered. At one side was a tap for drawing the necessary hot water from the boilers on the other side of the wall. There was no operating table, and there was nothing for it but to lie down on the smoothly cemented floor. The temperature, as far I could judge, would be about 150°. Our cook turned out to be a skilled shampooer, and he kneaded and rubbed, pushed and pulled, sat upon us, and rolled and tumbled us about with all the style of an old *hammum* hand. He failed not to give us a professional slap to mark the end of any particular operation.

The great affair of the evening, however, was the shampooing of Assor. Everybody was anxious to lend a hand, we, because for the moment he represented all Moorish Jews and their Mellahs, and our men because they saw he was frightened, and that here was an opportunity of paying off old scores long accumulating against the race of Israel. Seeing his protests to be in vain, he submitted to his fate on our promising to give him the treatment of a baby. Needless to say, our delighted followers pounced upon him right gleefully, with the most satisfactory results. If ever a man knew what it was to put off the 'old man' in the physical sense, that individual was David Assor, who at the age of forty-five got his first and probably his last Turkish bath.

On our return to the dressing and cooling room, the odour which had assailed our nostrils on entrance came upon us more overpoweringly than ever. A hasty examination revealed to us a most horrible open sewer. Sickened by both sight and smell, and heedless of possible colds, we hurried on the most necessary of our clothes and fled from the place.

The night was finished off by an exhibition of Moorish dancing. The dancers being women, they had to be smuggled in disguised in men's *jellabias,* otherwise they would have been watched and captured by the Kaid's soldiers. For the same reason it was necessary to bring them at night.

The dancing-women were introduced with a great air of caution and mystery, and showed much bashfulness in taking off their *haiks* and exhibiting their mature charms to infidel eyes. Finding, however, that we were not exactly ogres, and warming under plentiful libations of tea, they were soon quite at their ease. By and bye a wicked-looking wall-eyed individual who accompanied them strung up his native guitar or *gimbery;* one of our own men tapped on a brass tray, while the others kept time by clapping their hands. Thus invited to foot it on the carpet, one of the dancers stood up and circled round once or twice, accentuating the measure with her heel as she glided round. All at once she stopped and gave a sharp stamp with one foot. Next moment both feet were at work, much as if she had found herself on a hot plate from which she could not escape. This vertical rhythmical motion next developed into a sort of shake up of the whole body, every muscle being brought into play. The movement became faster and faster, till suddenly a climax was reached. The all round and up-and-down motion ceased, and she essayed with a wriggle to tie her legs in a knot before finally plumping down on one knee before us to receive the expected largesse.

The other girls next showed their skill, growing more lively and animated as they became accustomed to our unwonted presence, and the one-eyed Cyclops broke into a song on the pleasures of love, our men assisting in the chorus. The feat of the evening, however, was to load a brass tray with all the accessories of tea-drinking, including the filled-up, cups, poise it on the head, and then dance as before without spilling a drop of tea

ABOUT THE AUTHOR

JOSEPH THOMSON was born in Dunfriesshire in 1858, in the cottage built by his stonemason father. A fascination with geology and cartography took him to Edinburgh University (he walked the seventy-mile journey) and, before his twenty first birthday, he was taken on to assist with an expedition to Lake Nyasa (now Malawi) with Keith Johnston. Johnston died shortly after they left Zanzibar and Thomson took over going on to explore the lakes and rivers of the Great Rift Valley. He led further expeditions to Lake Tanyanyika and Lake Victoria, explored the Niger river, climbed Mount Elgon and had his name commemorated in Thomson's falls and Thomson's gazelle.

He made a remarkable exploratory visit to the closed world of Morocco's Atlas Mountains with just one companion, criss-crossing the ranges and making some ground-breaking ascents, and this is the adventure recounted in *Travels in the Atlas and Southern Morocco*. Part of this was spent in Marrakesh, plans for departure frustrated by medical problems and bureaucratic restrictions. Thomson's frustration is evident, but so is his attempt to make the best of the situation. He was a man of boundless enthusiasm but eventually his robust constitution was brocken by the years of tropical and desert travel and he died in 1895, aged only thirty-seven.

A Visit to Marrakesh

from *Adventures in Morocco* by Gerhard Rohlfs

Quite in contrast to Fez is the town of Morocco. The houses, almost without exception, are only one-storied and along the broad streets one often meets with large gardens. It is only in the trade centre of the town that the houses are close together and the streets narrower. The town has its Kessaria (bazaar – according to Lambert, a new one for foreign goods has recently been built), its Ataria, its large and small Funduks, its market places, the two principal ones being the one in front of the Djemma el Fanah, and the other outside the town before the 'Chamis' Gate. There is also a madhouse similar to that in Fez.

There are but few public buildings in the town. The Sultan's palace, though of great extent, is not in any way remarkable. The principal mosque is the Kutubia, so called from the Adulen (writers) and Ketabat (books), the former of which write and sell their books there. The tower of the Kutubia is about 250 feet in height according to Lambert and about 210 according to Maltzan; the latter prefers its architecture to that of the Giralda of Seville, though this last is spoken of by Lubke in his *History of Architecture* as one of the finest specimens of Spanio-Moorish architecture in existence. The interior of this mosque is very similar to that of the large mosque which is dedicated to the 'Archangel' in Fez. Here also are numerous pillars brought from Spain, and here also the charming fountains, though often enough unprovided with water, the once so splendid conduit which supplied the town with water from the Misfua and Mulei Brahim Mountains, being in ruins. The other mosques are unimportant. The most sacred place in the town is the Sauya of Sidi-bel-Abbes, situated in the northern part of the town. Sidi-bel-Abbes, who lies buried there in a small Kubba, is also the patron saint of the town. All strangers, particularly pilgrims, are boarded and lodged here three days gratis. As may be supposed this Sauya is also a place of refuge for criminals.

The Jewish Ghetto, called here as in all Moroccan towns, 'Milha', or the Salted Place, is, Lambert tells us, often jokingly called 'Messus', or the saltless place by the Mohammedans. The number of Jews is estimated at 6000. Moses Montefiore visited Morocco in 1864, in order to obtain a better postion for his unhappy co-religionists; but notwithstanding his rich presents, he was unable to obtain any redress for them, and they are still as miserable and oppressed as ever. For Christians, however, things seem to be looking a little better. Beaumier, though certainly he was a consul, in 1868 was allowed, with his wife, to visit all parts of the town; and H. Lambert, whom I have before mentioned, has lived in Morocco for several years past. But to be able to do this, it is necessary above everything to be well acquainted with the language, and further, to put up with the humiliations and vexations which the Mohammedans daily impose upon the Jews. But for all this I should be very loth to recommend – as Lambert does, at the end of his account ot the Paris Geographical Society, – 'tourists instead of following the old tracks, to visit the town of Morocco, to make it their head-quarters for excursions in the neighbourhood.' Such security as is implied in the above does not exist in the interior of this country yet.

With the exception of these one or two Christians and the Jews, the population of the town of Morocco consists of Berbers, Arabs and blacks, the latter being principally, as elsewhere in Morocco, Haussa and Bambara negroes, included under the name of Gnavi; they are all followers of Islam, but have preserved many of their ancient customs. One hears so much more Schellah than Arabic spoken, especially on market-days, when the country people flock in, that one is inclined to suppose that the Berber element predominates in the town, though this is really not the case. The townsman is nearly always of Arab origin, and prides himself upon it, though often enough he has other blood in his veins.

As in other towns of Morocco, so also here, there are numerous persons who have come from different parts of North Africa, and who remain for some years, sometimes settle down for good or after making a little money, return to their homes to enjoy it in their old age.

There is a separate village called Harrah, for lepers or 'unclean'. These only marry amongst themselves, and have their own Djemma (place of worship) and their own Medressen (schools), the priests and teachers in which are also lepers. They are never allowed to enter the town, but one sees them the whole day idling about the city gates, begging for alms. There are, however, persons of property amongst them, for they engage in various industries, and have their own ground, of which they form fields and gardens; and though the other Moroccans are not afraid of trading with them, Lambert exaggerates when he says that this fearlessness is carried so far that the townsmen eat out of the same dish, or sleep in the same room. In this Harrah there is a Milha for leprous Jews.

The trade of Morocco is small compared with that of Fez and the citizens are wanting in skill and enterprise. The once so famous leather tanneries (Corduan, Maroquin, Safian) lie in ruins; there are certainly whole streets where one can buy nothing but red and yellow leather, or shoes made of the same; but the finest leather is now made in Fez. The most important trade of Morocco is with the districts of the Southern Atlas and the Great Ued-Draa Oasis. From the latter place the town gets its stock of dates for supplying the numerous tribes of Arabs who do not care to undertake the tedious journey over the Atlas for this necessary.

We left the town on the third day, and I had seen about as much of it as the railway traveller does of a town in which he only stays a day. The market at evening, the Kutubia and the Sauya Sidi-bel Abbes were the only places I had been able to see.

ABOUT THE AUTHOR

GERHARD ROHLFS was born in Germany in 1831 and served in Algeria with the French army from 1855–60. It was directly after this tour of duty that he made the long journey through Morocco, including visits to places hitherto unvisited by Europeans, disguised as a penniless renegade, that would form the subject matter for his *Adventures in Morocco*. He was awarded the gold medal of the Royal Geographical Society and later became Consul General of Zanzibar. Gerhard Rohlfs died in 1896.

The Slave Market

from *Morocco* by S. L. Bensusan

As to your slaves, see that you feed them with the same food that you eat yourselves, and clothe them with the stuff ye wear. And if they commit a fault which you are not willing to forgive, then sell them, for they are the servants of Allah, and are not to be tormented.

from THE PROPHET MUHAMMAD'S LAST ADDRESS

In the bazaars of the brass-workers and dealers in cotton goods, in the bazaars of the saddlers and of the leather-sellers, – in short, throughout the Kaisariyah, where the most important trade of Marrakesh is carried on, – the auctions of the afternoon are drawing to a close. The *dilals* have carried goods to and fro in a narrow path between two lines of True Believers, obtaining the best prices possible on behalf of the dignified merchants, who sit gravely in their boxlike shops beyond the reach of toil. No merchant seeks custom: he leaves the auctioneers to sell for him on commission, while he sits at ease, a stranger to elation or disappointment, in the knowledge that the success or failure of the day's market is decreed. Many articles have changed hands, but there is now a greater attraction for men with money outside the limited area of the Kaisariyah, and I think the traffic here passes before its time.

The hour of the sunset prayer is approaching. The wealthier members of the community leave many attractive bargains unpursued, and, heedless of the *dilals'* frenzied cries, set out for the Sok el Abeed. Wool market in the morning and afternoon, it becomes the slave market on three days of the week, in the two hours that precede the setting of the sun and the closing of the city gates; this is the rule that holds in Red Marrakesh.

I follow the business leaders through a very labyrinth of narrow, unpaved streets, roofed here and there with frayed and tattered palmetto-leaves that offer some protection, albeit a scanty one, against the blazing sun. At one of the corners where the beggars congregate and call for alms in the name of Mulai Abd el Kader Jilalli, I catch a glimpse of the great Kutubia tower, with pigeons circling round its glittering dome, and then the maze of streets, shutting out the view, claims me again. The path is by way of shops containing every sort of merchandise known to Moors, and of stalls of fruit and vegetables, grateful 'as water-grass to herds in the June days'. Past a turning in the crowded thorough-fare, where many Southern tribesmen are assembled, and heavily-laden camels compel pedestrians to go warily, the gate of the slave market looms portentous.

A crowd of penniless idlers, to whom admittance is denied, clamours outside the heavy door, while the city urchins fight for the privilege of holding the mules of wealthy Moors, who are arriving in large numbers in response to the report that the household of a great wazeer, recently disgraced, will be offered for sale. One sees portly men of the city wearing the blue cloth selhams that bespeak wealth, country Moors who boast less costly garments, but ride mules of easy pace and heavy price, and one or two high officials of the Dar el Makhzan. All classes of the wealthy are arriving rapidly, for the sale will open in a quarter of an hour.

The portals passed, unchallenged, the market stands revealed - an open space of bare, dry ground with tapia walls, dust-coloured, crumbling, ruinous. Something like an arcade stretches across the centre of the ground of the market. Roofless is the outer wall itself, and broken down, as is the outer wall itself, and the sheds, like cattle pens, that are built all round, it was doubtless an imposing structure in days of old. Behind the outer walls the town rises on every side. I see mules and donkeys feeding, apparently on the ramparts, but really in a fandak overlooking the market. The minaret of a mosque rises nobly beside the mules' feeding-ground, and beyond there is the white tomb of a saint, with swaying palm trees round it. Doubtless this *zowia* gives the Sok el Abeed a sanctity that no procedure within its walls can besmirch; and, to be sure, the laws of the saint's religion are not so much outraged here as in the daily life of many places more sanctified by popular opinion.

On the ground, by the side of the human cattle pens, the wealthy patrons of the market seat themselves at their case, arrange their djellabas and selhams in leisurely fashion, and begin to chat, as though the place were the smoking-room of a club. Water-carriers – lean, half-naked men from the Sus – sprinkle the thirsty ground, that the tramp of slaves and auctioneers may not raise too much dust. Watching them as they go about their work, with the apathy born of custom and experience, I have a sudden reminder of the Spanish bull-ring, to which the slave market bears some remote resemblance. The gathering of spectators, the watering of the ground, the sense of excitement, all strengthen the impression. There are no bulls in the *torils*, but there are slaves in the pens. It may be that the bulls have the better time. Their sufferings in life are certainly brief, and their careless days are very long drawn out. But I would not give the impression that the spectators here are assembled for amusement, or that my view of some of their proceedings would be comprehensible to them. However I may feel, the other occupants of this place are here in the ordinary course of business, and are certainly animated by no such fierce passions as thrill through the air of a plaza de toros. I am in the East but of the West, and 'never the twain shall meet'.

Within their sheds the slaves are huddled together. They will not face the light until the market opens. I catch a glimpse of bright colouring now and again, as some woman or child moves in the dim recesses of the retreats, but there is no suggestion of the number or quality of the penned.

Two storks sail leisurely from their nest on the saint's tomb, and a little company of white ospreys passes over the burning market-place with such a wild, free flight, that the contrast between the birds and the human beings forces itself upon me. Now, however, there is no time for such thoughts; the crowd at the entrance parts to the right and left, to admit twelve grave men wearing white turbans and spotless djellabas. They are the *dilals*, in whose hands is the conduct of the sale.

Slowly and impressively these men advance in a line almost to the centre of the slave market, within two or three yards of the arcade, where the wealthy buyers sit expectant. Then the head auctioneer lifts up his voice, and prays, with downcast eyes and outspread hands. He recites the glory of Allah, the One, who made the heaven above and the earth beneath, the sea and all that is therein; his brethren and the buyers say Amen. He thanks Allah for his mercy to men in sending Mohammed the Prophet, who gave the world the True Belief, and he curses Shaitan, who wages war against Allah and his children. Then he calls upon Sidi bel Abbas, patron saint of Marrakesh, friend of buyers and sellers, who praised Allah so assiduously in days remote, and asks the saint to bless the market and all who buy and sell therein, granting them prosperity and length of days. And to these prayers, uttered with an intensity of devotion quite Mohammedan, all the listeners say Amen. Only to Unbelievers like myself,– to men who have never known, or knowing, have rejected Islam – is there aught repellent in the approaching business; and Unbelievers may well pass unnoticed. In life the man who has the True Faith despises them; in death they become children of the Fire. Is it not so set down?

Throughout this strange ceremony of prayer I seem to see the bull-ring again, and in place of the *dilals* the *cuadrillas* of the Matadors coming out to salute, before the alguazils open the gates of the toril and the slaying begins. The dramatic intensity of either scene connects for me this slave market in Marrakesh with the plaza de toros in the shadow of the Giralda tower in Sevilla. Strange to remember now and here, that the man who built the Kutubia tower for this thousand year-old-city of Yusuf ben Tachfin, gave the Giralda to Andalusia.

Prayers are over – the last Amen is said. The *dilals* separate, each one going to the pens he presides over, and calling upon their tenants to come forth. These selling men move with a dignity that is quite Eastern, and speak in calm and impressive tones. They lack the frenzied energy of their brethren who traffic in the bazaars.

Obedient to the summons, the slaves face the light, the sheds yield up their freight, and there are a few noisy moments, bewildering to the novice, in which the auctioneers place their goods in line, rearrange dresses, give children to the charge of adults, sort out men and women according to their age and value, and prepare for the promenade. The slaves will march round and round the circle of the buyers, led by the auctioneers, who will proclaim the latest bid and hand over any one of their charges to an intending purchaser, that he may make his examination before raising the price. In the procession now forming for the first parade, five, if not six, of the seven ages set out by the melancholy Jaques are represented. There are men and women who can no longer walk upright, however the *dilal* may insist; there are others of middle age, with years of active service before them; there are young men full of vigour and youth, fit for the fields, and young women, moving for once unveiled yet unrebuked, who will pass at once to the hareem. And there are children of every age, from babies who will be sold with their mothers to girls and boys upon the threshold of manhood and womanhood. All are dressed in bright colours and displayed to the best advantage, that the hearts of bidders may be moved and their purses opened widely.

'It will be a fine sale,' says my neighbour, a handsome middle-aged Moor from one of the Atlas villages, who had chosen his place before I reached the market. 'There must be well nigh forty slaves, and this is good, seeing that the Elevated Court is at Fez. It is because our Master – Allah send him more victories! – has been pleased to 'visit' Sidi Abdeslam, and send him to the prison of Mequinez. All the wealth he has extorted has been taken away from him by our Master, and he will see no more light. Twenty or more of these women are of his house.'

Now each *dilal* has his people sorted out, and the procession begins. Followed by their bargains the *dilals* march round and round the market, and I understand why the dust was laid before the procession commenced.

Most of the slaves are absolutely free from emotion of any sort: they move round as stolidly as the blindfolded horses that work the water-wheels in gardens beyond the town, or the corn mills within its gates. I think the sensitive ones – and there are a few – must come from the household of the unfortunate Sidi Abdeslam, who was reputed to be a good master. Small wonder if the younger women shrink, and if the black visage seems to take on a tint of ashen grey, when a buyer, whose face is an open defiance of the ten commandments, calls upon the *dilal* to halt, and, picking one out as though she had been one of a flock of sheep, handles her as a butcher would, examining teeth and muscles, and questioning her and the *dilal* very closely about past history and present health. And yet the European observer must beware lest he read into incidents of this kind something that neither buyer nor seller would recognise. Novelty may create an emotion that facts and custom cannot justify.

'Ah, Tsamanni,' says my gossip from the Atlas to the big *dilal* who led the prayers, and is in special charge of the children for sale, 'I will speak to this one,' and Tsamanni pushes a tiny little girl into his arms. The child kisses the speaker's hand. Not at all unkindly the Moor takes his critical survey, and Tsamanni enlarges upon her merits.

'She does not come from the town at all,' he says glibly, 'but from

Timbuctoo. It is more difficult than ever to get children from there. The accursed Nazarenes have taken the town, and the slave market droops. But this one is desirable: she understands needlework, she will be a companion for your house, and thirty-five dollars is the last price bid.'

'One more dollar, Tsamanni. She is not ill-favoured, but she is poor and thin. Nevertheless say one dollar more,' says the Moor.

'The praise to Allah, who made the world,' says the *dilal* piously, and hurries round the ring, saying that the price of the child is now thirty-six dollars, and calling upon the buyers to go higher.

I learn that the *dilal*'s commission is two and a half per cent on the purchase price, and there is a Government tax of five per cent. Slaves are sold under a warranty, and are returned if they are not properly described by the auctioneer. Bids must not be advanced by less than a Moorish dollar (about three shillings) at a time, and when a sale is concluded a deposit must be paid at once, and the balance on or shortly after the following day. Thin slaves will not fetch as much money as fat ones, for corpulence is regarded as the outward and visible sign of health as well as wealth by the Moor.

'I have a son of my house,' says the Moor from the Atlas, with a burst of confidence quite surprising. 'He is my only one, and must have a playfellow, so I am here to buy. In these days it is not easy to get what one wants. Everywhere the French. The caravans come no longer from Tuat because of the French. From Timbuctoo it is the same thing. Surely Allah will burn these people in a fire of more than ordinary heat – a furnace that shall never cool. Ah, listen to the prices.' The little girl's market– value has gone to forty-four dollars – say seven pounds ten shillings in English money at the current rate of exchange. It has risen two dollars at a time, and Tsamanni cannot quite cover his satisfaction. One girl, aged fourteen, has been sold for no less than ninety dollars after spirited bidding from two country kaids; another, two years older, has gone for seventy-six.

'There is no moderation in all this,' says the Atlas Moor, angrily. 'But prices will rise until our Lord the Sultan ceases to listen to the Nazarenes, and purges the land. Because of their Bashadors we can no longer have the markets at the towns on the coasts. If we do have one there, it must be held secretly, and a slave must be carried in the darkness from house to house. This is shameful for an unconquered people.'

I am only faintly conscious of my companion's talk and action, as he bids for child after child, never going beyond forty dollars. Interest centres in the diminishing crowd of slaves who still follow the *dilals* round the market in monotonous procession.

The attractive women and strong men have been sold, and have realised good prices. The old people are in little or no demand; but the auctioneers will persist until closing time. Up and down tramp the people nobody wants, burdens to themselves and their owners, the useless, or nearly useless men and women whose lives have been slavery for so long as they can remember. Even the water-carrier from the Sus country, who has been jingling his bright bowls together since the market opened, is moved to compassion, for while two old women are standing behind their *dilal*, who is talking to a client about their reserve price, I see him give them a free draught from his goat-skin water-barrel, and this kind action seems to do something to freshen the place, just as the mint and the roses of the gardeners freshen the alleys near the Kaisariyah in the heart of the city. To me, this journey round and round the market seems to be the saddest of the slaves' lives – worse than their pilgrimage across the deserts of the Wad Nun, or the Draa, in the days when they were carried captive from their homes, packed in panniers upon mules, forced to travel by night, and half starved. For then at least they were valued and had their lives before them, now they are counted as little more than the broken-down mules and donkeys left to rot by the roadside. And yet this, of course, is a purely Western opinion, and must be discounted accordingly.

It is fair to say that auctioneers and buyers treat the slaves in a manner that is not unkind. They handle them just as though they were animals with a market value that ill-treatment will diminish, and a few of the women are brazen, shameless creatures – obviously, and perhaps not unwisely, determined to do the best they can for themselves in any surroundings. These women are the first to find purchasers. The unsold adults and little children seem painfully tired; some of the latter can hardly keep pace with the auctioneer, until he takes them by the hand and leads them along with him. Moors, as a people, are wonderfully kind to children.

The procedure never varies. As a client beckons and points out a slave, the one selected is pushed forward for inspection, the history is briefly told, and if the bidding is raised the auctioneer, thanking Allah, who sends good prices, hurries on his way to find one who will bid a little more. On approaching an intending purchaser the slave seizes and kisses his hand, then releases it and stands still, generally indifferent to the rest of the proceedings.

'It is well for the slaves,' says the Atlas Moor, rather bitterly, for the fifth and last girl child has gone up beyond his limit. 'In the Mellah or the Madinah you can get labour for nothing, now the Sultan is in Fez. There is hunger in many a house, and it is hard for a free man to find food. But slaves are well fed. In times of famine and war free men die; slaves are in comfort. Why then do the Nazarenes talk of freeing slaves, as though they were prisoners, and seek to put barriers against the market, until at last the prices become foolish? Has not the Prophet said, 'He who behaveth ill to his slave shall not enter into Paradise'? Does that not suffice believing people? Clearly it was written, that my little Mohammed, my first born, my only one, shall have no playmate this day. No, Tsamanni: I will bid no more. Have I such store of dollars that I can buy a child for its weight in silver?'

The crowd is thinning now. Less than ten slaves remain to be sold, and I do not like to think how many times they must have tramped round the market. Men and women-bold, brazen, merry, indifferent-have passed to their several masters; all the children have gone; the remaining oldsters move round and round, their shuffling gait, downcast eyes, and melancholy looks in pitiful contrast to the bright clothes in which they are dressed for the sale, in order that their own rags may not prejudice purchasers.

Once again the storks from the saint's tomb pass over the market in large wide flight, as though to tell the story of the joy of freedom. It is the time of the evening promenade. The sun is setting rapidly and the sale is nearly at an end.

'Forty-one dollars – forty-one,' cries the *dilal* at whose heels the one young and pretty woman who has not found a buyer limps painfully. She is from the Western Soudan, and her big eyes have a look that reminds me of the hare that was run down by the hounds a few yards from me on the marshes at home in the coursing season.

'Why is the price so low?' I ask.

'She is sick,' said the Moor coolly: 'she cannot work – perhaps she will not live. Who will give more in such a case? She is of kaid Abdeslain's household, though he bought her a few weeks before his fall, and she must be sold. But the *dilal* can give no warranty, for nobody knows her sickness. She is one of the slaves who are bought by the dealers for the rock salt of El Djouf.'

Happily the woman seems too dull or too ill to feel her own position. She moves as though in a dream – a dream undisturbed, for the buyers have almost ceased to regard her. Finally she is sold for forty-three dollars to a very old and infirm man.

'No slaves, no slaves,' says the Atlas Moor impatiently: 'and in the town they are slow to raise them.' I want an explanation of this strange complaint.

'What do you mean when you say they are slow to raise them,' I ask.

'In Marrakesh now,' he explains, 'dealers buy the healthiest slaves they can find, and raise as many children by them as is possible. Then, so soon as the children are old enough to sell, they are sold, and when the mothers grow old and have no more children, they too are sold, but they do not fetch much then.'

This statement takes all words from me, but my informant sees nothing startling in the case, and continues gravely: 'From six years old they are sold to be companions, and from twelve they go to the hareems. Prices are good – too high indeed; fifty-four dollars I must have paid this afternoon to purchase one, and when Mulai Mohammed reigned the price would have been twenty, or less, and for that one would have bought fat slaves. Where there is one caravan now, there were ten of old times.'

Only three slaves now, and they must go back to their masters to be sent to the market on another day, for the sun is below the horizon, the market almost empty, and the guards will be gathering at the city gates. Two *dilals* make a last despairing promenade, while their companions are busy recording prices and other details in connection with the afternoon's business. The purchased slaves, the auctioneer's gaudy clothing changed for their own, are being taken to the houses of their masters. We who live within the city walls must hasten now, for the time of gate-closing is upon us, and one may not stay outside.

It has been a great day. Many rich men have attended personally, or by their agents, to compete for the best favoured women of the household of the fallen kaid, and prices in one or two special cases ran beyond forty pounds (English money), so brisk was the bidding.

Outside the market-place a country Moor of the middle class is in charge of four young boy slaves, and is telling a friend what he paid for them. I learn that their price averaged eleven pounds apiece in English currency – two hundred and eighty dollars altogether in Moorish money, that they were all bred in

Marrakesh by a dealer who keeps a large establishment of slaves, as one in England might keep a stud farm, and sells the children as they grow up. The purchaser of the quartette is going to take them to the North. He will pass the coming night in a fandak, and leave as soon after daybreak as the gates are opened. Some ten days' travel on foot will bring him to a certain city, where his merchandise should fetch four hundred dollars. The lads do not seem to be disturbed by the sale, or by thoughts of their future, and the dealer himself seems to be as near an approach to a commercial traveller as I have seen in Morocco. To him the whole transaction is on a par with selling eggs or fruit, and while he does not resent my interest, he does not pretend to understand it.

From the minaret that overlooks the mosque the *mueddin* calls for the evening prayer; from the side of the Kutubia Tower and the minaret of Sidi bel Abbas, as from all the lesser mosques, the cry is taken up. Lepers pass out of the city on their way to Elhara; beggars shuffle off to their dens; storks standing on the flat house-tops survey the familiar scene gravely but with interest. Doubtless the *dilals* and all who sent their slaves to the market to be sold this afternoon will respond to the *mueddins'* summons with grateful hearts, and Sidi bel Abbas, patron saint of Red Marrakesh, will hardly go unthanked.

ABOUT THE AUTHOR

SAMUEL LEVY BENSUSAN was born in 1872. Music critic, editor, journalist, poet and playwright, Bensusan was a prolific author whose last book was published at the age of eighty-three. He drew his experience of Morocco from his time there as a special correspondent. This extract draws on his rich descriptive powers and reveals the slave market of Marrakesh as a hardy institution that survived right through to the twentieth century. Samuel Bensusan died in 1958.

Gardens of Marrakesh

from *Moorish Lotos Leaves*
by George D. Cowan and R. L. N. Johnston

About half the area of the city, which is nearly nine miles in circumference, is occupied by gardens. The Moor believes not only that a garden was the original birthplace of mankind but also that the souls of virtuous Moslims will realise supreme beatitude in the radiant bowers of the Mohammedan paradise. There, amid golden groves adorned with kiosks of pearl and jacinth, towers the colossal Tuba tree, each bough laden with fruits of matchless flavour, each leaf filling with celestial melody the musk-scented air ever cooled by soaring fountains and crystal rivulets that flame with emeralds and rubies. Gorgeous flowers of richest odour, lustrous birds of sweetest song, banquets far surpassing the visions of the epicure, fragrant draughts of liquid ecstasy, together with the smiles of immortal beauty flashing undimmed through all eternity, 'shall make the spirit of the true believer almost faint with the soft burthen of intensest bliss.' Firm faith it was in such a paradise that, centuries ago, made each Mussulman a hero. The turbaned hosts that once menaced all Christendom with 'the Koran or the sword', owed their dauntless courage to – a strange idea – the dream of a garden. Wherefore many a Moorish Khalif strove to anticipate on earth some of the glories of his heaven, by lavishing on harem gardens all the art of Byzantium and half the spoils of Spain. Witness peerless Alhambra; witness the resplendent Garden of Zohra, where, amid a blaze of flowers, more than 4,000 slender pilasters of rarest marble upheld gold-fretted cedar pavilions and cool arcades aglow with brilliant arabesque and exquisite mosaic. In the shade of orange and citron groves, and stately palms brought from the East, and myrtle thickets where the trills of nightingales melted in the music of fountains and rustling leaves, there the caresses of magic loveliness ever invited voluptuous repose.

But all that remains to the Moor of today is the memory of the one time supremacy of his race in arms, in science and in art. Only in three or four towns of Marocco linger a few old Moresco families who have preserved the vaunted purity of their lineage. These descendants of the mighty ones, who reared the Giralda of Seville, the Palace of Granada, the Mezquita of Cordova, the Kitobeea of Maraksh, now reside in 'low-built, mud-walled, barbarian settlements', with crumbling battlements and squalid lanes – melancholy pictures of decay, framed in foliage and flowers – rose-wreathed skeletons.

It may be well to remark, in the words of Sir Joseph Hooker that;

> a garden in Marocco means something very different from what we understand by it at home. So far as any idea of enjoyment is connected with it, the paramount object is shade and coolness. Trees and running water, without which in this climate few trees will grow, are therefore the essential requisites. Beyond this the Moor, if he be rich and luxurious, may plant a few sweet-scented flowers; but otherwise no mere pleasure of the eye is dreamt of, and there seems to be among the natives a complete want of the sense of beauty. To the Moor the chief object of a garden is not pleasure, but profit.

Consequently, the gardens of Maraksh, containing no trim array of terrace, no neat symmetrical parterres, no close-clipped foliage, no box borders, no velvet lawns, no pomp of statuary or rockery, are merely green and teeming wildernesses, wherein botany runs riot in defiance of symmetry. Intersected by broad grass-grown avenues, overarched here with interlacing boughs, there with trellised vines, these sylvan retreats, brimful of sweet sounds, delicious perfumes, and rich colouring, are the favourite resorts of the lotos-eating Moor. Each garden contains one or more summer-houses, gay with arabesqued walls, painted ceilings, and tessellated floors, where merrymakers often wile away the afternoon with tea and music. But we choose to recline on the striped carpet spread in fig tree's ample shade while we feast our eyes on the bewildering colours worn by motley spring and inhale the sunny breeze which reeks with scents of orange blossoms, roses, jessamine and lilac blooms. Many a Christian captive has toiled to raise the high *tabya* garden-walls which form the burnt sienna background of this

> Popular solitude of bees and birds,
> And fairy formed and many-coloured things

Hark! The great tank is opened, and waters disbursed from Atlas's aerial treasury of snow babble through a score of tiny channels, adding their music to the wood-notes of blackbirds, doves and finches, accompanied at intervals by the chatter of magpie, the caw of crow, the hoarse croak of frog, the scream of the hawk poised high above innumerable swifts threading airy mazes in the cloudless blue; and once from a myrtle thicket the *Om el Hassan* or 'Mother of the Beautiful', as Moors appropriately call the nightingale, trilled forth in airily exquisite cadences her welcome to spring. An inexpressibly solemn stork on the margin of a little streamlet is attending in the same capacity of a hearse the funeral of a frog or of one of the tiny green lizards which peer at us from stony lurking places. White butterflies are paying afternoon-calls on the flower-fairies dwelling in rose, hollyhock, violent, scarlet poppy, yellow cornflower and white clover; the gauzy-winged dragon-fly skims sportively past in search of his afternoon blue-bottle, followed by a lustrous beetle humming as loud as any top. Wavering shafts of amber light quiver through foliage where the delicate grace of blue convolvulus entwines the fierce beauty of the pomegranate's blood-red flower. Lemon and lime blossoms here and there peep forth from amidst the leafage of white poplar, walnut, olive, mulberry almond, apricot, willow, aspen, and the evergreen Cyprus and myrtle. Towering above it all, the lordly date-palm waves its golden tassels.

A couple of cows browsing, closely tethered, on the rank grass were not altogether out of harmony; but it must be admitted that patches of barley, beds of pumpkins, melons, mint and other useful but unpoetic plants, considerably diluted the romance of the scenery. The Sultan himself, however, deigns to turn greengrocer, and realises many thousands of pounds by the sale of fruit and vegetables.

ABOUT THE AUTHOR

GEORGE D. COWAN was a merchant with twenty-five years of North African experience. His friend R. L. N. JOHNSTON was also another merchant, though he also served as vice-consul at Magador and as a foreign correspondent for several newspapers.

They shared a deep knowledge of Morocco, as can be seen from the deft familiarity with which they write of Marrakesh's gardens.

Writers in Context

A Haywire Winter – Gavin Maxwell

from *Gavin Maxwell; A Life* by Douglas Botting

Aristocrat, renegade, shark hunter, secret agent, racing driver, adventurer, naturalist, poet and painter, Gavin Maxwell was also one of the most popular authors of wildlife books in the twentieth century, and his classic account of life with otters in his remote refuge by the Hebridean sea – *Ring of Bright Water* – sold in millions around the world.

But never had the simple life been pursued by so complicated a man. Grandson of the Duke of Northumberland and a distant relative of Lord Byron and the Royal Family, Maxwell never knew his father (killed in battle in 1914, the year of his birth). His childhood was spent at his family's isolated Scottish ancestral home of ilrig, and after his wartime experience training SOE agents in small arms and survival techniques in the remoter corners of Scotland he set up a shark-hunting enterprise on the Hebridean isle of Soay – the subject of his first book, *Harpoon at a Venture*.

It was the explorer and Arabist Wilfred Thesiger who first introduced Maxwell to otters during a journey by traditional tarada canoe through the as yet unravaged Tigris Marshes of Iraq, then the traditional tribal home of the Marsh Arabs. Strangely for a dedicated Scottish naturalist, Maxwell had never come face to face with otters before, and as he was to admit later, he was to remain in thrall to these enchanting and highly intelligent creatures for the rest of his life - to the extent that when he finally returned home to Britain he took with him a young marsh otter called Mijbil. Before long 'Mij' was installed in Maxwell's idyllic Scottish hideaway by the sea at Sandaig Bay, the 'ring of bright water' (with stream or sea on three sides) to which he gave the name of Camusfearna (Gaelic for Bay of Alders) – a retreat where he could again live in close communion with nature as he had done when he was a child.

Not long afterwards, as a second bi-product of his Iraq journey, Maxwell met his future biographer – namely myself. Though I was still an undergraduate at Oxford at this time, I had already led an expedition to the little-known Yemeni island of Soqotra in the Arabian Sea and written a book about it, *Island of the Dragon's Blood*. When I read Gavin Maxwell's own highly acclaimed account of his journey through the Iraq Marshes, *A Reed Shaken by the Wind*, I immediately invited him to give a talk about it to the Oxford University Exploration Club, of which I was Chairman. It was then that, with exploration and writing in common, we decided to pool our respective talents. Gavin's first brainwave was characteristically zany. 'Why don't I go on a dangerous expedition and get lost,' he suggested to me, 'and you come out to look for me? If you find me I can write a book about the journey. But if you don't find me you can write a book about the search.'

Subsequently, at Gavin's behest, I planned two rather more soundly based joint ventures - the first a journey among the Nilotic tribes of the swamps of the Sudd in Southern Sudan, the second a winter mule trek across the breadth of the High Atlas Mountains of Morocco. The first proved impossible, and by the time Gavin was ready to embark on the second I was already on an expedition of my own round Lake Tchad (then still a lake) in the Southern Sahara. Gavin decided to go to Morocco alone.

He had first visited Morocco with his brother some years previously and had reported ecstatically on its 'splendours and horrors'. He had always planned to return, perhaps even to live there. Now, he reckoned, was the time. His primary object was to research a book – the exotic and horrifying story of the Glaoui of Marrakesh, the Lords of the Atlas, whose extraordinary reign had come to an end only five years before. Installed in a room in the Medina at Marrakesh, he wrote to me:

This really is one of the most fabulous cities left in the world . . . The stars have come out very bright, and the drumming has reached a crescendo and smells of mixed spice waft in at the window mingled with all the other smells that make a Medina in the olfactory sense. I looked at the Atlas with crimson sun on the snows from my rooftop this evening. They looked like the Himalayas! When and if we go we will need complete Alpine equipment. I see it all much more plainly now. And sometime we must do it together.

But Gavin's book, *The Lords of the Atlas*, was a more complex and time consuming task than he had envisaged and required several sojourns before its completion. By now he had taken up full-time residence in his West Highland retreat at Camusafearna, about which he had already published his best selling book *Ring of Bright Water*. Camusfearna was a complex and time-consuming establishment which normally comprised its gifted but temperamental and impractical tenant (Gavin himself), two boundlessly energetic and demanding young West African otters called Edal and Teko (successors to the short-lived Iraqi otter Mijbil, who had been killed by a local roadmender), and their keeper and general factotum, Jimmy Watt.

By the autumn of 1960 Gavin's mind turned increasingly to his impending return to Morocco. Worry about leaving Jimmy and the two otters on their own at Sandaig during the long, hard, dark winter months of a northern winter added to his many anxieties at the year's end. Finally he hit on a fortuitous solution. At this time I was looking for a remote and rent-free hideaway in which to write a book of my own during the winter. If I would care to come up and act in loco parentis for six months till the following spring, Gavin suggested, Sandaig was at my disposal, rent-free and all found. So the die was cast. Ahead lay a haywire winter for us both – for Gavin in distant Africa, for myself in a wintry Camusfearna buried deep in northern night.

On 17 December 1960, nearly six weeks after his departure from Sandaig, Gavin finally set off for North Africa in his brand new Land Rover, the first of his lavish purchases from the profits generated by the success of *Ring of Bright Water,* with a small Union Jack and the word 'Britannia' sign-painted in large Arabic letters on the back and sides.

Gavin's route took him by easy stages through France and Spain to Gibraltar, and thence south down the coast road of Morocco to the capital city, Rabat, and the ever-tumultuous apartment of Margaret Pope in the Place Lavigerle. He had barely had time to settle down and get his bearings, however, than circumstances dictated that he should fly back to England again. When I spoke to him on the telephone on New Year's Eve he was cryptic about his plans:

'I've had to come back to London to get a visa to go to Algeria,' he told me. 'I couldn't get one in Morocco. I'm also trying to fix up commissions for articles from *The Spectator* and *London Illustrated News.* But they're just my cover, really. I can't say any more on the phone. But I'm sure you know what I mean, Douglas. So wish me luck.'

Gavin left me in no doubt that he was going to Algeria on a secret mission of some kind. Since Algeria at that time was torn by a singularly intense and bloody war of independence, it had to be assumed that such a mission was not without its dangers. I could only guess that he was acting as an agent for some intelligence organisation or other. Only many years later did I learn from Margaret Pope the exact nature and purpose of his visit to Algeria.

Margaret Pope did not simply run a broadcasting department in Morocco. Her sparsely furnished and chaotic apartment in Rabat, with its avalanches of books and papers and its twelve-foot-long mattresses ranged against the walls, designed to accommodate all comers at all times, was a junction and clearinghouse for revolutionary partisans and representatives of unliberated or imperfectly liberated countries from all over Africa. 'Such men,' Gavin confessed;

'live in an atmosphere into which I am drawn as inexorably as a fly into the maw of an insect-eating plant, an atmosphere of intrigue and sudden death. In Africa, they warn me, a British author at large is a suspect figure. They advise me to inspect my car for bombs every morning; at this, while my more habitual proficiencies flag, I have become quick and unforgetful.'

All this was grist to the mill for Gavin, for no one ever grew up with a more deeply ingrained urge to be involved in high drama and great adventure - an urge complicated by an irresistible tendency to see a drama where there was none, or create one where he could not see one. Gavin's English friends in North Africa perceived this only too clearly. 'Gavin was an acute observer of certain things but not of political 'situations',' Margaret Pope noted;

'and in any case all his observations in my opinion were always subject to certain moods and even powerful emotive factors which at times amounted to hallucinations and very curious deviations of judgement. He was what one used to call a 'tortured soul' and I understood that – but he was always fighting against that and inventing reasons for not facing certain facts. I often had arguments with him about this tendency.'

238

For such a personality there was no more fruitful place to be sucked into the vortex of radical Third World politics and the anticolonial struggle than Margaret Pope's hospitable headquarters in the capital city of a country only recently liberated from the colonial yoke.

Among the activists who frequented Margaret Pope's flat were various high-ranking members of the Algerian FLN, or National Liberation Front, which had been fighting a long and savage war against the French. At this time the situation in Algeria had reached a critical stage. The French were not only fighting against the FLN but amongst each other, with the French Army split in two, one half siding with the French settlers, the colons, the other siding with General de Gaulle's government in France. What the outcome would be and where this would leave the FLN was unclear. 'The situation was so confused,' Margaret Pope recalled;

'that some of my FLN friends asked me to get some independent observers to fly over and report on the situation. I knew Gavin was not really sufficiently briefed on the Algerian question and I was doubtful if he could digest much of what he might observe. But at least he sympathised with the FLN and there was no doubt he would do the best he could. Anyway, he agreed to go and I did my best to put him in the picture.'

Gavin left London a second time on 8 January 1961, picked up a connecting flight from Casablanca to Algiers, and checked in at the Hotel Aletti, a renowned watering hole and meeting place in the centre of the city, next to the Prefecture. No doubt many of *Ring of Bright Water's* huge army of fans, fondly imagining their guru cosily ensconced with his wild creatures far from the cares of man, would have been greatly alarmed had they learned of his sudden metamorphosis from a latter-day St Francis into an alternative James Bond. Gavin's overt reason for visiting Algeria – the one listed in his visa application to the Algerian authorities – was to write some magazine articles about the new oilfields that had been opened up in the Algerian Sahara. These were dramatic enough in their own right, as Gavin wrote to Jimmy on his return:

I went down to Hassi Messaoud, the principal oilfield in the Sahara, which is really extraordinary. One flies there in a very old and leaky DC4 (the heating was stuck full on when we went down in the morning and stuck full off when we returned in icy starlight - the first was an oven, the second a fridge) over about three hundred miles of desert and suddenly Hassi Messaoud is THERE with the desert stretching away for hundreds of miles on all sides. One can see the perpetual flames of the burning gas and the great columns of black smoke from nearly a hundred miles away. They have made an artificial oasis, with trees and flowers and swimming pools and bars and jukeboxes and, of course, many million pounds' worth of machinery. In the sunset I drove across the desert itself for twenty miles to a lesser oilfield; when the sun got low everything was in shadow except the tops of the dunes we were passing among, and they were vermilion. I've never seen a sunset like it – the whole sky was tiger striped with every shade of red on the palette.

The rest of Gavin's time in Algeria was less agreeable, as he hinted in the same letter:

It was no fun there, needless to say . . . I discovered a microphone in a cunningly concealed position in my bedroom, and snored and farted at it for a bit to keep it occupied . . . I also had the slightly traumatic experience of seeing somebody's throat cut at close quarters. So traumatic I don't propose to write about it now or at any other time. I spent the whole ten days afterwards thinking it was my turn next . . .

In fact he did write about this particular incident later, in a vivid passage in his book *The Rocks Remain:*

Darkness on the waterfront in Algiers; a scuffle and a high bubbling cry. A burst of submachinegun close at hand and a window splatters somewhere overhead. I turn the corner; no one has moved him. He lies there, an elderly Arab with a beard jutting to the sky. There is more blood than I would have believed possible; I had not seen a slit throat before. A group of French parachutists swagger by; one kicks the corpse.

The handwritten draft of Gavin's report for the FLN which I found among his papers after his death, occupied twenty-four foolscap pages. It would appear to have been written on or about 21 January 1961. In essence it was a detailed profile of the state of the white business economy and the morale and political opinions of the middle-class French *colons* of Algeria at a point of grave crisis in the French-Algerian war – a point at which the French settlers were having to face up to the possibility that Algeria could become Algerian (and, worse, Communist). Here and there Gavin writes of the general atmosphere of tension and dread, the feeling of disillusionment and betrayal among some sections of the whites, the air full of plots and rumours and a widespread fear of an impending massacre, of British and American intervention, perhaps, even, of world war and a French nuclear bombardment ('a rumour', Gavin commented with evident relish, 'unconfirmed *but* uncontradicted'). Though his informants are identified only by initials, Gavin occasionally allows himself an aside at their expense. 'Military Intelligence Captain (bearded) attached Préfecture,' reads one such comment, 'lives at Hotel Aletti, has two Muslim mistresses, one of whom is known to be in the pay of FLN. General impression that French security is crazily bad and that given time any European could find out anything.'

Gavin's recommendations to the FLN (under the heading 'Personal Summary') were trenchant:

> True significance of events is not now but in the future. Action must be now; before delaying tactics allow the situation to become fluid again. Feel that key point is not withdrawal of French Army, but right of address by Ferhat Abbas to all Muslim Algerians, and similar right by French to *pieds noirs*. Both should broadcast to all, of both races. Now, not later. In the present psychological situation 90+ per cent all the Europeans would welcome this – they want to be led, want reassurance. In three months new movements will have formed, new allegiances, thinking will again have become blurred, new *culs de sac* will have taken shape. This is the moment. If it is not done now *it will be too late to prevent the long, final, extensive war which both sides dread.*

Gavin had done what he was asked to do and was anxious to put this troubled country behind him as quickly as possible. Privately, he was in no doubt how he felt about the colonial situation in Algeria and what he believed the final outcome should be. Later he was to write:

Morning, and the city under lashing rain; all along the waterfront the high waves rolled in, not Mediterranean blue nor nordic grey, but mud brown with dark Algerian sand, and when the crests curled over and the spume streamed back on the wind it too was brown. A French bar-tender looked out on it and said: 'It is an omen – the brown tide, the Arab tide that will sweep us all away, and unlike this tide it will not recede.' I ordered cognac; he poured two and raised his glass, 'Algérie Française'. He looked to me to respond; I raised my glass vaguely and said, 'Algérie!' What other answer could there be?

On 24 January Gavin returned to Morocco. In Rabat he handed his report over to Margaret Pope, who translated it into French and passed it on to the FLN. 'It was not of much importance in the long run,' she was to comment later, 'but the FLN boys were very grateful for his effort.' Then he drove down to Marrakesh and the decaying comforts of the Hôtel Centrale in the city's old quarter, 'with a sigh of relief', as he put it, 'and farewell, anyway, to microphones and murder'. From Marrakesh he sent me a postcard:

Returned from Algeria Tuesday night. Hardly reorientated yet. Not a healthy country, that! I sent my first press collect telegram from Algiers – *just* like Boot of the *Beast* in *Scoop*; it began 'Algeconomy moving crisiswards' and so on for two hundred words. Fun. Life in Africa is strange, don't you agree, or don't you? I do.' He had also got enough material for fifty articles, he said, and had sent one off to *The Spectator* already. 'It's so badly written that I daresay they'll decide not to use it.

The hotel in which Gavin had chosen to base himself for his winter in North Africa was a curious one for a bestselling author who was richer than he had ever been in his life. 'This hotel has practically fallen to pieces now,' he wrote to Jimmy.

Last year it had four people: a French manageress, two Arab maids, and an Arab porter. Now the Frenchwoman has left, and the porter (who only speaks Arabic) is the manager. The Arab owners have evidently decided to let it fall down, as the squalor and disrepair have increased a hundredfold. No one seems actually to live here except a very scruffy policeman, but there is a lot of coming and going all night and veiled ladies are to be seen leaving rooms early in the morning, so I think I know What Is Going On.'

The hotel lay off one of the narrow alleys that made up the infinite, bewildering complex of alleys of the antique Arab town, the earth-floored passage between the high mud walls full of the smells of spice, ordure, and impregnated dust. Gavin had a room in the garconnière (bachelors' annexe), which was somewhat removed from the main body of the hotel.

It was not a restful room, for all the welter of sounds of a teeming, closely confined Arab city poured into it by night and day. At sunset, above the endless plaint of the beggars, Gavin could bear the steady rhythm of drums and cymbals from the main square nearby and then the sudden siren that signalled the end of the Moslem fast of Ramadan for the day:

> The siren shrills high and thin, a violin-bow of sound arched over the wide confines of the fantastic city, and suddenly there is everywhere the smell of food where before the air held only the dry tang of spice. The voices of the beggars are silent; the predominant sound now is of dancers' drums. Turbaned figures eating bowls of thick harrissa soup sit huddled on my doorstep, for it is the only free seat above ground level. The light goes out altogether, and I linger on because I have become one of the alley's ghosts.

Gavin was often asked why he chose to live in such a shabby place when there were large and comfortable European-style hotels within a mile. In his Moroccan notebook he addressed himself to this point:

> It cannot be for financial reasons, for by my standards I am rich, horribly rich; I have never travelled with so much money before and my questioners know this. I answer with half-truths – that I dislike living in an atmosphere of conducted European tourists, that it is a question of habit, that when I go away for days or weeks I can keep the room and my things in disarray, for it costs so little. But the true reason is that I am one of the hotel's ghosts, for whom these four shabby walls once had meaning, and where I was happy; I linger here savouring an emptiness of whose reality I am unable to convince myself.

Gavin's first priority was to look into the circumstances surrounding the disappearance of his Berber friend, Ahmed, with whom he had hoped to travel in the mountains and the desert south. Ahmed's departure to Holland had hit Gavin hard. It also roused the wildest and most exaggerated suspicions on his part. Had Ahmed gone voluntarily, or had he been taken against his will? Had he betrayed Gavin's trust, or had he, as Gavin was strongly inclined to believe, been the victim of some dark Israeli plot, or even some sort of brown slave trade? Gavin had barely unpacked his bags before he sallied forth to find out. He gave his version of events in a letter to Jimmy Watt:

As soon as I got down here I saw Ahmed's father (an old man who can neither read nor write nor speak any language but his own) and realised very quickly that something pretty fishy was going on. Ahmed had been given a passport to go to Germany, not Holland, but his letters (not written by himself) came from a postbox number in Amsterdam. No one knew even the name of the man who took him away, and no one had ever had an address, only this postbox in Holland. So I began to suspect he had been kidnapped. His father wanted him back at once, so I cabled the postbox, and the only reply was, 'Ahmed's return impossible. Wolfgang'. (Which is a German not a Dutch name.) I then began to suspect that he was after all in Germany, but that the man who took him' had covered his tracks thoroughly by having only a postbox address in Holland. So I got Margaret on it, and she is now informing the Dutch and German Ambassadors and the Moroccan Ministry of Foreign Affairs. And I divide my time between interviewing passport police and sitting by a telephone and talking to Ahmed's father through an interpreter, who I don't think interprets anything I say.

Next day, after looking through three thousand photographs at the passport office in Marrakesh, Gavin found Ahmed's passport form – bearing a different name – and also the dossier, which revealed no name or address for the German or Dutchman who had taken him away. The same day Ahmed's father received a letter in reply to his demand for his son's return which claimed that he had now been sent to England. Gavin wrote:

I then found in the father's house the only thing ever really written by

Ahmed, a postcard from *Germany*. So I came to Rabat and put the whole affair directly in the hands of the Moroccan Chief of Police, who took a serious view of it and handed it over to Interpol, who are now searching three countries for Ahmed. So I've done all I can. Not, you must admit, a very happy situation, more especially as I'm so sick with worry about it all that I can't sleep no matter how many pills I take.

What with the spying and throat-cutting and kidnapping, Gavin's inveterate thirst for drama was being slaked to a remarkable degree. But he was rapidly tiring of it all. The loss of Ahmed was a mortal blow to his plans, for he was not just his friend and travelling companion, but his tongue and his ears as well, for he was fluent in Berber, Arabic, French and English and could arrange visits, fix introductions, facilitate Gavin's passage through local society, and tend to the practicalities of camels, mules, water and lodgings off the beaten track. Without the able Moroccan to guide him the impractical Scottish author was left stranded and alone, deprived of the expertise and means of functioning that would have made his travels possible and his visit to Morocco meaningful. Trapped in his wretched room in the medina, a prey to mounting anxieties that gradually overwhelmed him, Gavin grew ever more aimless, depressed and fearful, till his mental state degenerated into a full-scale crack-up – the personal paralysis that lay at the heart of what he was to call *The Haywire Winter*.

I don't know when I've enjoyed a journey abroad less than this one,' he wrote to Jimmy. 'Everything has gone wrong, and everything is in a state of complete chaos. Not the happy carefree life that no doubt most people think I'm leading! I came across a piece in *The Times Literary Supplement* about me and Patrick Leigh Fermor, Peter Fleming and Alan Moorehead in my luggage today, and managed to raise a sardonic smile at the words, 'They feel, fit, lucky, successful people in a world dominated by the petulant,' etc. Oh, they do, do they, I said to myself . . . Well, the drumming and dancing and snake-charming and so ON and so FORTH go on in the square outside, but somehow this year I feel a bit cut off from it all, and friendless. I'd like to get my work done and come home.

As week followed week Gavin's love-affair with the Maghreb began to wither; yet he could not bring himself to leave. He was like a sleepwalker, he recalled, or someone in a hypnotic trance, living in an evil dream from which he could not wake. At the beginning of March he wrote to me:

The recent happenings have put the final spokes in all my wheels. I've rarely if ever felt so low. I've had dysentery on and off for some time, which I've now cured myself of with chloromycetin, but it's left me very run down and what with one thing and another I'm groggy both mentally and physically. I project a book called *The Haywire Winter*.

And a few weeks later: 'I've got some awful 'flu in place of the dysentery and I'm so full of antibiotics I can't 'ardly breave . . . ' Added to his depression and mental confusion, his physical debility made it difficult for him to summon up the energy to complete even the basic routine of the day. 'Clinically, I recognised symptoms I had seen in others,' he wrote; 'they were those of multiple division of aim, for I no longer knew why I was there.' In his notebook he added: 'It is hard to admit one has failed in all that one has attempted.'

During this nightmare time, Gavin wrote to Constance McNab, giving expression to his feeling of lostness and despair:

Here it is hot and dusty and everything takes a long time to do . . . I am burnt up, used up, not knowing where my loyalties lie: I am a reed shaken by a wind (or a tree shaken by a tempest?). I have lost a symbol and I cannot find another – or perhaps don't want to. My life during the past two months has been a *bateau ivre* with the gamut of all emotion, despair predominating over incessant work sleepless nights and apparently efficient days. Some day, if we are ever in the right mood, I'll tell you about it, but it will be only words, because it's incommunicable.

With the letter he enclosed the draft of a poem he had just written which would, he said, 'explain a lot'. The poem was entitled '*Tiz'n Test*', after the high, windswept pass of that name that crosses over the High Atlas, and referred to an episode during Gavin's travels the previous winter and to its aftermath in this present winter. It spoke of the solace of human love in the deep dark of a bleak and lonely wasteland, and of the bitter nihilism of subsequent betrayal. The poem was clearly addressed to Ahmed, and written in the depths of despair. The imagery, drawn from the wild world of Tiz'n Test, is striking.

> The darkness and the storm,
> Wind-scream, clang of iron,
> The shuddering walls,
> Crash of falling stone,
> Your warm and living flesh against my own . . .
>
> Sunrise and a ruined inn,
> Far off a jackal's cry;
> Dawn, and the world's age
> A vulture in the sky.
>
> Sleeping, insentient, you became the giver
> Of a brief borrowed world –
> Snowthaw and the blood-red river,
> Windsurge of bird;
> Became the archetypal lover
> Knowing a forgotten world.
>
> These your betrayal takes away for ever:
> World without sin,
> Desert and mountain we explored together;
> Where has it led, that road that neither
> Knew? Only the broken inn?

Not all of Gavin's poetry was expressed in verse form. In their imagery and intensity of emotion, some passages in his book *The Rocks Remain*, in which he was to express his anguished experiences in Morocco during the Haywire Winter, are really poems too. Such passages are not statements of pure documentary fact; but nor are they mere inventions; rather they are extrapolations that start from a basis in fact and from that basis build a structure of thought and emotion that states a poetic truth rather than a documentary one. There is no clearer example of Gavin's prose-poetry – his narrative of extrapolation – than the incident at the salt-marsh at Rabat. Late one evening, while staying at Margaret Pope's flat, Gavin went out for a walk in the salt-marsh at the edge of the city. After an hour or two he returned to the flat. He did not talk about his walk and after a little while he went to bed. Later, in *The Rocks Remain,* he developed this straightforward and relatively brief excursion into a haunting and disturbing narrative – a poetic extrapolation that enabled him to come much nearer to the 'real' truth (about his state of mind) than the literal truth could have done:

> One night I wandered on a salt-marsh; I left the streets of the city in which I was living because without solitude I could not resolve the tangle of my thoughts. When I set out the moon was bright. Before me rose ghostly flocks of flamingos; they wheeled pale but colourless in the moonlight, and alighted always ahead of me, so that their numbers became illimitable and all-enveloping. After a long time the moon was hidden by a cloud and I could no longer follow their flight. The only possible paths were the now unlit causeways, running always at right angles to each other, and I had lost my bearings. In utter darkness I came upon a shack. A figure little darker than the sky was somehow beside me and drew me into the warm darkness of the shelter. A bellows fanned a charcoal brazier, a bearded face thus lit by firelight glanced at me without apparent curiosity. '*Min fdl'k,*' he said. '*Min fdl'k*' (make yourself at home), and leaving the brazier he spread a blanket on the floor. I drank mint tea and then slept; in the cold hour of the dawn I was aware that small children came and laid more coverings upon me. No one asked me any questions . . .

Gavin's hastily scribbled notes recording his unhappy domicile in the medina of Marrakesh, some of which were later published in shortened form in *The Rocks Remain,* include some of his finest, most savagely observed and emotionally disturbed and disturbing travel writing. He stares with unhooded eyes into the very heart of horror, the suffering and degradation of the Third World poor, a mirror image of his own private, privileged hell. Here he comes close to the vision of true, naked reality, uncluttered by romanticism, Christian optimism, or any other brand of wishful thinking. Gavin Maxwell's medina is Joseph Conrad's Congo jungle of the *Heart of Darkness;* it is the dying words of the mad, ailing Kurtz – 'The horror! The horror!' Gavin's Marrakesh home and the backstreets that envelop it are an exotic version of T. S. Eliot's *Waste Land,* holding for him a similar abyss, a similar void, a similar terror of the unknown. 'The essential advantage for a poet,' Eliot had written, 'is not, to have a beautiful world with which to deal; it is to be able to see beneath both beauty and ugliness; to see the boredom, and the horror, and the glory.' Gavin's prose description of the nightmare of Marrakesh as he perceived it during the late winter of 1961 is essentially poetic. The imagery, alternating between pity and horror, emptiness and fear, is the clearly focused, uncompromising imagery of the poet deranged, of the front-line soldier after close-quarter carnage, of the condemned to death and the dying. On previous visits Morocco had seemed to him an inordinately beautiful and wondrous land. Images of glory, however, are few now. Instead he sees:

> Two hooded figures squat in the dust of the alley outside my door slitting the throats of chickens over a small drain; there is a terrible commotion from the dying wings as the knife cuts through each neck. The dust soaks up the blood slowly, cats paw at it petulantly and lick their toes. One evening at the close of Ramadan . . . '

Gavin's world in the medina was inhabited predominantly, if not exclusively, by an army of beggars, whose cries filled both his waking and his sleeping hours, reaching their height towards sundown, when the siren sounded the end of the day's fast. He did not have to stir far to see them. They were beneath his window and outside his door.

Not even in sleep was he spared the horror of the suffering he saw all around him. 'One night,' he wrote in his notebook,

> I woke from a dream to hear the blind beggar's invocation from the street outside, and my own voice saying, 'Give me back my eyes.' But to whomever these words were addressed, they were no more heard than the beggar's, who asked for so little while I asked for so much. I put an Arab shawl round my shoulders and fumbled my way blindly down the stairs and found the beggar and gave him more, probably, than he had ever received in his life.

At dawn he would wake, or half-wake, from the tension of his dreams, slip his feet out of bed and remain sitting there for a long time, with his eyes resting unfocused upon some ancient obscene scrawl or a crevice in the crumbling plaster of his cell. Recalling his depressive state, he wrote: 'An Arab friend said to me: "You must go – otherwise you never will. People can die like this, without reason; they turn inward and they are against themselves." '

As the haywire winter dragged on, Gavin's depression deepened. Only his physical removal from the scene could save him from continuing decline. Buried deep in the high mud-walled maze of the medina, Gavin was like a man ensnared. In the daytime the narrow view of the sky above was simply a blue blank; but at night he could snatch a glimpse of wider bounds, of infinity and eternity together, the rectangle of brilliant stars hanging above the clamorous city like a studded belt of diamonds on dark velvet; and here and there he could catch an enfiladed view of a more attainable freedom – the snow-covered mountains of the High Atlas caught in the last rays of the sun as it sank towards the Atlantic, the flights of white egrets homing in over the palms and minarets from the open country beyond the city walls. 'Far to the south were the bright deserts where I longed to be,' he wrote, 'the deserts of shimmering castellated mirage and bounding gazelle, the flowering deserts where from waterless stone *jol* grew the miracle of mauve blossom upon pale thorn.'

Gavin's occasional forays away from his confining cell in the medina did little to ease his distress, for they took him as often as not into a realm of farce and chaos. Sometimes they led him westward to Rabat and the restless haven of Margaret Pope's apartment, seething as ever with the ebb and flow of African ambassadors and revolutionaries. 'He used to come with his horrible animals,' Margaret Pope recalled, 'gigantic lizards and things from the desert. He tied them to my lampstands and tried to feed them flies – dead ones at first, then live ones. Once a lizard bit him, right through the quick of his fingernail, when he tried to force its mouth open to feed a live fly to it. So I took the thing to the kitchen and I was going to cut its head off but Gavin wouldn't let me. 'You don't know anything about animals,' I scolded him. 'You're just *emotionally* involved with them.

In Margaret Pope's flat Gavin found some distraction in the occupational therapy afforded by the domestic chores to which he and the politicians were assigned – sewing buttons, mending gloves, and other millinery diversions. For a few weeks he took part in a radio programme called 'Answers to your Questions' which was broadcast on Margaret Pope's English-speaking service of Moroccan Radio. Listeners' questions ranged from space travel to speleology, and the answers were provided by experts from UNESCO in Paris and the Science Division of OECD in London. To present these answers in a manner suitable for popular broadcasting, Margaret Pope conceived the idea of casting

Gavin in the role of 'Professor Svenski' – 'a miraculous combination of Bronowski, Russell, Huxley, and all the great specialised scientists of the decade'. Speaking with a stateless middle-European accent of the kind he had perfected in SOE during the war, Gavin solemnly held forth on every learned subject under the sun. Only when it was felt that to continue the deception would risk exposure was Gavin's role in the programme discontinued; listeners were told that Professor Svenski had left for Indonesia, while Gavin himself returned to his lonely rented room in Marrakesh.

From time to time there were other distractions. Much to the gratification of his highly developed sense of drama, he was caught up in the excitement of the street demonstrations that followed the death of the King of Morocco, Mohammed V in February 1961 – first in Casablanca and then in Marrakesh, where an armed guard was placed at the door to his quarters in the medina. Once, at the instigation of his official mentor in Morocco, His Excellency Moulay Ahmed el Alaoui, the mercurial Minister of Information, Tourism and Fine Arts, a one-eyed cousin of the late King and intimate of the heir apparent, he accompanied a party of fifty Berber beaters and two English sportsmen, *grands chasseurs* with a special permit to shoot the rare moufflon, the giant wild mountain sheep of the Atlas, on a hunting expedition in the foothills of the southern mountains, where he despatched a running boar with his only shot at three hundred yards.

Gavin's Moroccan notebook contains brief, cryptic references to other incidents and encounters in Morocco during that distracted winter:

> The tire aux pigeons
> Lady Steele Maffland – Marquise – visit – blank
> The duck shoot at Larache
> Murder of Ghouié
> The angry bull at Sodom and Gomorrah
> Visit by stately negro at night to explain cause

and so on. Since no fuller account was forthcoming later, these episodes must remain for ever enigmatic spoors in the sand.

Gavin realised that the only solution for his helpless condition, for the inertia and depression that held him prisoner, was to leave the country altogether and go home. But time and again he postponed his departure, unable to break away, unable to burst through the barrier which confined him, the nature of which he could not understand.

> I would try sometimes to think of Camusfearna in March sunshine, of the waterfall and the budding birches of primroses among dead bracken, of the soft mountain distances and blue sea, but always the image would dissolve before it was complete. Before it was strong enough to draw me from where I was.

Finally Gavin wrote home suggesting that Jimmy Watt should come out to Morocco to help him with his return journey. Jimmy arrived in the last week of March, and the hypnotic spell was broken. But the unpredictable twists and turns of the Haywire Winter persisted to the very end, for Gavin's exit from Morocco was both farcical and triumphal, a source of hilarity that belied the tortured months that had gone before. He had booked a passage home on a freighter from Casablanca, but the day he and Jimmy were due to deliver the Land Rover at the docks turned out to be the day that Marshal Tito, the President of Yugoslavia, was to begin a state visit to the city. The road to the port – the processional route – was sealed off by army and police roadblocks and decorated with flags and bunting and lined with great crowds of spectators, including tribesmen trucked down from the hills. All traffic had been diverted and there was not a single vehicle on the broad, mile-long avenue when Gavin drove up to the police point that barred further progress.

As it happened, Moulay Ahmed had furnished him with a number of highly official documents to facilitate his travels around the country, including a government *laissez-passer* and a police *coupefile* which allowed him, to all intents and purposes, to ignore any police order or regulation that got in his way. Presenting these papers to the officer in charge, Gavin was astonished to be waved through the roadblock. Ahead lay the empty avenue and a great, expectant crowd lining both sides as far as the eye could see. The Land Rover was evidently the first vehicle that had passed along this route all day, and as Gavin swept along it the crowd pressed forward. Some, taking him for an outrider, clapped and raised a ragged cheer. Others, the Berber tribesmen from the hills, mistook Gavin, if not for Tito, then at least for one of his entourage. They burst out drumming and dancing, they sang and swayed to the rhthym of their age-old tribal dances. Thus honoured and acclaimed, Gavin and Jimmy passed through the serried ranks of Arab well-wishers and Berber mountain-men, their faces fixed in discreet smiles, their arms raised nonchalantly in a gesture halfway between a wave and a salute, till they safely reached their journey's end.

The next day they shipped the Land Rover on board a small freighter full of oranges and tortoises and headed home across the Bay of Biscay. Ahead of Gavin lay another year at Camusfearna and a new life as a famous author; behind him the Haywire Winter withered and died on the Maghreb shore. 'I have buried the rest of it in the compost heap of my subconscious,' he was to write later, 'and now it only returns to me in the poignancy of dreams, urgent and febrile, in which are implicit the sense of some task unfinished, some goal unattained – sometimes I have thought it was death.'

On 11 April 1961 Gavin arrived back in Britain. From Sandaig I sent him a letter reassuring him that the otters were well and happy, and warning him about the smoke that sometimes emerged from behind the panelling in the kitchen-parlour. From the pathologist at London Zoo I received a letter: 'I was delighted to hear that Edal is now almost normal again. The recovery of this animal is a fantastic success story. I think you should all be extremely proud of the way that you have saved her life.'

A couple of days later, at the end of nearly half a year at Camusfearna, I set off on my long journey south. Through the dark days and stormy winds of the Haywire Winter, Avalon and its wild creatures had prevailed. But these had been the final months. With the coming of summer, Avalon was to prevail no more.

So in due course Gavin and I changed places and went home, and the year finally ended for both of us in improbable ways – for Gavin the last fairy-tale days of his old life at Sandaig prior to his giant wedding bash at Claridge's, for me a late-night New Year's Eve knees-up at the Karimjee Club in Zanzibar and a wander through the moonlit narrow alleys of Zanzibar's ancient Stone Town arm in arm with an extraordinarily pretty Zanzibari princess, both of us carolling the tropic New Year night with such appropriate seasonal ditties as 'My old man's a dustman, he wears a dustman's hat, he wears gorblimey trousers, what do you think of that . . . ?'

For both Gavin, looking out over the moonlit North Atlantic from Sandaig Bay, and for myself looking out over the moonlit Indian Ocean from a beach in Zanzibar, the future seemed uncertain and obscure. None of us knew where, literally or metaphorically, the wind would blow us. In Zanzibar it was literally still blowing due south, towards the Antarctic, not Africa. For Gavin it was metaphorically driving him towards wedlock and prospects that seemed no less perilous than ours.

But for the moment it was still a world of magic. That New Year's Eve at Sandaig the snow fell thickly and laid a pristine white mantle two feet thick right down to the sea's edge. It turned intensely cold, so that the burn froze over, followed by the waterfall itself, with icicles more than seven feet long and as thick as a man's arm.

Those last days of Gavin's old life at Sandaig were fairy-tale days, the hills a crisp, blinding white, the sea blue, the night skies starlit and bare. A toboggan was improvised for Teko the otter to slide down the hill, and as it slowed he would kick ecstatically with his hind legs to keep the contraption in motion. With the roads blocked by snow, Gavin took to the sea in his motor launch. 'The winter sun was just up in a bare blue sky,' he was to record of one enchanted voyage, 'and the green white hills all about us were salmon-pink above a smooth enamel sea of beetle-wing blue.' But three days after Gavin left Camusfearna, Teko attacked Jimmy Watt – an act of savagery that would soon lead to the confinement of the last of the famous otters and mark the end of the Camusfearna idyll.

If the savagery of the otters destroyed the myth of Camusfearna, the failure of his shortlived marriage would be the first stage in the destruction of Gavin himself, and other stages were soon to follow – the destruction of Camusfearna by fire and the death of Edal in the smoking ruins, followed not long after by Gavin's own mortal sickness and death from cancer.

On Thursday, 18 September 1969 – under a clear, singing sky and a dry east wind, the trees just touched with autumn gold, the Skye hills still green across the dancing waters of the Sound, Gavin's ashes were laid to rest at the exact spot where his writing desk had once stood, the desk on which he had written *Ring of Bright Water,* before a small assembly of family and friends, who had gathered to pay their last respects. Two weeks later, Teko, the last of the Camusfearna otters, drowned after suffering an epileptic fit.

And so it was ended, everything had vanished, swept away as if it had never been: the man, the otters, the house, the vision of Camusfearna. Only the ring remained, the waterfall ceaselessly tumbling, the burn winding round to the sea.

Avalon was lost. Or was it, then, truly gained at last ?

Sleeper beneath the rowan tree,
You have become your dream,
Sky, shore, and silver sea.

ABOUT THE AUTHOR

DOUGLAS BOTTING is a writer and biographer whose previous books reflect his interest in travel, exploration and wild places. After reading English at Oxford, he accompanied scientific and filming expeditions to Socotra and Southern Arabia, the Sahara and Lake Tchad, the Amazon, Mato Grosso and Andes, Arctic Siberia and Central Asia, and many parts of north, east, west and central Africa. He was for a time BBC Special Correspondent in Moscow and has worked on assignments for BBC TV, Time-Life, *Geographical Magazine* and other UK and US publications in various parts of the world. He became a full-time author with the publication of his highly praised biography of the German explorer-naturalist Alexander von Humboldt (*Humboldt and the Cosmos*) and has subsequently written three other biographies – *Hitler's Last General, Gerald Durrell: The Authorised Biography* (shortlisted for the BP Natural World Book prize), and more recently *Dr Eckener's Dream Machine* (the story of the round-the-world Zeppelin). 'The Haywire Winter' is taken from perhaps his most engaging biography – *Gavin Maxwell: A Life*. Douglas Botting is a Fellow of the Royal Geographical Society and a Member of the Royal Institute of International Affairs and the Biographers' Club.

Wheels within Wheels – Gavin Maxwell

Hamish Brown

One evening towards the end of the Sixties I was standing watching the scene on the Jema el Fna when a gentleman in a smart *djellaba* standing beside me turned to ask, 'Excuse me, are you English?'

I replied, 'Depends how you mean it. I'm actually Scottish'.

He laughed. 'Of course. I know the differences too. I have been to Scotland. Stayed near Doune.'

We talked a bit more then he rather diffidently broached the subject of his optimistic curiosity in the first place.

'I wonder, oh it's such unlikely, and, oh silly to ask really, but you wouldn't, by any chance, perhaps, know of a Scottish writer by the name of Gavin Maxwell?' Now, it takes something to shock any Moroccan into silence, but I did with my reply.

'Oh yes, I was staying with him a couple of weeks ago.'

Not surprisingly we shifted to a café for mint tea and talk and then I was carried off through a bewildering number of alleys to his house buried deep in the medina. Those blank walls with plain doors do not lend themselves to easy navigation but I coped with all the rights and lefts to find my way out, and back again, on several occasions, to enjoy Mohammed's generous hospitality. Initially he had had a motive, seen in his Fna question which, like an arrow loosed at random, found gold.

He was the one-time secretary to the notorious Glaoui Pasha of Marrakesh who, from such power under the French, virtually ruled the Atlas and helped to depose the sultan, the grim, fascinating story Maxwell wrote about in *Lords of the Atlas*. With the sultan's return the house of Glaoui fell ('and great was the fall of it'), with the villain dying shortly after his humiliation; death almost as an act of diplomacy. His palaces and kasbahs of course were devastated so this was not a good period to be associated with the name. Si Mohammed El Khizzioui lived very discreetly in the Marrakesh Medina. He had been present throughout the final dramas.

Maxwell, researching in Morocco, found Mohammed and of course he was a primary source of information. Although *Lords of the Atlas* had been published Mohammed had received no copy, nor had many important papers been returned. Would I help when I next visited Maxwell?

There seemed no reason why I shouldn't, but in the end I never did find the opportunity. Maxwell's home had gone up in flames (January 1968) so any documents would have been destroyed and it was simpler just to give my kind Marrakesh host some books myself – which I did. (Maxwell died in 1969.)

Though Mohammed was naturally disappointed at the loss of the papers his home was still mine to visit. A couple of years later I arrived at his door in the middle of the celebrations for his sister's return from the *haj* and, when I tried to excuse myself, he would not hear of my going away. The graciousness of Moroccan hospitality is something the west could learn from.

Came the year I headed across the Fna towards the medina and Mohammed's house -and couldn't find it. I spent *hours* wandering in the maze, no doubt making things worse at every step. I tried several times over the next few months, and the year after, I haunted the Fna and its cafés but the thread was broken. I never saw Mohammed again. This may seem incredible but those who know the medina will understand – and sympathise.

I had known Maxwell for some years and we also coincided in Morocco, he researching his book, friends and myself exploring the mountaineering richness of the High Atlas. Some of the book I'd read in manuscript in Scotland and just how we became acquainted is a story in itself.

I was teaching in Fife and had a school historical project on the drovers, the hardy men who could drive cattle from Skye to London. The climax of our studies was to go and trek a drovers' route from Killin to Skye, crossing from Glenelg where, in those days, the beasts were swum across the narrows to the mainland. With a day to spare we explored south down the coast but stopped short of Maxwell's 'Camusfeama' (the setting of the *Ring of Bright Water)* for we knew his peace was much disturbed by unwanted visitors.

However, our dixi, intended for lunchtime tea-making, was filled with marine life including one extraordinary looking creature I'd never seen before, and I knew my western seaboard. So risking Maxwell's ire we eventually invaded his house seeking the identity of this fish. He was a naturalist after all. None of his books helped so the poor creature was sent off to the Natural History Museum. (It proved a Cornish sucker fish whose normal range was round the Scilly Isles!) Maxwell enjoyed the boys' visit and it led to subsequent visits with school parties to stay at that magical spot.

There was to be a coda to the Marrakesh connection. When the splendid biography of Maxwell was being written the reason for the coolness with Mohammed appeared. He had thoroughly ripped off Maxwell over visits to Telouet and so on, disagreements that even involved solicitors. But then, Maxwell struck me as something of an innocent abroad, full of romantic dreams and never very practical in situations where money was involved. I found this *post scriptum* more ironic than sad.

Well, it's all a long time ago now. Mohammed was an old man when I met him and must have died many decades ago, Maxwell didn't long survive his dreams going up flames and, today the sultan's grandson is King of Morocco and the Dar Glaoui at Telouet crumbles away. Some monuments remain.

Maxwell's *Lords of the Atlas* has just been re-published and remains as well read as ever.

ABOUT THE AUTHOR

HAMISH BROWN is a writer, traveller and photographer who, since 1965, has spent a couple of months each year exporing the Atlas Mountains. In 1995 he made an end-to-end Atlas trek of 96 days, from Taza to Manri, and has used this as the basis for a book *The Mountains Look on Marrakesh*. He has written or edited over twenty books, ranging from children's stories and poetry to classic mountaineering tales, for which he was awarded a D.Litt from St Andrews University in 1997 and most recently an MBE. He still organises and leads small exporatory treks and climbs, cultural tours and flower and birding trips in Morocco.

Birds of Marrakesh

Horatio Clare

My first overseas trip for the BBC, though put together in a hurry, and done on the cheap, nevertheless took me to the old heart of Marrakesh. Suddenly, we needed a radio feature about the story-telling cultures of Morocco. After three days on the phone, I was strapping myself into a slightly tatty old McDonnell Douglas in Milan Malpensa. We flew along the Cote D'Azur, above Barcelona and down, over Granada, across the Med again, the Atlantic, and into Casablanca. Casablanca! A white city, with racing traffic, Art Deco cinemas like space ships and corner cafes where old France still lurks like an undercoat behind peeling mint walls. I took the train to Marrakesh. First the land was bright green and soft, like a sponge. There were no fences, just rolling grass. Here and there red tracks cut irregular shapes through the sward, occasionally supervised by men in rust-coloured djelebas, cloaked figures with pointed hoods. I fell asleep. When I woke the land was orange and brown, hills of sand and shale. Here, as in so many places in Morocco, battles were fought. Here invaders and sultans attacked and defended Marrrakech. Night fell. Some lights appeared, bobbing about beyond the windows, more lights, then a platform, and the train stopped. According to the station clock, we had arrived seventeen seconds early.

My Petit Taxi driver had a sense of occasion. 'Your first time in Marrakesh?' (Many Moroccans say it with a certain relish, accelerating through the syllables, so the middle becomes a sort of growl and the end a satisfying woosh.)

' I have been twice before – I am lucky.'

'So, you like?'

'I do!'

The Jamma al Fna was thronged. White smoke and ruddy yellow light rising ragged into the night sky, crowds of people, many of them dark, sub-Saharan men in white robes, swaying back and forth. The image was almost hallucinatory, an effect I had only ever experienced before when looking across great flocks of flamingos; hundreds go one way, hundreds the other, until the frame of your vision starts to shimmer. Above and behind it, the drums, a particular syncopation, in strange harmony with a thin hullabaloo of pipes.

My hoped-for hotel was full but I was met in the lobby by a teenager, Laila, who led me through a maze of medina streets to a riad hotel, run by a Frenchman, who appeared to be enjoying a mid-life crisis and a very beautiful girlfriend half his age. The riad had only recently opened for guests – the paint in the shower was still wet and stained the soles of my feet bright blue.

I woke at quarter past five with the cries of *muezzin* echoing through the house. I vowed to prepare for it, next time, with my minidisc recorder, and slept again.

When I emerged onto the roof for breakfast the air was warm, and infinitely blue, and filled with swifts – in March. I started recording that morning. Listening now I can hear collared doves, (beautiful, lavender-brown pigeons which rule the rooftops) cockerels and the marvellous, mousy squeaking of swifts.

At half-past eleven I was in the Cafe de France with Spain's greatest living novelist, Juan Goytisolo. The Cafe de France, one of those legendary establishments which exist more in literature than in life, where one might well encounter Spain's greatest living novelist, or anyone else, is divided into distinct spaces, territories, which are observed by all cogniscenti. Goytisolo had been specific – inside, not on the terrace. When later I met Sharif, whose capacity to conjure magical reality from the alleys of the city matched the prowess with which the Senor created fictional events, he too insisted on the interior. Peter Mayne wrote there, not outside. Outside, on the terrace, is the place to watch the world, and be seen by it. Inside, in cool, green shadow, one does business.

I arrived early and waited, fiddling with my equipment. A man came in and I met his eye, leapt to my feet and covered the distance between us in an easy stride. I offered my hand, clasped his and gave him a heartfelt smile. 'Senor Goytisolo!' I said, gratefully.

'I don't understand,' said the man, in French, smiling around, suspecting he had been set up.

'Merci,' I said solemnly, and returned to my seat.

When he arrived, on the stroke of half past eleven, the old writer was entirely unmistakable. He was small and wore a sludge-green linen suit. His hair has receeded under time and sun, the brown pate neatly framed with a shadow of what once must have been thick hair, sculpted with a razor, the way Marrakeshi barbers do. The long nose curled dramatically down, like a parrot's beak. Couched below drooping lids, the eyes regarded me with an almost pained good humour. A sophisticated and infinitely benign old vulture. A vastly accomplished, former exile, bisexual, surrealist widower in a mournful air and photo-sensitive green sunglasses, he reminded me of a distinguished politician, a public figure in state service. One of the Good, but tough. Like a pistol wouldn't phase him much.

He leads the way to an alley behind the Cafe de France, pausing to greet a small, lined old man with a huge open mouth. This man's expression is awed and delighted. They shake hands, touch their hearts, exchange a few words before we move on.

'My friend is a very great story teller,' Goytisolo says quietly, 'one of the best. He was very patient, very kind to me.'

He speaks with a Spanish slipped lisp, slowly. The grammar is almost perfect, the vocabulary good, but he is very unsure of it, apologises more than once.

'I have used it only for one week, fifteen years . . . ago . . . In New York, at Columbia.'

The riad behind the door in the wall which he opens is quiet, even for Marrakesh. The courtyard is filled with a great tree beneath which we sit. We drink water. People, two women cleaning and a child, move around at the edge of the microphone's range. We begin.

In the tree above us, a beautiful thrush-like bird begins to call, a loud, musical chiiieeew! performed over and over with animal gusto. I edge closer to Goytisolo.

I am clumsy, ignorant. I try to draw him into general descriptions of the Jamma al Fna, overviews, summaries. He replies slowly, sometimes answering, sometimes ignoring the question. I try wide open invitations, questions about his life. Sometimes I think he misunderstands, but he has heard these questions before, answered them – he gives me the name of his English translator. There is no impatience about him, but we are frustrated, I am not giving us a chance.

We get on to the storytellers. He tells me he saw them in 1976 and vowed he would not leave until he could understand them. He learned, with their help. He tells me the story of the storks, men and women who have chosen to become birds in order to see the world, returning to Morocco if and when they will. Goytisolo wrote a story based on the Berber tale. 'It was published here. One of the storytellers asked me to translate it to colloquial Arabic – to tell it again.'

'As if fired by a premonition I went to see my oldest brother: I told him I'd decided to go to Europe and handed my children over to him for their temporary care and education. That fretful phase of my life was abruptly at an end.

'The following day I was aloft with a flock of storks in an ineffable state of bliss and delight. The world was at once miniature and immense: toy towns and landscapes, seas gleaming like mirrors, white mountains . . . My altitude, lightness and speed of movement granted me a feeling of superiority over humans, slow as turtles, tiny like insects.'

We talk about the relationship between storytelling and literature. He refers to the work of Walter Ong, and what Ong calls 'secondary orality': oral traditions carried into print.

'Not only in poetry, where evidently rhythm is of huge importance, fundamental, but also in prose. James Joyce . . . is a magnificent example, in English; Celine, in French – Ardo Schmidt, in German – Cabrera Infante in Cuban – have you read *Three Trapped Tigers*? Magnificent. There is a close relationship between traditional orality and the Avant Garde novel in the twentieth century.'

I press him on the links between Moorish and Arabic stories and European literature. Where, in whose works, can we see the stories crossing from one continent, one faith, to another?

'The first novel to be influenced by The Thousand and One Nights is Don Quixote. It's very close . . . he knew (Cervantes) . . . Then there are the Sarasine Chronicles, there is Flaubert, Orientalism, Richard Burton . . .

'One of my friends, the story teller Sarouk, – he is very fine, a very fine person – he was never being serious, always making comic criticisms of Moroccan society, customs and attitudes – I heard him telling a story in the square which was also written in Castillian in the fourteenth century. I was amazed!'

We circle the square (I am still trying to get him to sum it up with some perfectly chosen words) and return to it again.

'When I first came to Jamma al Fna, I found here everything I had been reading in Bakhtin, the carnival.'

One of Bakhtin's ideas was that a carnival can be taken as a metaphor for the playful, lawless aspects and effects of literature. The critic and scholar dubbed his theory 'Carnivalesque', he might have described it, in the manner of my faux-academic territorialisation of the Cafe de France deployed above, as a model of resistance to, play against and subversion of officialdom and the everyday world.

'I found all the things he describes. The magicians, acrobats, the dubious (he charms me unaware with his pronunciation 'dub-ioos') elements of society . . . '

'One of the great influences on Spanish literature, on European literature, was the Arch Priest of Hita. He wrote in the fourteenth century. One day I was in the square and I heard one of the storytellers tell the same story which is told by L'Arceprieste D'Hita.'

By implication, the story originated in Africa and has lived as long in minds and mouths on the Jamma al Fna as it has in European books. The roots of 'our' literature are alive, exposed and flourishing in the noisy square 100 metres away.

'There is a huge Moorish influence on Europe, but today there is much hatred and racism towards Moroccans in Spain, particuarly in the south of Spain.'

Goytisolo remains engaged with hatred and racism. Weeks after I saw him he went to the West Bank, one of the PEN delegation which included Wole Soyinka.

So what is the secret of the haphazard square, that it should nuture and maintain men, traditions, stories, through time and change? A triangle, explains Goytisolo, conceding to my appeals for simplification.

'In the west, such spaces are the aim, the future. People come here to try to discover how it works, how to recreate it in the world elsewhere. They did a study to discover why the Jamma al Fna is as it is, a study with questionnaires. They found three reasons. People come for the market, to sell and buy, for entertainment, and to eat. That is all. Change one thing and it will all disappear.'

It is a researcher's conclusion, a tiny, stunted answer compared to those Goytisolo reached years ago, and has published. The final section of his novel 'Makbara' is a chapter entitled 'A reading of space in the Xemaa-El-Fna' which would be definitive, were it not concerned with a site which is itself the very definition of elusive, permanent change. A kaleidoscope of repeating pattern, fractal, never and always the same.

> Survival of the nomad ideal as a utopia: a universe without government or a leader, the free circulation of persons and goods, land owned and used in common, the tending of flocks, sheer centrifugal force: the abolition of private property and hierarchy, of rigid spatial boundaries, of domination based on sex and age, of the ugly accumulation of wealth: emulating the fruitful freedom of the gypsy who respects no frontiers.

So much for the theory. I was anxious not to repay Senor Juan's kindness with a test of his patience. The hour had gone, too fast, of course. He escorted me to the door. There in the alley was a small child with dark hair and eyes who kissed Goytisolo's cheek, then mine. I left them there, the old man smiling and occasionally commenting on the boy's chatter.

I think of him often in his quiet riad; a widower's home, where the shadows remember his wife, whom he still loves, whose whole name he used: 'I used to come to Marrakesh for six months of every year until my wife, Monique Lange, died. Since then I have lived here all the time.'

Apart from the flamingo flock in which I waver, of journalists, parodists, derivers, and autobiographers, students of one kind or another, he is another thing, an artist whom accomplishment and endeavour have set free, even from fascism and exile. When he said 'James Joyce' it seemed to me that I sat with a rare descendant, of equivalent intellect and vision to the writers he named. It was at the time a star-struck, uncritical reaction, but having since read 'Makbara' and 'Landscape after the Battle', I defend it. I mean to follow his work and progress, if not all his example. 'I find I re-read more as I get older,' he said. The rest of it, the peace mission, the writing, the efforts to tear down Spanish and European racism – he down-plays, though it is almost the most a man can do.

Lunch was in the new town with an highly charming and very witty Marrakeshi whose number I had been lucky enough to obtain in London; Richard Lawson. 'I'll be standing outside the pizza place. I'm wearing all black – and bright yellow slippers, actually.'

'Hello, he said as we met 'You look like you're looking for someone.' He looked like a Hollywood producer hiding under a metalhead t-shirt and much hair.

Over pizza Richard talked about the Sahara, the High Atlas, Hamish Brown and Marrakesh, among other things. I asked about the city's economy. 'You can get anything you like in Marrakesh,' he said, reflectively. 'Half the wealth of the Sultans came from prostitution.'

He was surprised that I was surprised. One wonders what goes on behind the doors of Marrakesh, but it would be a persistent visitor who obtained the merest clue. Which is why, as a real journalist once said, 'When you arrive somewhere in the middle of something you know nothing about, you pray for someone like Sammy.' In that instance Sammy was a Zanzibari midget with a landrover and two friends who could clearly sort you out. Lucky me, Richard was a friend of his equivalent in Marrakesh – Sharif.

It was agreed that my third appointment should be in the Cafe de France at four – inside, not on the terrace. 'Well, he looks a bit like a bear, I suppose. Shambling. Doesn't have many front teeth. I'll be interested to hear how it goes,' Richard said. He also mentioned that Sharif enjoyed unparalleled access and freedom within the town walls – the one and only official unofficial guide. 'Knows everyone. When I met him he was living in a garage – I think it's his office now.'

Sharif and I recognised each other almost instantly. We left the cafe by the back door (I am deplorably easily impressed) and in a few moments, really very quickly, I had explained what I was doing and what we needed, and we were in the street of scribes.

The shop are open-fronted and divided by tables. At each, scribes, mostly women, sit typing. On the other sides of their typewriters sit their customers, mostly men, who talk and idle, waiting for their words to be written. We stopped and sidled into one such scene. With Sharif translating, the typist, who wore white and had curling oriental eyes, said she could type wills, business, letters, contracts – anything. 'Love letters?' I demanded, which got smiles but no answer. Which did she prefer? Contracts, because they are most lucrative, at 100 Dirhams a time (£7). I wondered about the relationship, the trust between writer and customer. My questions met frowns and mistranslations. There was no issue of trust – 'What you say, she write it. What you don't say, she don't write it!' Sharif put it.

There is plenty of work for these writers. Morocco's illiteracy rate is about forty per cent. Given a modest amount of money, illiteracy would be the least of one's problems – nothing, compared to losing that small capital. Among the coming generations, employment is the exception – and even a university degree, statistically, no help. While the educated population grows, wealth and influence remain with the elite. Miserable, dusty poverty is everywhere, especially, it seemed in the streets, among older men and single mothers. The country's history has never been dull, and shows ominous promise of interesting times ahead.

Typewriters have their beauty, especially those which write Arabic, but my generation are fortunate to have avoided them. On the disc, you can hear the hammer-chatter as the lady in white works. We stand a while, recording. After a couple of lines you hear me say, idiotically struck, 'It's pretty hard work, isn't it?'

Sharif assents with feeling.

We returned to the Jamma Al Fna, in search of storytellers. Sharif produced three, in a line, each with a small crowd around him. Sharif winced at the microphone; I covered it with the flap of my bag. This muffled ambient sound, focusing the effective field into a tight cone off my right hip, and added a mission-wrecking 'thump' to the soundtrack, every second pace.

The first we came to was the old friend of Goytisolo's, haranguing his audience. I asked Sharif to translate, but all he gave me were half lines 'old stories, some old stories . . . ' and 'old Kings . . . all kinds of things . . . '

How seized Goytisolo must have been, that first time. Imagine him, following every word, watching every flinch on the listeners' faces, watching the storyteller's eyes, his hands. And the irresistable impulse, the demand of himself and them. I will learn to understand you.

Then, suddenly, the storyteller stops. The audience remonstrate with him but he rebuffs them. I am still trying to get the bag, and Sharif, closer. 'What happened? How did it end?'

'It hasn't ended,' growls Sharif. 'He won't say – wants money.' Some of the crowd, particularly those crouched near the old man's feet, sound quite frustrated by the tactic, torn between demanding and trying to wheedle the rest from the raconteur.

I felt the License Payer would well understand this pay-to-view predicament, and pitched in with the Dirhams. The story resumed, ended with much emphasis and many rough and beautiful words, not one of which I understood, and nor would Sharif translate them for me.

The second talker squatted on the ground, which made his voice easy to record. (Dangling from a hand, the bag got everything perfectly, at knee level.) These were Koranic stories and commentaries, the Hadiths. We did not linger, drawn to the largest of the three crowds.

The man at the centre of this circle was kneeling beside a small mat, on which stood a phial containing yellow liquid and a sprig of what appeared to be Rosemary. He was chanting out his words at some speed, his voice rich, swooping theatrically, like a livestock auctioneer.

'What is he saying?'

Sharif was very taken, almost transfixed. 'About a man. A sick man . . . '

'Yes?'

'He is very ill, very weak . . . cold..'

'Ok, yes?'

'He takes this pill . . . this . . . aphrodisiac . . . '

'Aphrodisiac!'

'Yes it stops cold, stops tired.'

All the while the crowd grew, and it seemed the yellow phial must surely boil in the heat of attention turned upon it, when, joy of joys, I understood a phrase, isolated French in the torrent of colloquial Arabic. It was spoken fast and with some derision: 'Il a achete un valioom!' As if some shop-bought valioom could compare with a yellow phial and sprig.

I am in no doubt that had I wanted hidden treasures, counterfeit currency, false papers, drugs or forty whores Sharif could have pointed me in the right direction. I utterly failed to exploit him, but his telephone number and the location of his office remain prized souvenirs of our encounter. I spent the evening on the roof, gazing at the blue and white Atlas and listening through the recordings. The remaining tasks were clear: Saturday night on the Jamma Al Fna, then, later, the muezzin.

Over dinner I had the gratifying experience of being accused, by the other guests, a young German couple and an elderly Dutch couple, all and any of whom could have been spies, of being a spy. I made such a fool of myself, delightedly denying it, that I thought for a moment I might have accidentally double-bluffed them.

I talked to the teenager, Laila, the Riad's receptionist and caretaker-manager. She wore tight, western clothes and pink lipstick. She envied my return ticket, my freedom. Yes, she could apply for a visa, but the waiting, the questions, the money, the endless forms. She shrugged and pouted, insulted, as many Moroccans are, by the anachronistic prejudice against them among Europeans.

'I just want to go to France to see how people are there, what they do, how they are.'

'How they are?'

'How the women are with men. It is very important for me, I think. To see how people live there.'

She shook her head. 'I do not think I will go. I don't think so.'

'What, then?'

'I will live here in Marrakesh. Marry a man, if I am lucky!'

Later, dined, miced and hyped, I made my way through the alleys towards the light and noise. The sound comes on with a thump, voices, scooters, the night, music, conversation outside a mosque. We head for the music, dancing through the traffic stream, the way one crosses the road in Marrakesh, with great circumspection, trying to strike instant and cautious bargains with the drivers of taxis, bikes and mule carts. Through a line of orange juice sellers, and on, into a crowd, who are clustered around a Gnaoua band. A fiend and a gypsy girl are dancing. The crowd mills closer – on the disc you can hear the space tightening around the microphone.

The gypsy danced, spinning, first on one foot, then the other, and the fiendish character of the old violinist was a delight to see, as he sawed and sliced the bow across his instrument's throat. The violin was grasped behind the head, and planted butt-down on a block, pinned upright and wailing. The crowd was male and we were all near hypnotised by the dancer, who wore her hair in braids and rustled with silver – one of the very few whites in the middle of the square.

'Harups! Harups!' shouts someone near by, passionate and dead on mic. Then the band's hats come round and, cravenly, I join the dance of the non-paying guest. The population shifts and shuffles in ripples, sometimes great waves, after a finale. An old man bust into song beside me, 'Ooh–Ayy Mellou!' he sang. I lingered, looking elsewhere, sucking his sound into my bag. Then on to another crowd, this time everyone singing, a hundred or more, 'Whoaa–

oah–oah–ooaaah, oah–oah–ooaaah, oah–oh–OH!' A wonderful rolling tune, small boys and old men alike, holding it, belting it out, smiling with their eyes over the top of their open mouths. Then there is a growling sound and you hear me apologise. Then the growl returns, louder, and transforms itself into an unmistakable offer. 'Grroaoa . . . Hashisch?!' My answer, relatively high-pitched, sounds comical. 'C'est gentil, mais non merci!' I pipe. I would like to have cut it in alongside Goytisolo's description of the 'dubi-oos' elements – the most blatant dope peddling ever transmitted on Radio 3 – but lacked the nerve.

After an hour of acrobats (not great radio) more drums, dancers and all manner of random sales pitches, I withdrew to the hotel and turned in, setting the alarm for 5 a.m. When it woke me the house was silent, and I climbed the stone stairs as if in a dream. Up top it was raining. Red Saharan sand and sprays of drizzle blew down over the Atlas, veiling and smearing what lights were visible. On the rooftops all around things waved and creaked in the wind, and on the sound horizon there was a kind of moaning, as if devotees were doing Salaams in their sleep. I switched on the mic and started the recording. It is obvious on the disc: the sound is men, tuning their voices, their thoughts, their very souls. An overture in complete surround sound – in Marrakesh one is encircled by minarets. The greatest, the Koutoubia, was the one bright light, a pale flame towering above the black nodding heads of the palms.

I wish I had had a camera as well as the minidisc. Above the Koutoubia, clear in the light of the vertical spotlights which illuminate the tower, a great hawk was hovering. It looked like one of the kestrel family, but much larger than any I have ever seen. It was absolutely stationary apart from shivering wings, and appeared to hang directly over the point on top of the four golden balls. It was almost unbelievable, yet it was not an hallucination. The rain rose and died, rose again and died, and then, from the Koutoubia there was a single clicking sound and a great voice filled the night. 'Allah Akbar!' Slow, old and electrifying, my heart jumped and the wind began to blow again. As the repeated phrase ended, the cry was answered from another minaret, then another, and all of them, and the sound rolled and hollered over the city. The rain and wind swelled again, the night answering the voices, and I found myself doubling over the microphone, shielding it against the gusts, almost prostrate, and facing East!

With the wuther of the wind, the hissing rain and the crying, declaiming voices, it was as intense an experience as I have ever had. At once physical, auditory and visual, it was also unsettlingly, arrestingly spiritual. As the skirls of rain rilled around the few orange lights and things flapped on the flat roofs, and the muezzin called their God by name, I felt myself to be standing in an outlying town of a great Empire, and wondered how a civilisation based on materialism, such as ours, can even engage a civilisation founded upon faith, unless it be through a common memory of a time when we all believed in God.

I was very sad to leave the next day. I had resolved to walk through town to the station, so packed my things and prepared to go in good time. Farewells were said: the maid, the Frenchman, his girl. There was no sign of Laila so I left her a 'goodbye' with the maid and set out. The rush hour was taking place in a picture-peach evening, the city walls glowed and you could smell flowers where the road passed the Menara gardens. Arriving at the station with ten minutes to spare, I was amazed to find Laila waiting by the main door. She had taken a taxi. 'You didn't say goodbye!'

We sat on a bench on platform one. I offered apologies which were slowly accepted. I was not supposed to be smoking at the time but cigarettes seemed to be called for. I offered Laila one, knowing she smoked. She accepted, hesitantly, and we lit up. Every time a man walked past us Laila cupped her cigarette in her hand and stared into the distance. The men came often, passing and re-passing, their assumption plain in their frowns. An obviously unmarried Marrakeshi girl and a single male tourist taking awkward leave. Laila was discomforted by the situation but she stoked it nevertheless, all reproachful looks and loud shrugs. I tried to write my innocence and respectability large across my expression, and failed like a fool. You felt that anything, Laila's cigarette, could tip the silent disapproval into public outrage and shouting. A similar sensation, ironically, to that which one experiences upon lighting up in public in California.

She toughed it out. Took my telephone number very carefully, made sure I wrote hers down correctly. We resolved to get in touch whenever we were in the other's city. I urged her to call – whenever, as soon as she arrived in Britain or France – and she smiled assent with heroic sarcasm.

Predictably, the train to Casablanca left precisely on time.

ABOUT THE AUTHOR

HORATIO CLARE was born in London in 1973 and raised on a sheep farm in South Wales. Educated at Atlantic College and York, he was a trained lifeboatman, journalist and bartender when he joined BBC radio in 1998, expecting to be sacked within a year. He has since worked as a researcher and producer on many programmes, including *Front Row*, *Night Waves* and *The Verb*, Radio 3's language and literature programme. When the latter was launched in 2002 he had the good fortune to return to Marrakesh, the most beguiling city he has ever visited. Horatio Clare's writing has appeared in various publications, including the *Guardian*, *The Spectator* and the *New Statesman*. In the spring of 2006 his memoir of a childhood in Wales, *Running for the Hills*, was published by John Murray and in the summer Eland published his collection of the travel literature of Sicily.

Sources and First Texts

Introduction

Barnaby Rogerson

For the first five centuries of the British Moroccan relationship Marrakesh was not known – or at least not described – by any writer in English. Our partial knowledge came from such indigenous North African historians and writers as Ibn Battuta and Leo Africanus. The first English descriptions, when they come in the 16th century, are concerned not with culture, religion or architecture but with the common ground of trade. This was the period when such merchant-men as the SS *Lion* sailed to the 'harbours' of Marrakesh – Safi and Agadir – selling English cloth and northern gemstones like amber, jet and coral in exchange for sugar, dates, almonds, wax and goatskins. All – in the excitable short-hand of the day – considered to be very 'vendible'. This was the time when Elizabeth ruled England from London and Ahmed el Mansour ruled the vast Saadian Empire of Morocco from Marrakesh; when England could still match Morocco in romance: the Directors of the Barbary Company claimed the right to escort the Moroccan Ambassador from his ship in a mounted torch-light parade through the streets of London to the Queen's audience hall.

These two sovereigns had much in common, they were both highly literate and multi-lingual and had known what it is like to become a non-person, either as an impoverished exile or an imprisoned princess. They also shared a fear of the Spanish and Portugese Empires and certain mutual deficiences in armaments. Morocco was short of ships' timber and iron, England was chronically short of saltpetre – the vital component of gunpowder. Although it was illegal for a Muslim power to sell weapons of war to a Christian power, and vice versa, in 1576 there is the first recorded shipment of English cannonballs for saltpetre. Soon there was enough of this secret trade in armaments to be going on for John Williams to be appointed local agent. He reported back that the Sultan Abdal Malik was 'well experienced in the Scriptures, as well in the Old Testament as in the New' and passed on his request for some English musicians.

In 1577 it was recorded that Francis Drake anchored in Safi. The Moroccan populace so far from being kept ignorant of foreign affairs thought he was the advance guard of an English fleet that would help Morocco against Spain. And indeed this was what the Saadian and Tudor courts had been secretly discussing. A number of such joint ventures were discussed, many 'too complex and important to be committed to paper'. The ones we know about include backing Don Antonio for the throne of Portugal and joint attacks on Spain and her possessions in south America. They were hampered by lack of trust between the two canny old operators, Queen Elizabeth and Ahmed el Mansour, who were also clearly spying on each other's technical know-how. Both died in 1603, the Queen in March, the Sultan in August. They clearly missed out on a real opportunity, for in his own piratical raids through the Caribbean Drake found that the Moorish captives of the Spanish would on their own initiative come to his aid and help him in his attack on the city of Cartagena.

After the death of the two great sovereigns a number of 'common ventures' did in fact occur. We know that in the midst of the Saadian civil war between the heirs of Ahmed el Mansour, some 200 English mercenaries under the command of a Captain John Giffard helped Moulay Zidan seize power in Marrakesh in 1613, although a smaller group of English mercenaries had failed in 1603. At about this time a secret agent from the Court of King James I, Sir Anthony Sherley was plotting (with the knowledge of the Holy Roman Emperor) to launch a Moroccan army against the Ottoman Empire. But this far-fetched scheme was quickly undermined by a very real and practical alliance between the dreaded power of Habsburg Spain and one of the least promising of the Saadian princes. In exchange for Spanish military support, prince Muhammad al-Sheikh handed over the two Moroccan ports of Larache (on the Atlantic coast) and Badis (in the middle of the Rif mountains on the Mediterranean). Although Muhammad al-Sheikh was able to force himself onto the throne of Fez in 1610, he only held onto it at the barrel of his Spanish garrison. His ruthless treason totally discredited the entire dynasty, even his rival brother Moulay Zidan whose authority only extended to the gates of the al-Badi palace in Marrakesh.

To make matters even worse, this was the period when the Spanish enemy embarked on the wholesale expulsion of all those of Moorish descent from Spain – be it that they had been practicing Christians for generations. In the end some 300,000 Moors were forced out of Spain. Many of them settled in Morocco and their desire for revenge fuelled the success of the Barbary corsairs, who operated out of every anchorage and estuary along the Moroccan coast. The most successful fleets were based on Salé-Rabat and at Mehdiya. The latter were joined by a squadron of English pirates which under the loose command of Henry Mainwaring (who would later make good as MP for Dover, constable of Dover Castle and receive a knighthood) made many a profitable descent on the trading ships that shadowed the Moroccan coast on their way to Cape Horn or the Americas.

England's shipping was not however immune to the attacks of the 'brethren of the sea'. This was especially true during the collapse in authority of the Royal Navy during the Civil War when some 300 British ships were 'taken' between 1622 and 1642. So much so that the ransoming of English captives and the accounts of those who converted to Islam and became renegades provides us with our first great body of travel literature. Twenty-two such accounts have survived though in terms of swash-buckling adventure all must cede place to that of the Cornish cabin boy turned Moroccan cavalry officer, Thomas Pellow that was published in 1739. Not that this period was short of characters, such as Captain Harrison who became 'Our Man in Morocco' and who would make eight separate bartering expeditions to Morocco to pick up English captives. In 1627 he records that he swopped 4 brass and 2 iron cannon, 150 pikes, powder and shot for 190 prisoners. In his book The tragical Life and Death of Muley Abadal Melek, the late King of Barbarie published in 1633 he records how the Sultan had liberated 18 Englishmen and then offered them employ as gunners. On one occassion the Sultan even gave one of these gunners a lift on his horse but asked him not to sit too close as he was afraid of catching lice.

In 1637 Harrison was succeeded in his role by one Giles Penn who became the first resident British consul amongst the Barbary Corsairs at Salé-Rabat. He was the grandfather of William Penn, the founder of Pennyslvania. Interestingly it is now thought that in 1620 there were more Englishmen in North Africa, some 8,000 merchants, captives or mercenaries, than in all the states of North America whose British population then stood at some 5,000. Robert Blake restored some of Britain's lost prestige with a naval tour of Barbary during Cromwell's Commonwealth. He seems to have made happy use of the Moroccan harbour at Tetouan, so much so that he even appointed a consul Nathaniel Luke from amongst the resident merchants, his salary to be paid for by a 2% tax on English trade. The Restoration of Charles II proved to be a decisive turning point in British-Moroccan relations. The old, familiar pattern of two mutually tough trading partners joined in convenient friendship was to be replaced by the first whiff of Imperial aggression as Britain attempted to fortify Tangier which fell under English possession as part of the dowry of Charles II's Portugese bride – along with Bombay.

The Travels of Ibn Battuta

Ibn Battuta

I went with them to Asilah, where I stayed some months, then to the city of Sala. From Sala I travelled to the city of Marrakush.

It is one of the most beautiful cities, spacious and extending over a very wide area, and has ample resources. It has magnificent mosques, like the principal mosque, which is known as the Kutubiyin Mosque [Mosque of the Booksellers]. This has a wonderful awe-inspiring minaret, which I climbed and from which the whole town can be seen. However, ruin has overtaken the city and I can compare it only with Baghdad, except that the bazaars of Baghdad are better. In Marrakush is the wonderful *madrusa* distinguished by the beauty of its site and the excellence of its construction, which was built by our master the Commander of the faitful Abu 'l-Hasan, God be pleased with him.

Ibn Juzayy remarks: 'The qadi of Marrakush, the imam and historian Abu l-Ausi Abdullah Muhammad b. 'Abd al-Malik, said of it:

> "God's be the illustrious town of Marrakush
> How splendid are the noble sayyids who live there!
> If a stranger from afar arrives there
> It consoles him with its friendliness for his people and home
> What one hears and sees of it
> Gives rise to envy between the eye and the ear."

ABOUT THE AUTHOR

IBN BATTUTAH is probably the most famous Islamic traveller ever, and rivals Marco Polo in any consideration of medieval explorers. Having set off from Tangier in 1325, aged only twenty-one, Battutah's pilgrimage to Mecca became an epic journey that was to last twenty-nine years and cover three times the distance of Polo's travels. Battutah was to visit countries from Morocco to China (claiming the position of ambassador in the latter) before returning to Fez in 1349 to write up his adventures at the bidding of Sultan Abun Inan.

As a native of the area it is understandable that Battutah's references to Marrakesh are slight, but nonetheless leave an impression of his sense of wonder and eye for a colourful scene.

Leo Africanus

In the said citie of Maroco is a most impregnable castle, which, if you consider the bignes, the walles, the towers and the gates built all of perfect marble, you may well thinke to be a citie rather than a castle. Within this castle there is a stately temple, having a most loftie and high steeple on the top whereof standeth an halfe moon, and under the halfe moon are three golden spheares one bigger than another which all of them together weigh 130,000 ducates. Some kings there were, who being allured with the calue, went about to take down the saide goldern sphears: but they had alwaies some great misfrtune or other, which hindered their attempt: insomuch that the common people thinke it verie dangerous, if a man doth but offer to touch the said sphears with his hand. Some affirme that they are there placed by so forcible and influence of the planets, that they cannot be remooued from thence by any cunning or deuice. Some others report that a certain spirite is adiured by Arte-magique, to defend those sphears from all insults and iniuries whatsoeuer. In our time the king of Maroco neglecting the vulgar opinion, would haue taken down the said sphears, to vse them for treasure against the Portugals, who as then prepared themselues to battell against him. Howbeit his counsellours would not suffer him so to doe, for that they esteemed them as the principall monuments of all Maroco. I remember that I read in a certaine historiographer, that the wife of King *Mansor*, to the ende she might be famous in time to come, caused the three spheares to be made of the princely and pretious iewels which her husband *Mansor* bestowed vpon her, and to be placed vpon the temple which he built.

ABOUT THE AUTHOR

AL-HASSAN BIN MOHAMMAD AL-WAÛZAN ALZAYYATI was born in Granada between 1489 and 1495, his family exiled to Fez after the Moorish expulsion from Spain in 1492. In his youth he worked as a diplomat and businessman, traveling great distances through Islamic North Africa and the Levant. In 1518 he was captured and enslaved by Christain corsairs off the Island of Jerba, and his erudition and intelligence led his presentation to Pope Leo X (Giovanni de Medici).

Baptised with the name of his patron, GIOVANNI LEONE (or LEO AFRICANUS as he was commonly known) was freed and given a pension. He went on to write up in Italian the many rough notes he had made on the various countries he had visited on his travels. These were eventually published in 1550, the year of his death, as *Le descrizione dell'Africa*. The English translation appeared in 1600. This work was to remain a prime source for European knowledge of inner Africa for the next two hundred years.

Sultan Abd al Malik to Elizabeth I

Official Correspondence
from *Letters from Barbary, 1576–1774*

I put my trust in my Creator.

In the name of God, the Merciful, the Compassionate; and God bless our lord Muhammad and his Family and his Companions and give them peace.

From the slave of God, the Protected by God (*al-muctasim bi-llah*), the Commander of the Faithful Abu Marwan Abd al-Malik son of the Commander of the Faithful Abu Abd Allah Muhammad al-Shaykh, the *sharif* of the line of Hasan (may God favour him and confer on him His benefits without cease).

To the mighty, the celebrated, the distinguished, the honoured, the high-born *sultana* Elizabeth daughter of the mighty, the most famous, the high-born, the favoured, the distinguished, the most glorious *sultan* Henry (may God bestow His benefits on you and grant you unceasing favours): We write to you from our illustrious capital Marrakush (God preserve it with every benefit and universal benevolence). Great praise be to God.

The motive for this letter is to inform you that God (who is blessed and exalted) has given the realm of my father my lord the *sultan* ([God] have mercy on him) into my power. I have taken possession of all his territories and the hearts of all the people of my kingdom are united in love for me. Such is God's favour towards me. When I was in the East I ever took your Majesty's part and believed in your affection. Now, therefore, when (God be praised) I have reached my country and succeeded to my estate I have held it to be one of the most important and urgent matters to inform you and write to you, so that you may be aware of this affection for you. If ever you have any desires in our country, they will be satisfied in a manner pleasing to you, except with respect to that which our Law forbids, for we stand by its prohibitions. Nevertheless, your Majesty is held in the affection due to you. Pray, do not refrain from sending to us news of you, or informing us of your purposes.

Written in Raiab al-fard in the year 984.

John Smith

from *The Adventures and Discourses of Captain John Smith*

Being thius satisfied with *Europe* and *Asia* understanding of the warres in *Barberie*, hee went from *Gibralter* to *Guta* and *Tanger*, thence to *Saffee*, where growing into acquaintance with a French man of warre, the Captaine and some twelve more went to *Morocco*, to see the antient monuments of that large renowned Citie: it was once the principall Citie in *Barbarie*, situated in a goodly plaine Countrey, 14 miles from the great Mount *Atlas*, and sixtie miles from the *Atlanticke* Sea; but now little remaining, but the King's Palace, which is like a Citie of it selfe, and the *Christian* Church, on whose flat square steeple is a great brouch of iron, whereon is placed the three golden Bals of *Affrica*: the first is neere three Ells in circumference, the next above it somewhat lesse, the uppermost the least over them, as it were an halfe ball, and over all a prettie guilded *Pyramides*. Against those golden Bals have been shot many a shot, their weight is recorded 700-weight of pure gold, hollow within, yet no shot did ever hit them, nor could ever any Conspirator attaine that honor as to get them downe. They report the Prince of *Morocco* betrothed himself to the King's Daughter of *Aethiopia*, he dying before their marriage, she caused those three golden Balls to be set up for his Monument, and vowed virginitie all her life. The *Alfantica* is also a place of note, because it is invironed with a great wall, wherin lye the goods of all the Merchants securely guarded. The *Inderea* is also (as it were) a Citie of it selfe, where dwell the Iewes: the rest for the most part is defaced: but by the many pinnacles and towers, with Balls on their tops, hath much appearance of much sumptiousnesse and curiositie. There have been many famous Universities, which are now but stables for sowes and Beasts, & the houses in most parts lye tumbled one above another; the walls of Earth are with the great fresh flouds washed to the ground; nor is there an village in it, but tents for Strangers, *Larbes* & *Moores*. Strange tales they will tell of a great Garden, wherin were all dorts of Brids, Fishes, Beasts, Fruits and Fountaines, which for beautie, Art and pleasure, exceeded any place knowne in the world, though now nothing but dung-hills, Pigeon-houses, shrubs and bushes. There are yet many excellent fountains adorned with marble, and many arches, pillars, towers, ports and Temples; but most only reliques of lamentable ruines and sad desolation.

When *Mully Hamet* reigned in *Barberie*, hee had three sonnes, *Mully Shecke*, *Mully Sidan* and *Mully Befferres*, he a most good and noble King, that governed well with peace and plenty, till his Empresse, more cruell than any beast in *Affrica*, poisoned him, her owne daughter, *Mully Shecke* his eldest sonne borne of a Portugall Ladie, and his daughter, to bring *Mully Sidan* to the Crowne now reigning, which was the cause of all those brawles and warres that followed betwixt those brothers, their children and a Saint that start up, but he played the Devill.

King *Mully Hamet* was not blacke, as many suppose, but *Molata*, or tawnie, as are the most of his subjects; every way noble, kinde and friendly, verie rich and pompous in state and Majestie, though he sitteth not upon a Throne nor Chaire of Estate, but crosse legged upon a rich Carpet, as doth the *Turke*, whose religion of *Mahomet*, with an incredible miserable curiositie they observe. His Ordinarie Guard is at least 5000 but in progresse he goeth not with lesse than 20000 horsemen, himselfe as rich in all his Equipage, as any Prince in Christendom, and yet a contributor to the *Turke*. In all his Kingdome were so few good Artificers, that hee entertained from *England*, Gold-smiths, Plummers, Carvers and Polishers of Stone, and Watch-makers, so much hee delighted in the reformation of workmanship, hee allowed each of them ten shillings a day standing fee, linen, woollen, silkesm and what they would for diet and apparel, and custome-free to transport, or import what they would; for there were scarce any of those qualities in his Kingdomes, but those, of which there are divers of them living at this present in *London*. Amongst the rest, on Mr *Henry Archer*, a Watch-maker, walking in *Morocco*, from the *Alfantica* to the *Inderea*, the way being verie foule, met a great Priest, or a *Sante* (as they call all the great Clergy-men) who would have thrust him into the durt for the way; but *Archer*, not knowing what he was, gave him a box on the eare, presently he was apprehended, and condemned to have his tongue cut out and his hand cut off: but no sooner was it knowen at the Kings Court but 300 of his Guard came, and broke open the Prison, and delivered him, although the fact was next degree to Treason.

Concerning this *Archer*, there is one thing more worth noting. Not farre from *Mount Atlas*, a great Lionesse, in the heat of the day, did use to bathe herself, and teach her young Puppies to swimme, in the river, *Cauzeff*, of a good breadth, yet she would carrie them one after another over the river; which some *Moores* perceiving, watched their opportunitie, and, when the river was between her and them, stole four of her whelps, which she perceiving, with all the speed shee could, passed the river, and coming neere them they let fall a whelpe (and fled with the rest) which she took in her mouth and so returned to the rest: a Male and a female of those they gave Mr *Archer*, who kept them in the Kins Garden, till the Male killed the Female, then he brought it up as a puppy-dog lying upon his bed, till it grew so great as a Mastiffe, and no dog more tame or gentle to them hee knew: but being to returne for *England*, at *Saffee* he gave them to a Merchant of *Marsellis*, that presented him to the French King, who sent him to King *Iames*, where it was kept in the Tower seven yeeres: after one Mr *Iohn Bull*, then servant to Mr *Archer*, with divers of his friends, went to see the Lyons, not knowing anything at all of him; yet this rare beast smelled him before hee saw him, whining, groaning and tumbling, with such an expression of acquaintance, that being informed by the Keepers how hee came thither; Mr *Bull* so prevailed, the Keeper opened the grate and *Bull* went in: But no Dogge could fawne more on his Master than the Lyon on him, licking his feet, hands and face, skipping and tumbling to and fro, to the wonder of all the beholders; being satisfied with his acquaintance, he made shift to get out of the grate. But when the Lyon saw his friend gone, no beast by bellowing, roaring, scratching, and howling, could expresse more rage and sorrow, nor in foure days after would he either eat or drinke.

In *Morocco*, the Kings Lyons are all put togetherin a Court, invironed with a great high wall; to those they put a young Puppy-dogge: the greatest Lyon had a sore upon his necke, which the Dogge so licked that he was healed: the Lyon defended him from the furie of all the rest, nor durst they eat till the Dogge and he had fed; this Dog grew great and lived among them many yeeres after.

Fez also is a moste large and plentifull Countrey, the chiefe Citie is called *Fez*, divided into two parts; old *Fez*, countaining about 80 thousand households, the other 4000 pleasantly situated upon a River in the heart of Barbarie, part upon hills, part upon plaines, full of people, and all sortes of merchandise. The great Temple is called *Carucen*, in bredth seventeene Arches, in length 120 borne up with 2500 white marble pillars: under the chiefe Arch, where the Tribunall is kept, hangeth a most huge lampe compassed with 110 lesser, under the other also hang great lamps, and about some are burning fifteene hundred lights. They say they were all made of the bels the *Arabians* brought from *Spaine*. It hath three gates of notable height, Priests and Officers so many, that the circuit of the Church, the Yard and other houses, is little lesse than a mile and a halfe in compasse; there are in this Citie 200 Schooles, 200 Innes, 400 water-mils, 600 water-Conduits, 700 Temples and Oratories; but fiftie of them most stately and richly furnished. Their *Alcazar* or *Burse* is walled about, it hath twelve gates, and fifteen walks covered with tents, to keep the Sun from the Merchants, and them that come there. The Kings Palace, both for strength and beautie is excellent and the Citizens have many great privileges. Those two countries of *Fez* and *Morocco* are the best part of all *Barbarie*, abounding with people, cattell, and all good necessaries for mans use.

ABOUT THE AUTHOR

JOHN SMITH is best known for his reputed relationship with the Native American princess Pocohontas. However, according to his, rather colourful, memoirs, his early life was a swashbuckling adventure of espionage, piracy, slavery and adventuring, including a time spent searching for mercenary work in Morocco.

He claims to have travelled to Italy, been branded a Huguenot and thrown overboard before being rescued and employed by pirates. He went on to travel through Italy and join the forces of the Archduke of Austria, playing a vital part both in the raising of the siege of Limbach and the capture of Stühlweissenberg from the Turks. He gained a coat of arms for victorious single combat against three separate Turkish champions before being captured and sold into slavery. Held in Constantinople before being rescued by a Turkish woman, Smith was kept as a slave by a Pasha in Varna on the Black Sea. He killed his tyrannous master and escaped, wandering through Europe and Morocco, from which travels he drew the material for the extract printed here, before sailing back to England on a British warship.

His remaining years were no less exciting. As one of the founding members of Virginia, Smith proved skilled at foraging for and scavenging food, eventually presiding over the fledgling colony. It is in this period that his contested rescue from the wrath of native tribes at the hands of Pocohontas took place.

After leaving Virginia, Smith went on to develop fishing settlements along the coast of New England, participating in exploration of the region and spending another period of captivity fighting the Spanish on a French warship before settling in London to produce maps and pamphlets of and about America, until the end of his life in 1631.

Thomas Pellow of Penryn

from *The History of the Long Captivity and Adventures of Thomas Pellow*

NOW I am again in the City of *Morocco*; of which I do not doubt, but it may be expected that I should give a particular Description, and an Account of all its Curiosities; which I could readily, and would as willingly do, did I not think it altogether inconsistent with my main Point, and would enlarge my History to very little Purpose, by only repeating what has been, without Doubt, before made publick; therefore I shall, by Way of Digression, mention only two of the most agreeable Curiosities, which my own Fancy was struck with, the one within, and the other without the Walls, and refer my Readers for the rest to the several Books already printed; and first, of that within the Walls, which was four golden Globes of a large Size and Value, fixed on the Top of the Tower of the Emperor's Palace, and which, according to common Fame, were set up many hundred Years ago, on the following Occasion:

LULLA OUDAH, Daughter and Widow to two of their antient Emperors, happened one Day to see in a Woman's Basket some very very tempting Peaches, and being at the Time with Child, she took one of them, and after biting off a small Part of it, and putting the Remainder into the Basket again, she went away, saying, *She had but just nick'd the Time*; of which some of the By-standers taking Notice and pondering thereon, it soon came into their Minds, that it must be very near the Time of the Commencement of their *Ramadam*, which is a very strict Fast they observe every twelfth Moon; and during which, if any are known to eat or drink from an Hour before the Breaking of the Day, till the Appearance of the Stars, it is Death by their Law; and they are not only obliged to abstain from all Manner of Food, but likewise from Smoaking, washing their Mouths, taking Snuff, smelling Perfumes, or conversing with Women.

THOSE who are obliged to travel, may drink a little Water; and such as are sick, may borrow a few Days of their Prophet; but they must, and do repay punctually, when they recover Strength. In the Towns they run about the Streets, and wake all those people they think are asleep, that they may eat, and so be the better able to support themselves in the Day; they rise three or four Times in the Night, and sleep again. Such as are Libertine and used to drink Wine, abstain from it at this time.

IT is usual in the Towns, every Evening, when the Fast of that Day is ended, for a Trumpet to be sounded from the Castle, to give Notice of it, before which Time it is pleasant to see the Posture of the *Moors*, one holding a Pipe ready fill'd, while he impatiently expects the Sound of the Trumpet; another with a Dish of *Cuscassooe* before him, ready to run his Hand in; some got close to the Fountains, to be first that shall drink. On the Eve of their Lent, they make great Rejoicing, shouting and repeating the Name of GOD, and watch for the Appearance of the Moon, at which they fire their Muskets, then fall to saying their Prayers, the Emperor himself sometimes at their Head; who, to persuade the People of his great Regard for Religion, keeps this Fast four Months every Year; but they are obliged to observe it only during that one Moon.

THE poor longing Queen was, by a due Enquiry into the Moon's Age, found to have transgressed in it by three Hours, and immediate Sentance was passed upon her, which put her under a grievous Agony, as not knowing (though she was exceeding rich) how to get off; though at the last (on her promising to set up those Balls, and to build four several Bridges over two very rapid Rivers, *viz*, three on *Murbia*, and one on *Wadlabbid*, wherein abundance of People had been before drowned, in their attempting to cross over) she obtained a Pardon; and these Promises were in her Lifetime accordingly performed, together with several large Buildings and Donations for Scools, Alms-Houses, &c. over and above her very extraordinary and chargeable Obligation.

THESE four Globes are, by Computation, seven hundred Pounds, *Barbary* Weight, each Pound consisting of twenty-four Ounces, which make in all 1050 Pounds *English*; and frequent Attempts had been made to take them away, but without success; for, as the Notion ran, any attempting it were soon glad to desist from it, they being affrightened and especially at their near Approach to them, in a very strange and surprising Manner, and seized with an extraordinary Faintness and Trembling, hearing at the same Time a great rumbling Noise, like as if the whole Fabrick was tumbling down about their Ears so that, in great confusion, they all returned faster than they advanced.

THIS I did often hear, yet had I a very strong Itching to try the truth of it; and to gratify my Curiosity, I one night (having before communicated my Intentions to two of my Men, and persuaded them to go with me, and provided myself with Candles, Flint, Steel and Tinder) entered the Foot of the Tower, lighted my Candles and advanced with my Comrades close at my Heels till I had gained at least two thirds of the Height, I still going on; when really, to my Seeming, I both felt and heard such a dismal rumbling Noise, and Shaking of the Tower, (my Lights at that very Instant, quite going out) as I thought far surpassed that of common Fame; yet was I resolved to proceed, and called to my Comrades to be of good Courage; but having no Answer from them, I soon found they had left me in the Lurch; upon which, falling into a very great Sweat, I went back also, and found them at the Bottom in a terrible Condition: And so ended my mad Project; and which was, I think, a very mad one indeed, for had I obtained the Globes, in what could it have bettered my deplorable Condition, being always obliged to follow my Emperor's Pleasure, and with whom it was a most sufficient Crime to be rich; And so much for my foolish Attempt on the golden Globes.

WHAT I was most delighted with, without the Walls of *Morocco*, was a most curious and spacious Garden for the King's Pleasure, when he came to that City, it being by far the finest of all I had ever seen before, being kept in the most exquisite Manner, as to its curious and regular Walks and Arbours, and laid out with large Collections of most kinds of Fruit and Flowers, the Fruit Trees being very large,and dressed and pruned in a very elegant Manner; so that their wood, and especially that of their Orange-Trees, was always in a prosperous Condition, almost ever green, blooming and bearing Fruit. In this Garden I saw the Trunk of an old Tree (which I was told was that of a very large Orange Tree) with great spreading Branches which, when in its Prosperity, was the Death of *Maley Archid*, the Emperor's Brother, (who, about seven Years before killed *Mulley Emhamet*, his elder Brother, with his own Hand, to make Way for himself to the Empire:) He being one Day in this Garden on Horseback, and his Horse running suddenly out with him, so that he could by no Means stop him, carried him under this Tree, in a moment appearing on the other Side, without his Rider; and notwithstanding the quick Approach of his Attendants, they found him quite dead, hanging by his Head in a forked Limb; on which Account there was no Doubt, no little Hurry all over the Empire, he being reckoned one of the most famous Conquerors in those Parts having made himself Master, by the Sword, of the kingdoms of *Tafilet, Fez, Morocco* and *Sus,* and by this Means the old Tyrant (whom I was obliged to serve) came to the Throne: However, this Accident was by all reckoned a just Judgement.

ABOUT THE AUTHOR

THOMAS PELLOW provided one of the earliest intimate descriptions of life in eighteenth century Marrakesh. He was born in 1704 and raised in Cornwall, attending the Latin School in Penryn. However, he tired of this life and, in 1715, persuaded his uncle, a merchant, to take him on one of his sea voyages. On return from Genoa, the ship came under attack from Moroccan pirates and was forced aground and the crew captured and sold into slavery. Pellow converted to Islam under pressure from his master, and was taken into the service of the emperor Moulay Ismail, working in the imperial palace before fighting in the army alongside other renegade former-Christians. After heavy involvement in the chaotic civil war that followed Moulay Ismail's death in 1727, Pellow finally returned to England in 1738. His memoirs were published two years later and provide a fascinating insight, albeit one somewhat skewed by the overly-enthusiastic editor of the first edition. His references to Marrakesh, extracted here, are perhaps of greatest interest in that Pellow – like so many travellers after him – focuses on the golden spheres on the Katoubia Mosque as being of primary interest in the city.

Timeline

Dates at which the respective authors were in Marrakesh

Pre-1500	1325	Ibn Battuta
1500	1526	Leo Africanus
1550	1576	Sultan Abd al-Malik
1600	1606	John Smith
1650		
1700	1720–36	Thomas Pellow
1750		
1760		
1770		
1780	1789	William Lempriere
1790		
1800	1803–7	Ali Bey
1810		
1820		
1830		
1840		
1850		
1860	*c.1860*	Gerhard Rohlfs
1870		
1880	*c.1883*	Johnston/Cowan
1886–*c.*1926		Walter Harris
1888		Joseph Thomson
*c.*1884–90		Budgett Meakin
1890	1897	R. B. Cunninghame Graham
1900	*c.1904*	S L Bensusan
1905		

1910	*c.1911*	Donald Mackenzie
1915	1917	Edith Wharton
1920		
1925		
1930	*c.1930*	Henriette Celarié
		Wyndham Lewis
1935	1930–79	Leonora Peets
	1938–39	George Orwell
	1939	Sacheverell Sitwell
1940		
1945		
1950	*c.1950*	Peter Mayne
1955		
1956–present		Juan Goytisolo
	c.1958	Nina Epton
1960	1960–1	Gavin Maxwell
	c.1960s	Elias Canetti
		Esther Freud
		Christopher Gibbs
		Anthony Gladstone-Thompson
		John Hopkins
		Hamish Brown
2000 and after		Horatio Clare
		Justin McGuinness
		Tahir Shah

Bibliography

Africanus, Leo, *A Geographical Historie of Africa* trans. Jon Pory (George Bishop, London; 1600) – written in Italian, translated into Latin and translated from that into English

Battuta, Ibn, *The Travels of Ibn Battuta AD 1325–1354, Volume IV* translated by H. A. R. Gibb & C. F. Beckingham (Hakluyt Society, London; 1994)

Bensusan, S. L., *Morocco* painted by A. S. Forrest (Adam and Charles Black, London; 1904)

Bey, Ali, *Travels of Ali Bey in Morocco, Tripoli, Cyprus, Egypt, Arabia, Syria and Turkey Between the Years 1803 and 1807* (Longman, Hurst, Rees, Orme and Brown, London; 1816)

Botting, Douglas, *Gavin Maxwell; A Life* (Harper Collins, London; 1993)

Canetti, Elias, *The Voices of Marrakesh* trans. J. A. Underwood (Marian Boyars, London/New York; 2001) translation first published 1967

Celarié, Henriette, *Behind Moroccan Walls* trans. Constance Lily Morris (Books for Libraries Press, New York; 1970) First published 1931

Cowan, George D. and R. L. N. Johnston, *Moorish Lotos Leaves; Glimpses of Southern Morocco* (Tinsley Brothers, London; 1883)

Cuninghame Graham, R. B., *Mogreb-El-Acksa* (Century, London; 1988) first published 1898

Epton, Nina, *Saints and Sorcerors; A Moroccan Journey* (Cassell, London; 1958)

Freud, Esther, *Hideous Kinky* (Penguin, London; 1992)

Goytisolo, Juan, *Cinema Eden* (Eland, London; 2003)

Harris, Walter, *Morocco That Was* (Eland, London; 2002) First Published 1921

Hopkins, John, *The Tangier Diaries 1962–1979* (Arcadia Books, London; 1997)

Hopkins, J. F. P., translated and annotated, *Letters from Barbary, 1576– 1774,* (Oxford University Press; 1982)

Lempriere, William, *A Tour from Gibralter to Tangier, Sallee, Mogodor, Santa Cruz, Tarudant and thence over Mount Atlas to Morocco Including a Particular Account of the Royal Harem etc.* (London; 1791)

Lewis, Wyndham, *Filibusters in Barbary* (London; 1932)

Mackenze, Donald,*The Khalifate of the West; Being a General Description of Morocco* (Simpkin, Marshall, Hamilton, Kent, London; 1911)

Mayne, Peter, *A Year in Marrakesh* (Eland, London; 2002) first published as *Alleys of Marrakesh* (1953)

Maxwell, Gavin, *Lords of the Atlas: The Rise and Fall of the House of Glaoua 1893-1956* (Eland; 2004)

Meakin, Budgett, *The Moors* (Swan Sonnenschein, London; 1902)

Orwell, George *Collected Essays, Journalism and Letters* (London, 1968)

Peets, Leonora, *Women of Marrakesh; Record of a Secret Sharer, 1930–1970* trans. Rein Taagepera (C. Hurst, London; 1988)

Pellow, Thomas, *The History of the Long Captivity and Adventures of Thomas Pellow In South Barbary* (London; 1740)

Rohlfs, Dr Gerhard, *Adventures in Morocco and Journeys through the Oases of Draa and Tafilet* (Sampson Low, Marston, Low & Searle, London; 1874)

Sitwell, Sacheverell, *Mauretania; Warrior, Man, and Woman* (Duckworth, London; 1940)

Smith, John *The True travels, adventures, and Observations of Captaine John Smith, In Europe, Asia Africa and America, from Anno Domini 1593 to 1629* (Thomas Slater, London; 1630)

Jérome et Jean Tharaud, *Marrakech ou les Seigneurs de l'Atlas* (Paris; 1920)

Thomson, Joseph, *Travels in the Atlas and Southern Morocco; A Narrative of Exploration* (George Philip, London; 1889)

Wharton, Edith, *In Morocco* (Century Publishing, London; 1984) first published 1920

And featuring contributions from Hamish Brown, Horatio Clare, Christopher Gibbs, Anthony Gladstone-Thompson, Justin McGuinness and Katri Skala

Acknowledgements

We would like to thank the following:

Douglas Botting and his literary agent Andrew Hewson at John Johnson for permission to quote from *Gavin Maxwell: A Life*; Marion Boyars Publishers for granting permission to reprint an extract from Elias Canetti's *The Voices of Marrakesh*; Lady Jean Polwarth and her literary agent, Andrew Hewson at John Johnson for permission to quote from Cunninghame Graham's *Maghreb el Aksa*; Esther Freud for giving us permission to quote from *Hideous Kinky*; Gary Pulsifer of Arcadia Books for granting permission to quote from John Hopkins' *Tangier Diaries*; Gavin Maxwell Enterprises for granting permission to quote from *Lords of the Atlas*; Ben Mason at the A. M. Heath Agency for arranging permission with Bill Hamilton, literary executor of the estate of the late Sonia Bronwell Orwell and the publishers Secker and Warburg to re-print George Orwell's 1939 essay 'Marrakesh'; Christopher Hurst for granting permission to reproduce a chapter from Leonora Peets's *Women of Marrakesh*; Sir Reresby Sitwell and Francis Sitwell and their literary agent Bruce Hunter at David Higham Associates for permission to quote from Sir Sacheverell Sitwell's *Mauretania: Warrior, Man and Woman*; the estate of Wyndham Lewis, for permission to quote from Wyndham Lewis's *Filibusters in Barbary*; Rose Baring at Eland Books for granting permission to quote from Walter Harris's *Morocco that Was* and Peter Mayne's *A Year in Marrakesh*; and especially Christopher Gibbs, Justin McGuiness, Katri Skala, Anthony Gladstone-Thompson, Douglas Botting, Hamish Brown and Horatio Clare for their original contributions.

Every effort has been spent to trace the holders of copyright and to acknowledge permissions where appropriate. If we have inadvertently failed in this mission, we would be pleased to hear from any literary heirs, and correct this admission in future editions.

One of the pleasures in preparing this collection has been to hunt down rare copies of out of print (and out of copyright) travel books amongst the specialist dealers. Although they were unwitting colleagues in the search it has always been a pleasure to be on the receiving end of the unsung scholarship behind the catalogues regularly despatched by Adab Books of Cambridge, Joppa Books and Francis Edwards at Hay on Wye. Of the many dealers in London who also assisted I would like to thank James Tindley at 4 Cecil Court, Mohammed ben Madani of the Maghreb Review and the Maghreb Bookshop, Fine Books Oriental at Museum Street, Griffiths & Partners in Great Ormond Street and Reg and Philip Remington when they were based at 18 Cecil Court.

ELAND

61 Exmouth Market, London EC1R 4QL
Tel: 020 7833 0762   Fax: 020 7833 4434
Email: info@travelbooks.co.uk

Eland was started in 1982 to revive great travel books that had fallen out of print. Although the list has diversified into biography and fiction, it is united by a quest to define the spirit of place. These are books for travellers, and for readers who aspire to explore the world but who are also content to travel in their own minds. Eland books open out our understanding of other cultures, interpret the unknown and reveal different environments as well as celebrating the humour and occasional horrors of travel.

All our books are printed on fine, pliable, cream-coloured paper. Most are still gathered in sections by our printer and sewn as well as glued, almost unheard of for a paperback book these days. This gives larger margins in the gutter, as well as making the books stronger.

We take immense trouble to select only the most readable books and therefore many readers collect the entire series. If you haven't liked an Eland title, please send it back to us saying why you disliked it and we will refund the purchase price.

You will find a very brief description of all our books on the following pages. Extracts from each and every one of them can be read on our website, at www.travelbooks.co.uk. If you would like a free copy of our catalogue, please telephone, email or write to us.

ELAND

'One of the very best travel lists' WILLIAM DALRYMPLE

Memoirs of a Bengal Civilian
JOHN BEAMES
*Sketches of nineteenth-century India
painted with the richness of Dickens*

Jigsaw
SYBILLE BEDFORD
*An intensely remembered autobiographical
novel about an inter-war childhood*

A Visit to Don Otavio
SYBILLE BEDFORD
*The hell of travel and the Eden of arrival
in post-war Mexico*

Journey into the Mind's Eye
LESLEY BLANCH
*An obsessive love affair with Russia and
one particular Russian*

The Devil Drives
FAWN BRODIE
*Biography of Sir Richard Burton,
explorer, linguist and pornographer*

Turkish Letters
OGIER DE BUSBECQ
*Eyewitness history at its best:
Istanbul during the reign of Suleyman
the Magnificent*

My Early Life
WINSTON CHURCHILL
*From North-West Frontier to Boer War
by the age of twenty-five*

Sicily: through writers' eyes
ED. HORATIO CLARE
*A selection of the best travel writing on
Sicily: a guidebook for the mind*

A Square of Sky
JANINA DAVID
*A Jewish childhood in the Warsaw
ghetto and in hiding from the Nazis*

Chantemesle
ROBIN FEDDEN
*A lyrical evocation of childhood
in Normandy*

Croatia: through writers' eyes
ED. FRANKOPAN, GOODING & LAVINGTON
*A selection of the best travel writing on
Croatia: a guidebook for the mind*

Travels with Myself and Another
MARTHA GELLHORN
*Five journeys from hell by a
preeminent war correspondent*

The Weather in Africa
MARTHA GELLHORN
*Three novellas set amongst the
white settlers of East Africa*

Walled Gardens
ANNABEL GOFF
An Anglo-Irish childhood

Africa Dances
GEOFFREY GORER
*The magic of indigenous culture
and the banality of colonisation*

Cinema Eden
JUAN GOYTISOLO
*Essays from the Muslim
Mediterranean*

A State of Fear
ANDREW GRAHAM-YOOLL
*A journalist witnesses Argentina's
nightmare in the 1970s*

Warriors
GERALD HANLEY
Life and death among the Somalis

Morocco That Was
WALTER HARRIS
*All the cruelty, fascination and
humour of a pre-modern kingdom*

Far Away and Long Ago
W H HUDSON
A childhood in Argentina

Holding On
MERVYN JONES
*One family and one street in
London's East End: 1880-1960*